The
Improbable
Era

The
Improbable
Era   *The South since*
World War II

Charles P. Roland

The University Press of Kentucky

ISBN: 0-8131-1335-0

Library of Congress Catalog Card Number: 75-12082

Copyright © 1975 by The University Press of Kentucky

A statewide cooperative scholarly publishing agency
serving Berea College, Centre College of Kentucky,
Eastern Kentucky University, Georgetown College,
Kentucky Historical Society, Kentucky State University,
Morehead State University, Murray State University,
Northern Kentucky State College, Transylvania
University, University of Kentucky, University of
Louisville, and Western Kentucky University.

Editorial and Sales Offices: Lexington, Kentucky 40506

To Doll Aycock &
to the memory of Frank Aycock

Contents

Tables

Acknowledgments

I am indebted to my wife Allie Lee Roland for invaluable assistance in the research, editing, and indexing of this book; to Dorothy Leathers for efficient and cheerful service in typing the manuscript; and to the American Philosophical Society and the University of Kentucky Research Foundation for financial support of the project.

Prologue

The South was fated to be changed almost as much by World War II as by the Civil War. Both conflicts brought toil, sacrifice, social chaos, and grief along with an exhilarating sense of patriotic purpose. But here the comparison ends. Instead of being invaded by hostile and destroying northern soldiers, during the recent struggle the South was host to millions of allied if not entirely friendly northern troops in training; it was strewn with armament and equipment factories built or subsidized by the federal government; its cities were beehives of commerce, manufacture, and transportation. In 1865 the South was crushed, bankrupt, demoralized; in 1945 it was intact, prosperous, confident.

Yet in countless ways the South came out of World War II very much what it had been at the beginning: the most close-knit and consciously distinctive region in the country. It was still what Wilbur Cash had called it on the eve of the war: not quite a nation within a nation, but the next thing to it.[1] More than any other section it gave expression to its sectionalism; for instance, its greatest novelist, William Faulkner, in 1948 caused one of his characters to say the southern people were the only truly homogeneous people left in America.[2]

History helped both to explain and to perpetuate this sectional consciousness, for the South bore the mark of a different past reinforced by a widespread awareness and interpretation of it. All southerners knew, however imperfectly, that the South was once a country set apart by plantations and black slavery; that it attempted through arms to gain independence and was defeated on the battlefield; that the bondsmen were emancipated and made citizens against the regional will; that the land was occupied by federal troops and subjected to rule by northerners, freedmen, and disaffected southern whites; that the redemption of local white government was the result of Ku Klux Klan violence and white solidarity in the Democratic party; that the southern people even after the Reconstruction endured exploitation, poverty, and national scorn.

To be sure, the actual record of events was distorted in the southern mind, embellished by time and telling, by prejudice and pride. The Old South became a place of moonlight, magnolias, and mint juleps: an idyllic land enjoyed almost as much by the slaves as by their masters. The Civil War was an epic in southern valor against overwhelming numbers; Reconstruction, an exercise in northern tyranny and African barbarism. The South emerged from these ordeals triumphant in spirit, but it remained a misunderstood and maligned minority within the nation. Despite a persistent malaise from their heritage of slavery, secession, defeat, and poverty, southerners looked upon themselves as defenders of the ancient American virtues. From this unusual historical experience and from the southern perception of it arose much of the South's continuing distinctiveness as a region.

But southern distinctiveness was not altogether a product of the past or of the southern image of the past. Obviously the section remained physically different from the rest of the nation, and this difference had always exerted a profound influence on the attitudes and behavior of the population. The weather was especially influential. A historian of early Virginia attributed the indolence of his fellow colonists to their being "climate struck." Where God does so much for people, he said, they never work for themselves. And Professor Ulrich B. Phillips opened his discourse on life and labor in the Old South with the sentence: "Let us begin by discussing the weather, for that has been the chief agency in making the South distinctive."[3]

Summer in the South after World War II was still summer, when for fifty or more humid afternoons a year the thermometer would reach ninety degrees in the shade, a point sometimes followed by shattering thunderstorms and torrential downpours. The day of artificially cooled homes, offices, libraries, stores, and factories was still in the future. Moderate exertion, or none at all, brought drenching sweat; vigorous exertion brought visions of the Inferno. What southerner now over forty years old does not recall with a mixture of relief and nostalgia the stifling, restless nights filled with the smell of dust and flowers through the open windows and with the myriad sounds of insects in the darkness. On the other hand, southern winters were comparatively brief and mild—too mild in the lower South to kill grass or cockroaches. Growing seasons for field crops, fruit, and vegetables were twice as long as in the extreme North.

Inevitably, the climate of the South affected the rhythm of life, slowed its beat. Farmers could hardly be blamed for taking naps on shady porches or under sheltering oaks at the height of the sun; nor city dwellers, for pausing frequently to sip iced drinks under the fans. To other Americans the southern temperament seemed relaxed and easy, representing a nearly tropical lassitude, but, like the southern thunderstorm or hurricane, capable of demonic rage or energy when aroused. The sun, rain, and wind of the South continued to make their peculiar imprint on the land and its inhabitants.

To outsiders the South of World War II was an archaic rural area. In fact, almost two-thirds of the entire population as late as 1940 was still defined by the federal census as being rural. The countryside was full of cotton, corn, hay, tobacco, or sedge fields, vast stretches of tangled woods, isolated dwellings, and occasional small towns and villages. It had many well-tilled farms set off by neat and commodious country homes. Here and there stood great old white-columned plantation houses, monuments of a legendary past. But compared with the tidy communities and farms of New England, the great-barn country of Pennsylvania, or the geometrically sectioned face of the Midwest, the rural South was irregular and unkempt, a bushy, weedy land of unpainted farmhouses, dog run cabins, sharecroppers' huts, tumbledown barns, and makeshift sheds. The presence of throngs of black field workers, of loitering white farmers in overalls and battered hats, of barefoot children white and black, and of mules instead of tractors at the plows gave an exotic appearance to the scene.

Such regional cities as Atlanta, Memphis, and Richmond were in many ways indistinguishable from cities elsewhere. They had moderately tall skyscrapers, apartment houses that substituted for homes, endless rows of close-packed and almost identical residences, and a constant snarl of automobile and pedestrian traffic and noise. Yet to persons accustomed to New York, Chicago, or Philadelphia, the southern cities were remarkably uncongested and casual, more like overgrown country towns than genuine urban centers.

The most noticeable difference between the southern people and those elsewhere was in the attitude of the white and black races toward each other. Despite the exodus by mid-century of millions of blacks, the South was still the home of two-thirds of all the nation's blacks. They made up more than a fourth of the entire southern population and in parts of the lower South, the Black Belt, they were a majority. Handicapped by an alien cultural origin and by slavery and discrimination, they formed a caste at the bottom of the regional social and economic scale. Racial segregation was grounded in local statutes —the so-called Jim Crow laws—as well as in seemingly immutable custom. Institutionally the color line was absolute. Black teachers taught black pupils; black ministers preached to black churches; black physicians treated black patients; black undertakers buried black corpses. In business and industry blacks got only those jobs disdained by whites; most working black women were servants in white homes. The behavior of individual southern whites toward the blacks varied from contempt and brutality to paternalism and indulgence. Unquestionably, many whites and blacks developed ties of honest affection in spite of the barriers. But all classes of whites were agreed that the blacks as a group must "stay in their place."

That the South was the poor cousin of the affluent American society was no mere figment of the southern imagination. As the most rural of American regions, it was obliged to sell the bulk of its natural resources to stoke the national industrial machine, while importing from the North most of its manufactured wares: automobiles, refrigerators, radios, and the like. Discriminatory rail rates until abolished in 1945 by the Interstate Commerce Commission favored established industries, most of which were outside the South, and played at least a minor role in perpetuating the regional imbalance. Economically, the South was as much a part of the colonial world as Ireland, Algeria, or Korea, in an arrangement not calculated to benefit the colonies. The per capita personal income of Florida, the richest but most non-southern of southern states, was 88 percent of the national figure; that of Mississippi, the poorest and most southern of southern states, was less than half the national figure. A survey taken in the late 1930s moved President Franklin D. Roosevelt to call the South the nation's "No. 1 economic problem." The warborn regional prosperity did not alter this unenviable ranking.

Southern politics operated to preserve the region's traditional interests and prejudices. Local politics took many forms. For example, in predominantly agricultural Mississippi a kind of Populist white democracy representing the hill country farmers contended for supremacy with the Bourbon bossism of the plantation Delta. Relatively industrialized North Carolina was a "progressive plutocracy" run by an "enlightened oligarchy." In history-conscious Virginia a seemingly invincible state organization gave the appearance of a political museum piece that performed with eighteenth-century grace but machine-age precision.[4]

In national as in state politics southern leaders espoused programs that were a blend of Populism, Progressivism, and Bourbonism (or agrarian radicalism, middle-class reformism, and economic conservatism). Captivated by the idealistic fervor of President Woodrow Wilson—the first southern-born chief executive in more than half a century—southerners formed the vital core of political support for his New Freedom. Panicked by the havoc of the Great Depression, they played a similar role in the early stages of President Roosevelt's New Deal, although from 1938 they led the opposition against an expansion of it. Traditionally quick on the military draw, they were the political vanguard of American participation in both world wars. Senator Carter Glass of Virginia seriously explained this regional military-patriotic impulse as being the result of "superior character and understanding of the problem."[5] Still, southern spokesmen generally were politically conservative, frequently even reactionary; they stood for reduced taxation, a balanced budget, and noninterference by the federal government in local problems, especially the race problem. Senator Harry Flood Byrd, political boss of Virginia, was the "watchdog" both of the United States Treasury and of southern "state rights."

Diversity in southern politics failed to destroy an even greater unity. Whether Populist, Progressive, or Bourbon, the vast majority of southern voters were Democrats. The Democratic primaries, which in most of the region were "lily white," closed to blacks, were in effect the final elections; in many states the Republican party did not bother to put up candidates. The elemental characteristics of southern politics through World War II were Democratic solidarity and white supremacy.

Southern religious life was almost as distinct from that of the rest of the nation as were its racial attitudes and its politics. Church membership was more common in the region than elsewhere, and it was overwhelmingly orthodox Protestant, heavily concentrated in the southern white and black branches of the Baptist church, the southern jurisdiction of the Methodist church, the southern Presbyterian church, the Churches of Christ, and the various Pentecostal and Holiness sects. The South was the nation's strongest center of biblical literalism, or fundamentalism, as it was named early in the twentieth century. Theologically, the region was indeed what Henry L. Mencken once called it in derision: the Bible Belt.

Regional religion showed little of the radicalism or reformism that leavened southern politics. The churches were primarily interested in saving souls for a life of eternal happiness in the beyond. Although they gave their blessing to the liberal political programs of the New Freedom and the New Deal, and although they did many philanthropic works, they did not embrace the Social Gospel as proclaimed by prominent theologians of the North. Southerners rejected the dream of human perfectibility and the promise of an earthly utopia. The leading character of Robert Penn Warren's novel *All the King's Men* spoke for the region in saying he had thoroughly understood the sinful nature of man since his childhood Sunday school training. Religion was the "mighty fortress of the status quo" in the South of World War II.[6]

Nothing reflected more sharply than formal education the contrast between the aspirations and the limitations of the region. By the turn of the twentieth century most southerners uncritically accepted the dogma that formal education was a panacea for the ills of society. Long before World War II the South was spending on its schools a higher proportion of its wealth than any other region. Yet its hope of coming educationally abreast of the rest of America remained unfulfilled. The South was too poor and had too many children for this to be possible. The average annual expenditure per pupil in its public schools in 1945 was only 53 percent of the national average. Southern schools at all levels still lagged seriously in teachers' salaries, training, and scholarship; in size and quality of libraries and laboratories; and in strength of curricula. Not a university within the former Confederate states ranked among the top twenty universities of the nation. Undaunted, the South was resolved to catch up.

The most acclaimed of southern cultural achievements was a body of imaginative literature produced in the Southern Renaissance of the quarter-century preceding World War II. It reached a peak in the Southern Gothic novels of William Faulkner of Mississippi, who in

1950 would receive the Nobel Prize for Literature. Faulkner exposed the most dreadful traits of the southern character, especially its bigotry and cruelty. Still, one could find in Faulkner an equally severe condemnation of northern materialism and commercialism, as well as a yearning for a way of life that reflected the nobler southern ideals. Nor did all southern literature run to Southern Gothic. An extraordinary group of writers and critics at Vanderbilt University remained traditionalists in their views of southern society and the southern past. Led by a poet who was also a distinguished professor of English, John Crowe Ransom, they embraced the New Criticism, a search through textual analysis for the intrinsic qualities of literature and life. Calling themselves The Fugitives they wrote urbane poetry contrasting the shortcomings of modern ways with the virtues of the old. Some of them joined a group of southern writers called The Agrarians to publish a volume of essays entitled *I'll Take My Stand* (1930), a manifesto against unrestrained industrialism and the American worship of progress.

That the romantic mode remained strong was evident also in Stark Young's *So Red the Rose* (1934) and in Margaret Mitchell's *Gone with the Wind* (1936), both calling up myths of the Old South and the Confederate Lost Cause. Eudora Welty of Mississippi avoided both romanticism and Southern Gothic. In *Delta Wedding* (1946) she described the Mississippi that Faulkner ignored: in Rubin's words, "a tidy, protected little world, in which people go about their affairs, living, marrying, getting children, diverting themselves, dying, all in a tranquil, pastoral fashion."[7] Southern writers regardless of genre laid unusual emphasis on the very points most emphasized in southern life: history, family, sense of place, race, religion, and the imperfectibility of man. Southern literature was a mirror of these institutions and ideas, often calling attention to them through exaggeration or distortion.

Southerners were unable to achieve in the fine arts a success comparable to that in literature. Just why this was so cannot be satisfactorily explained. In any case, painting, sculpture, and what may be called serious music had not affected the life of the Old South to the depth that oratory, journalism, and fiction had affected it; hence the painters, sculptors, and musicians of the modern South lacked the sort of regional artistic traditions that the contemporary writers drew upon. Although the architecture of the Old South was imaginative and resourceful, if not in the true sense original, that of the New South was largely dependent upon restorations or adaptations of earlier forms, or upon functional designs imported from the North. Southern drama came the nearest to rivaling southern literature in its vigor and originality. The affinity of the two art forms is obvious and perhaps explains the similarity of their appeals. The most regionally distinctive productions were the historical dramas written by the North Carolinian Paul Green for outdoor presentation at or near the sites of the actual events, accompanied by music, dancing, and offstage narration.

The South's relative lack of originality and distinctiveness in the classical art forms was in part balanced by its contributions in folk music. Early in the twentieth century, Negro spirituals, blues, and jazz began to be hailed as the freshest and most expressive types of American music. The Fisk University Jubilee Singers became famous for their performance of such spirituals as "Swing Low, Sweet Chariot"; William C. Handy's "Memphis Blues" and "St. Louis Blues" became national favorites; such black jazz musicians as pianist Ferdinand "Jelly Roll" Morton and cornetist Louis "Satchmo" Armstrong became legendary. White folk music was less acclaimed by critics, but in the form of hillbilly music it became immensely popular. The Grand Ole Opry in Nashville was its most publicized center. Uncle Dave Macon with his twanging banjo, Roy Acuff with his nasal rendition of "The Great Speckled Bird" or "The Wabash Cannonball," and dozens of other performers became national radio celebrities.

Southern homogeneity reflected also a bond of sympathies and customs that together heightened the regional sense of community. Because the area was only lightly affected by the waves of European immigration either before or after the Civil War, the population was longer settled than elsewhere in the country. Ties of blood were stronger in the South. Bemused outsiders said that, given time, any two southerners could establish kinship. Moreover, the South had a way of assimilating its relatively few newcomers and remaking them into southerners; in sectionalism as in religion the convert's zeal was the strongest of all. Historic sectional loyalties were stretched to include such modern activities as beauty contests and athletic events. Southerners were convinced that the South produced the nation's most beautiful and most lovable women. Students and alumni of southern colleges supported their athletic teams in intersectional rivalries with a spirit resembling that of Confederate patriotism. Indeed, they employed the very symbols of the Confederacy—Rebel flags, Rebel yells, and the music of "Dixie"—to cheer the efforts of their favorites.

The South kept its peculiarities of tone and taste. In spite of a generation of the crisp stage diction of both southern and nonsouthern radio announcers, southern speech remained as distinctive as ever. For example, southerners invariably said "y'all" instead of "all of you" when addressing more than one person. In spite of the exhortations of nutritionists, southern cuisine continued to feature hot biscuits, grainy corn bread, fried chicken and other fried meats, and vegetables cooked with salt pork. These were manifestations of what Grady McWhiney suggests as the sensually unique South, a region and a society engaging the human senses with a set of impulses and preferences of its own.[8]

Southerners still held to a cult of good manners and practiced a politeness that had waned in many other parts of the country. Women were still called ladies unless disqualified by their behavior. Men still rose to offer women seats on trolleys; women still accepted such offers without suspicions of condescension or exploitation. The ideal southerner conducted his everyday affairs with a due regard to the amenities. Even the southern poor, said Cash, demonstrated a level-eyed courtesy and ease of port presumably borrowed from their social betters.

Obviously the southern way represented a medley of beliefs and traits. In 1946 Norman Foerster, a northern-born scholar at the University of North Carolina, recorded his observations of southern distinctiveness in saying: "People of the region impress one at once with their different voices, different accent, their sense of manners, the courtesy that appears in all classes, their organic folksiness (as if all of one family), their awareness of the past as a force both hampering and helping."[9] In this "organic folksiness" lay the key to the southern character. David M. Potter interpreted the quality as a "folk culture" derived from the South's exceptionally long and intense experience as a rural society: a force that in part repudiated the mass culture of modern, urban, industrial America.[10] In retaining closer ties with nature the southern people retained closer ties with one another.

World War II released immense energies and kindled grand aspirations in the South. Prosperity whetted an insatiable appetite for goods and services; the burgeoning war factories promised to convert the South into an industrial empire. At the height of the conflict the national director of the Office of War Production, Donald M. Nelson, predicted that within the generation the region would become "the vanguard of world industrial progress."[11]

The war also challenged the region's traditional values, customs, and prejudices, especially in race relations. Southern blacks were significantly affected by the conflict. Following the example of northern blacks, they made tentative protests against the color barrier on public conveyances and in places of public accommodation. For the time being these efforts were futile. But black servicemen received pay and allowances equal to those of whites, and black civilians got employment and compensation on an unprecedented scale. A desire for better things stirred among the black rank and file. In the words of Howard W. Odum, "It was as if some universal message had come through to the great mass of Negroes, urging them to dream new dreams and to protest against the old order."[12] Vast changes were in store for the postwar South.

I.

The Postwar
Economic Drama

The southern economy during the postwar years fulfilled the hopes of those who had forecast a booming future for the region. Factories arose everywhere to take advantage of the South's raw materials, hungry markets, favorable tax laws, and cheap and plentiful labor. Cities tripled in population as millions of rural inhabitants thronged in from the farms and took jobs in trade and industry. Southern agriculture flourished through mechanization, crop diversification, and the merging of small holdings into giant commercial farms. The southern people as a whole enjoyed the greatest prosperity of the region's history. By the 1970s the South was aware of the darker aspects of industrialization and urbanization: overcrowding, traffic congestion, land despoliation, air and stream pollution, and depletion of resources. Moreover, the South still lagged behind many other parts of the nation in industrial and agricultural production and in wealth; it remained the seat of the nation's most widespread poverty. But these problems were subordinated to the southern resolve to enter the mainstream of American affluence.

In large measure the new regional prosperity was merely a part of the national prosperity of the times. The immediate impulse for industrial activity came from the conversion of war plants and their backlog of skilled and semiskilled workers to peacetime needs. The disposal at nominal cost of government establishments and machinery to private industry combined with the accumulated wartime savings and hunger for civilian goods to help keep the wheels of southern factories spinning. They now turned out such commodities as refrigerators, cultivators, air conditioners, and pleasure craft instead of guns, shells, airplane parts, and torpedo boats.

But new plants also sprang up across the South. Many of these were regionally owned and managed, but a large portion represented the shift of northern industry drawn south by the lure of lower expenses and increased profits. Regional employment, wages, and incomes remained almost as high as at wartime peaks; the streets of southern cities and towns milled with people eager to buy; stores, shops, and residences were better painted and in better repair than ever before; the inhabitants drove newer and larger automobiles and were more modishly dressed than before. Observers returning after a few years' absence invariably exclaimed about how the South had changed.

The growth of industry both in the South and in the rest of the nation drastically altered the nature of southern society as it encouraged a great migration from country to city. More than 100,000 blacks annually left the region altogether; other multitudes of rural folk of both races moved into the swiftly expanding cities of the South. Once-stagnant places such as Charleston, South Carolina; Wilmington, North Carolina; Alexandria, Virginia; and Augusta, Georgia, swelled in size and hummed with trade and industry. Greater Atlanta, as the commercial and transportation hub of the Southeast, rose in population from 438,000 in 1940 to almost 1.2 million thirty years later. Greater Houston, with nearly 1.7 million people in 1970, was the center of a southwestern domain of oil, agriculture, industry, and shipping. Other cities experienced comparable growth.

Southern governors, legislators, mayors, and members of industrial commissions and chambers of commerce worked as zealously as the southern Bourbon politicians of the late nineteenth century to attract outside capital and persuade national companies to establish branches in their areas. Influenced by a Mississippi program begun in the 1930s under the slogan Balance Agriculture with Industry, the other state governments began to offer inducements in the form of tax suspensions, free plant sites, special training programs, and rail and highway spur lines. Governor Luther H. Hodges of North Carolina set the pace in "selling" his state to industrialists and investors. During 1959 alone he traveled more than 67,000 miles in this effort, one spectacular venture being a trip to Europe with the North Carolina Trade and Industry Mission. Among the more imaginative North

Carolina measures for appealing to foreign capitalists was a booklet describing in German the state's industrial opportunities and bearing the captivating title, *Nordkarolina, Der "Tar Heel" Staat*. In 1970 the Georgia Department of Industry and Trade became so modern as to open a computer data bank with economic profiles of 600 Georgia communities. Industrial companies seeking plant sites were invited to submit lists of requirements, to which the computer replied with printouts describing the advantages of various locations.

A favorite device for attracting industry was the industrial park, a tract of land purchased by a local development corporation for lease on favorable terms to new factories. Georgia, with more than a hundred of these organizations in 1960, led the way; but perhaps the most noteworthy such development was the Research Triangle Park created in 1959 in North Carolina. This was a 5,200-acre plot approximately equidistant from Durham, Chapel Hill, and Raleigh. The trained staffs and research facilities of the universities located in these cities, Duke, North Carolina, and North Carolina State, helped to attract industries primarily concerned with research. By the 1970s the park had nineteen such industries, including a branch of International Business Machines making data communication terminals and computer components, the headquarters and research laboratory of pharmaceutical manufacturers Burroughs Wellcome Company, the Chemstrand research center of Monsanto Chemical Company, the main research center of the Federal Air Pollution Control Administration, and a major environmental health science complex of the United States Department of Health, Education and Welfare (HEW). Research Triangle Institute, a subsidiary of the fostering research foundation, was founded and administered by the three participating universities. It carried out research on contract in education, population and family planning, air pollution, medicinal chemistry, health care, traffic safety, and economic planning.

To overcome the handicaps of the archaic system of rural southern county governments in attempting to attract and develop industry, a group of Georgia planners in the 1950s devised the "local development district." A cluster of a dozen or more counties would band together to form a development district, which then set up its own planning staff to survey local resources, to recommend needed improvements in schools, hospitals, recreational facilities, and public utilities, to negotiate with national companies for the establishment of branch plants, and above all to acquire federal development grants; for "milking the feds" quickly became an art, especially through the influence of southerners holding strategic committee positions in Congress. Supported by the Nixon administration in the 1960s and 1970s, the concept of the rural development district spread to other southern states and to a number of nonsouthern states also.

Much of the southern industrial expansion was in the construction of small plants in towns and villages—a garment factory here, a shoe factory there, an electrical appliance factory somewhere else. The most notable increases occurred in the processing of the area's farm, forest, and mineral products—the same kinds of extractive industries that had traditionally distinguished the region. Significant gains also took place in the manufacture of such durable goods as furniture, machinery, primary metals, and transport equipment. The oldest of southern industries, tobacco processing and the production of cotton textiles, enjoyed the greatest boom in history, and the synthetic textile industry made even more spectacular growth.

The South continued to profit from the manufacture of military equipment and supplies and from the location of military posts within its borders as the Korean and Vietnam wars increased the demand for arms and troops. In 1969 the region had more than 1,200 plants turning out goods worth $1 million or more annually for national defense; together that year their shipments amounted to almost $33 billion. The Lockheed-Georgia Company, a division of the Lockheed Aircraft Corporation of California, employed almost 33,000 workers making planes for the government at its giant Marietta, Georgia, factory.

Southern climate and topography, along with southern political influence, caused a disproportionate number of training camps and National Aeronautics and Space Administration (NASA) installations to be placed in the region. In some rural parts the Army Post Exchange sales accounted for a great portion of the local county's entire volume of retail sales—in one Alabama county for about 60 percent. Among the southern space installations were the Marshall Space Center at Huntsville, Alabama; the manned spacecraft center at Houston; and the famed launching site at Cape Canaveral, Florida. Almost one quarter of all annual NASA expenditures were made in the southeastern states alone, amounting to more than $700 million.

Every southern state contributed to the region's industrial expansion. Mississippi by 1972 could point to 1,386 establishments that had come into existence since its program of attracting industry was launched. Textile and clothing mills operated in every state, though a majority of them remained concentrated in the Piedmont area stretching from Virginia into Georgia. Aluminum plants were located in Baton Rouge, Louisiana; Bauxite, Arkansas; Mobile and Sheffield, Alabama; and in Alcoa, Tennessee. Major refineries had been built in Baton Rouge, New Orleans, Lake Charles, Houston, Beaumont, Port Arthur, and Texas City. The entire stretch along the Mississippi River from New Orleans to Baton Rouge promised to become one unbroken chain of petrochemical and metals plants, and the Gulf Coast from Biloxi to Galveston could truly be called an industrial and agricultural empire. Florida's sunshine and beaches worked in combination with its low corporation tax to make it the second-fastest-growing state in the nation. Great companies such as General Electric, Glenn Martin Aircraft, United Aircraft, and Sperry Rand and Minneapolis-Honeywell instruments manufacturers located plants there. The invention of a successful method of concentrating frozen citrus juices added a new and lucrative industry to the peninsular state.[1]

The Tennessee Valley Authority (TVA) with its vast system of dams, reservoirs, and electrical generators helped to industrialize much of the upper South. By 1972 the Tennessee River was carrying annually 3.5 billion ton-miles of barge traffic and TVA was turning out about 10 percent of the nation's electricity—almost 20 million kilowatts, with plans for an additional 10 million. Scores of plants producing and processing chemicals, synthetic fibers, fertilizers, pulp and paper, meats, prepared feeds, and cement were scattered along the waterway, and close by were such government defense establishments as the Oak Ridge Atomic Laboratory in Tennessee; the Air Force's Redstone Arsenal at Huntsville, Alabama; an atomic energy plant at Paducah, Kentucky; and the Arnold Air Force Research Laboratory at Tullahoma, Tennessee. By 1970 a comparable government-sponsored navigational and hydroelectrical system—the McClellan-Kerr Arkansas River Navigation System—was in operation in the Southwest; four years later work was under way on a ship channel to connect the Tennessee River to the Gulf of Mexico through the Tombigbee River in Mississippi and Alabama.

Table 1

SOUTHERN MANUFACTURES 1939, 1972

	Number of establishments		Number of employees		Value of products 1939 (millions)	Value of shipments 1972[a] (millions)
	1972	% change since 1939	1972 (thousands)	% change since 1939		
Alabama	4,929	140	321	155	$575	$11,200
Arkansas	2,864	143	180	362	160	6,400
Florida	10,168	388	328	456	242	11,500
Georgia	7,540	139	463	172	677	18,300
Louisiana	3,646	96	181	126	565	11,500
Mississippi	2,680	107	198	296	175	6,400
N. Carolina	8,578	166	751	163	1,421	24,200
S. Carolina	3,691	177	345	159	398	10,700
Tennessee	5,680	148	467	224	728	16,200
Texas	14,235	165	740	403	1,530	36,800
Virginia	4,809	86	377	158	989	12,800
Total South	68,820	161	4,351	215	$7,460	$166,000
United States	316,336	72	18,919	112	$56,800	$752,800

Source: U.S., Bureau of the Census, *Statistical Abstract of the United States*, 1941 and 1974, pp. 879–80, 730–31.

Note: Figures are based on preliminary estimates for 1972 and have been rounded.

aValue of shipments is not the exact equivalent of value of products, but the two are corresponding items in their respective census listings.

Between 1939 and 1972 the South had added more than 40,000 new manufacturing establishments, many of them representing investments of hundreds of millions of dollars. It was now building plants worth $1 million or more at the rate of almost 300 a year. The region's proportional rate of industrial expansion throughout the entire period was significantly higher than that of the rest of the country. On the eve of World War II the South had produced, by value, less than 14 percent of the nation's annual manufactures; by the early 1970s it was turning out over 22 percent of them.

Southern industry and southern labor preserved a historic relationship of regional hostility to unions. In 1946 the proportion of the region's organized textile workers was less than one-third that of textile workers elsewhere. A determined effort during the late 1940s and early 1950s by the Congress of Industrial Organizations (CIO) to organize southern nonagricultural laborers failed signally. A perceptive observer commented that fifteen years of prosperity had made vast changes in the condition of the textile workers without altering their sense of class distinctions or their suspicion of labor organizers. The decade of the 1950s brought no radical change in this situation. In 1961 another analyst said the South remained a "new frontier" for organized labor, though eighty years had passed since the first organizing campaign in the region.[2]

This plaintive remark would still have been essentially justified in the 1970s. The proportion of organized nonfarm laborers in every former Confederate state was below the national average of 27.9 percent. Tennessee with 20.6 percent had the highest level in the South, while in a number of nonsouthern states union memberships ran as high as 36 to 43 percent. North Carolina with only 7.8 percent was the South's and the nation's lowest. Local industrial commissions and chambers of commerce still appealed to new industries with offers of a good supply of nonunionized labor.

The customary southern obstacles to the wholesale unionization of labor still prevailed. The suspicion and hostility of the public took political form in "right-to-work" laws that were enacted by ten southern state legislatures during the 1940s and 1950s and remained on the statute books in the subsequent years. These laws were designed to prevent the "closed shop" practice of requiring all workers in a factory to be members of the union if a majority voted in favor of unionization. A number of southern communities supplemented the right-to-work laws with local ordinances obliging union organizers to register and pay license fees. Many southern churches still looked upon unions as sources of mischief, unrest, and worldliness. A general atmosphere of disapproval in the southern society created among the workers a fear of retaliation and of the loss of jobs and security.

Resistance to organization remained strong among the workers themselves. Fond memories of paternalistic proprietors of the past lingered in the minds of many older laborers, while the younger ones tended to respond favorably to the "human relations" programs of the new management. A persistent individualism rendered impossible the delivery of bloc votes that was often achieved by the leaders of immigrant or ethnic groups in the North. Antiunion propaganda struck effectively at the national, regional, religious, racial, and family pride of a notoriously proud and conservative people. One caricature represented the union agent as a drooling apelike creature of Negroid features holding a carpetbag with a CIO label on it. The caption of the cartoon read, "I've come down here to organize you bastards."[3] Finally, the relatively great prosperity of the South during the entire post–World War II era tended to deter laborers from joining unions. For southern workers had always been fickle in their affections for unions, embracing them in lean years and shunning them in fat times.

Many signs pointed to increased unionization of southern workers in the future. The quickened pace of industrialization in the South seemed likely to have this effect, especially with the growing numbers of outsiders moving into the region to work in the industries and the tendency of southern branches of the national industrial corporations (usually representing the largest of the local factories) to adopt the company labor policy prevailing outside the South. Also, there was the ultimate prospect of the disappearance of the regional surplus of unskilled and semiskilled workers. But signs of imminent union triumph in southern labor had been seen for decades, always to recede into the indeterminate future when the time for fulfillment arrived. Progress in unionization was still outweighed by regional resistance.

By the early 1970s southerners were beginning to be aware that modern industry demands a price in more than money. Stream and air pollution were now serious problems in the region. The Tennessee River was tainted with mercury; environmental experts warned that without abatement of stream pollution the Gulf of Mexico could become a dead sea. The effects of strip-mining coal in Kentucky and other states were especially severe and highly visible. Kentucky author Harry M. Caudill wrote eloquent indictments of strip-mining in *Night Comes to the Cumberlands* (1963) and *My Land Is Dying* (1971). Ironically TVA, which had long been applauded as an agent of conservation, was now accused of being one of the chief offenders in its heavy purchase of strip-mined coal. Shortages of water, sewage disposal facilities, and public services in Florida provoked some of this state's leaders to complain of "people pollution." "Florida no longer desires to be known as the fastest-growing state," said the president of the Florida Senate. "We have our hands full now taking care of more than 6.8 million permanent residents."[4]

Public alarm caused a number of industrial projects in the South to be stopped: President Nixon halted construction on a barge canal designed to cut across the upper part of the Florida peninsula; plans for damming and dredging the Red River of Texas and Louisiana into a system of lakes comparable to the Arkansas River system fell dormant; plans were temporarily held up on a $200-million petrochemical plant supposed to be built on the South Carolina coast; a federal court ordered work to cease for a time on the Tennessee-Tombigbee Waterway.

By 1971 every southern state had a pollution control agency or board and required permits to construct and operate new, expanded, or modified industrial plants. They provided penalties in fines or damage suits for pollution, and they granted tax concessions on investments for installing devices to control the problem. Whether these measures would bring significant improvement remained to be seen. Frank E. Smith, director of TVA, identified the dilemma facing both his own organization and the region generally when he said, "We cannot achieve a satisfactory quality of life for all Americans, let alone the South, from our present inadequate economic base. To expand that base, we are going to have to continue to develop our natural resources. That, in turn, requires a completely candid appraisal of our environmental condition."[5]

More damaging to the economy than environmental pollution was the worldwide energy crisis of the 1970s. The South with its vast deposits of oil and coal would have had enough energy for itself, but these resources were largely controlled by the corporations exploiting them; and with the regional economy integrated as it was into the national economy, the South shared the burden of shortages with everyone else. In some ways it may have suffered more acutely than others. Southern factories were reported to be curtailing operations more sharply, possibly because they had expanded faster during the preceding years, or because of the decrease in military orders, or because many of the regional plants were mere branches of industries located mainly outside the South. At least temporarily, the energy shortage appeared to have killed the greatest industrial boom the South had ever known.

Stimulated by the insatiable demands of the growing factories and cities, regional agriculture after World War II prospered as never before. An observer in 1953 was at least partially justified in writing: "Agriculture's big story in the South will continue to expand and grow in magnitude. . . . [It] is no fairy tale either, for it is built on a more stable and solid foundation. Like Cinderella . . . , however, the agricultural South has kept her glass slippers, has found her prince charming and will live happily ever after!!!"[6]

Southern agriculture profited greatly from the adoption of effective measures for erosion control and from the application of improved fertilizers. The hilly and sandy nature of much of the region's soil made it highly vulnerable to erosion by the prevailing heavy rainfall. In addition, the cultivation of cotton and other crops in straight rows created innumerable ditches that drained off the topsoil and turned wide areas into gullied and useless wastes. The introduction of new crops and of the practices of contour plowing and terracing went far toward solving this problem. At the same time, the region's soil was enriched by the superior mineral and synthetic fertilizers that were developed in the state agricultural colleges and experiment stations and, especially, in the National Fertilizer Development Center of TVA at Muscle Shoals, Alabama.

The region's most important recent agricultural development—the increased investment in tree farming, cattle growing, and poultry culture—was in a sense a return to nature and to earlier ways of making a living in the South. Responding to the soaring demand for lumber and pulpwood, and aided by tax concessions, southern farmers now increasingly turned from tillage to tree farming. By the mid-1960s the region led the nation in the number and acreage of these establishments and was producing nearly one-third of the nation's lumber, including some of the finest of its hardwood and more than three-fifths of its pulpwood.

Grazing was even more widespread than tree farming. Awakening in the 1940s to the advantages of their long pasturage season, southern farmers began to shift from cotton to cattle production, a change greatly accelerated by the exodus of tenants and laborers from the farms. As the traveler of the 1970s rode north from New Orleans to Virginia, he saw about him vast stretches of green fields and grazing cattle, broken only by tracts of timber, where a few years before he would have seen cotton fields and pine barrens. More than 35 percent of the entire cropland of Virginia, Tennessee, Mississippi, Alabama, and Florida was in pasture, without counting the large areas of grassy woodland that provided additional grazing and forage. Smaller but significant proportions of the cropland of all other southern states were now in grass. The South's annual income from beef cattle multiplied five times in the years after World War II. It was now more than three times the regional income from cotton.

The growth of southern poultry farming was almost as spectacular as that of cattle raising. Influenced by studies published through the extension services of the state departments of agriculture, large numbers of southern farmers, and in some instances even physicians, lawyers, bankers, and college professors, turned to the commercial production of chickens. By the mid-1950s the southern uplands were filled with establishments featuring elongated buildings of metal, cement block, or wood sheltering hundreds or sometimes thousands of bright-feathered broilers or layers. Georgia, Arkansas, Alabama, and North Carolina led the South in the 1970s, producing almost 90 percent of the nation's broilers and over 40 percent of its eggs. Perhaps no one now would have repeated the exclamation uttered earlier by an Arkansas farmer who said: "Who'd a thought that a dad-burned chicken could scratch cotton off the land!"[7]

Paradoxically, southern agriculture was changed more radically than southern industry by mechanization. Before World War II most southern farms used men and mules as their primary sources of power. By the 1970s virtually all farms were wired with electricity and equipped with tractors. Approximately 96 percent of the area's cotton was now picked by mechanical pickers or strippers. Multiple-row plows and disk harrows cultivated most of the land; chemical sprays controlled weeds and insects; electric pumps supplied water; electric machines milked most of the cows; mechanical conveyors loaded trucks and lofts; combines and reapers harvested crops; and automatic feeders and push-button silos fed cattle. A great majority of the farm homes had television sets linking them to the outside world. The isolated, dirt-grubbing farmer had almost disappeared.

Through improved cultivation, fertilizers, and seed, southern farmers were able to increase significantly the yield of all kinds of crops. Despite government restrictions during most of the period on the growing of such venerable southern crops as tobacco and cotton, they remained a highly important part of the region's agriculture, though both now represented only a fraction of its total dollar value. The South still grew about 80 percent of the nation's cotton and almost all its tobacco. The bulk of the cotton now grew west of the Mississippi River; most of the tobacco grew in such states of the upper and border South as North Carolina, Virginia, and Kentucky. The region also grew almost 80 percent of the nation's rice, with Louisiana, Texas, and Arkansas the leading states in its production. Sugar continued to be the major crop of southern Louisiana and of the Lake Okeechobee area of Florida. Hogs, corn, hay, sorghum, peanuts, and an increasing variety of fruits and vegetables poured forth in abundance from southern farms. The nineteenth-century advocates of agricultural diversification in the South—such prominent publishers as J. D. B. DeBow of New Orleans and Henry W. Grady of Atlanta—would have marveled at the change.

The most significant new southern crop was soybeans. An important source of protein, they also provided fiber for the manufacture of synthetics, and their vines made nourishing forage and hay for livestock. The plant grew luxuriantly in the southern soil and climate; southern farmers also favored it because it required relatively little labor and was not subject to government acreage restrictions. Planted in rotation with rice, wheat, or corn, the beans replaced cotton in many parts of the region, especially in the Mississippi River Delta states of Arkansas, Tennessee, Mississippi, and Louisiana, where they now accounted for more than 40 percent of the entire area of harvested cropland. That the exotic soybean, Asiatic in origin, had been fully adopted by the South was obvious in the names given to the favorite strains grown here, including Davis, Lee, Jackson, and Rebel.

Ironically, the rise in southern agricultural production coincided with a steady decline in the farming population as the exodus of southerners from the farms to the cities and factories continued unabated. The lure of favorable wages, the promise of a richer or more exciting life, the mechanization of agriculture, and the conversion of land to uses requiring less labor all combined to hasten the flow of tenants and impecunious proprietors from the country into the teeming urban centers. The number of farms in the Confederate South shrank from almost 2.5 million in 1940 to fewer than 1 million in 1969. By 1970 only about 2.3 million persons in the South actually lived on farms, approximately 4.6 percent of the population. As the farmers gave up farming, many of them sold part or all of their land to the larger landowners, thus causing the average farm to more than double in size during the period. An ever-increasing proportion of the agricultural production of the South now came from large commercial farms, many of which would have stirred the envy of a pre–Civil War planter.

These developments brought vast changes in the quantity and nature of southern farm labor. More than a million families were displaced altogether during the twenty-four years after the war. Tenantry seemed on its way to extinction, along with the family-sized subsistence farm. By 1969 there were only 91,693 white tenant farmers and 16,863 black tenant farmers left in the region, or approximately 12 percent of the entire body of farmers. Aside from the remaining independent farmers, most southern farm workers were now wage earners operating the tractors and other machines that characterized the agriculture of the region. Exceeding 500,000 in numbers, these workers were largely unorganized and were unaffected by federal minimum wage laws. On the average, they received less than $1.40 an hour. Their lot represented the modern sequel of plantation slavery.

The operations of one of Mississippi's greatest plantations, the Delta and Pine Land Company of Scott, Mississippi, offered dramatic evidence of the forces shaping agriculture in the modern South. The plantation in the 1930s had 16,000 acres in cotton and employed 1,200 tenant families that furnished about 5,000 laborers. In 1969 the company had 25,000 acres in cultivation: 7,200 acres in cotton, the rest in

Table 2

Southern Agriculture

	Number of farms 1969 (thousands)	% change since 1940	Population on farms 1970 (thousands)	% change since 1940	Value of produce sold 1969 (millions)	% change since 1940	Value of produce sold 1973ᵃ (millions)	% change since 1940
Alabama	72	−69	160	−88	$670	+670	$1,283	+1,374
Arkansas	60	−72	174	−84	973	+600	2,143	+1,441
Florida	36	−42	73	−76	1,132	+875	1,868	+1,510
Georgia	67	−69	172	−87	1,040	+627	1,929	+1,249
Louisiana	42	−72	114	−87	496	+428	1,166	+1,140
Mississippi	73	−75	210	−85	685	+552	1,528	+1,355
N. Carolina	119	−57	375	−77	1,195	+500	2,277	+1,044
S. Carolina	40	−71	113	−88	362	+266	747	+655
Tennessee	121	−51	317	−75	623	+391	1,102	+768
Texas	214	−49	386	−82	3,293	+546	5,551	+988
Virginia	65	−63	193	−80	570	+363	879	+615
Total South	909	−63	2,284	−83	$11,039	+534	$20,473	+1,075
United States	2,730	−55	8,282	−73	$45,609	+444	$83,450	+896

Source: U.S., Bureau of the Census, *Sixteenth Census of the United States, 1940: Agriculture*, vol. 1, pts. 3–5 and *Population: Characteristics of the Population*, pts. 1–7; *Census of Agriculture, 1969*, volumes for individual states; *Statistical Abstract of the United States, 1974*, p. 601.
ᵃEstimate.

pasture, soybeans, rice, silage corn, green beans, and miscellaneous other crops. There were 3,200 head of cattle. The agricultural machinery included 150 tractors, 9 combines, 31 mechanical cotton pickers, most of them rented, and a variety of additional equipment. The entire working force was 510; and not a tenant remained.[8] The most historic and venerable form of southern agriculture, the plantation, seemed ordained to outlast all others.

In 1973 the agricultural yield of the former Confederate states brought a sum estimated at almost $20.5 billion, more than eleven times that of 1940. During the intervening period the South's share of the country's annual farm production rose from about 20 percent to about 25 percent. The role of southern farming seemed destined to grow even greater as the worldwide threat of famine and the American energy shortage combined to enhance the importance of all American agriculture.

Table 3

MISSISSIPPI AGRICULTURE 1940, 1969

	1940	1969	% change
Number of farms	291,092	72,577	− 75
Number of farms, 1,000 acres or more	1,062	2,758	+160
Number of farms, 500 to 1,000 acres	2,420	3,773	+ 56
Average farm acreage	65.8	221	+236
Number of persons living on farms	1,399,884	210,042[a]	− 85
Percentage of population on farms	64.1	9.5[a]	− 85
Number of tenant farms	192,819	6,580	− 97
Percentage of black tenant farmers	70	40	− 43

Source: U.S., Bureau of the Census, *Statistical Abstract of the United States,* 1943, p. 574; *Sixteenth Census of the United States, 1940: Characteristics of the Population,* pt. 4; *Census of Agriculture, 1969,* vol. i, pt. 33; *Census of Population: Characteristics of the Population,* vol. 1, pt. 26, p. 151.
[a]Figure for 1970.

The postwar expansion of southern agriculture along with the immense gains in southern industry formed the base for a continuous and unprecedented regional prosperity. Various other means of producing or attracting wealth augmented the primary sources. The tourist industry was an outstanding example of a secondary but important supplement to the sectional income. Drawn south by any number of attractions—the mildness of the climate, the beauty of the landscape and beaches, the historic sites and houses, the glamorously staged intersectional athletic contests, or the simple pleasures of fishing or relaxing—millions of northern visitors yearly spent money in the area. Billions of tourist dollars flowed into the tills of southern motels, gasoline stations, restaurants, entertainment and recreation establishments, curio shops, and stores. Every southern state maintained a system of parks with living accommodations designed, in part, to attract out-of-state visitors and cash. A combination of favorable location, spectacular scenery, and skilled management and advertising caused Kentucky's parks to be especially successful in this enterprise. Florida's image as a tropical paradise made it the tourist mecca of the South. The Florida Department of Commerce reported that tourists spent more than $3.6 billion in that state during the single year 1970.

Sales of agricultural produce and employment in industry and the various trades and services ran high for more than a quarter-century after World War II. The wages of southern workers rose proportionally nearer and nearer the national wage level; a combination of good prices and government subsidies kept the farmers' returns favorable. The gap between the per capita personal income of the South and that of the nation generally continued to narrow. In 1959 the southern per capita personal income, excluding Texas and Oklahoma, was 69.1 percent of the national level; in 1963 it was 73 percent; in 1972 it was 80 percent. The per capita personal income in Texas was now 89 percent of the national figure; in Oklahoma it was 85 percent.

Yet despite the undeniable gains of the South, it remained a poor cousin of the affluent American society. It still had a significantly higher proportion than the rest of the nation of families living in poverty and a significantly lower proportion of families living in abundance. With more than 20 percent of the nation's population, eleven states of the Southeast possessed less than 15 percent of the nation's long-term savings and less than 13 percent of its bank deposits. The per capita personal income in the southeastern states in 1972 was $745 below the national level; the southeastern figure was the lowest of all the major United States regions; it was $1,245 below that of the richest United States region, a group of states in the Northeast. The per capita personal income of the citizens of Florida, the South's richest state, was $114 below the national figure and almost $1,000 below that of Connecticut, the nation's richest state. The annual income of the average citizen of Mississippi, the South's and the nation's poorest state, was $1,355 below the national average and more than $2,000 below that of Connecticut. One could of course live in the South less expensively than elsewhere; thus in a sense the region's lower living costs offset lower income. This was partly the result of the milder climate, which required less fuel and clothing and made easier the growing of food. But the lower living costs were the result also of the same conditions that made them possible in rural Mexico or other poverty-stricken areas—the depressed wages and marginal living standards of much of the population.

Table 4

SOUTHERN PER CAPITA PERSONAL INCOME 1940, 1972

	1940	1972	% change
Alabama	$282	$3,420	1,113
Arkansas	256	3,365	1,214
Florida	513	4,378	753
Georgia	340	3,909	1,050
Louisiana	363	3,543	876
Mississippi	218	3,137	1,339
N. Carolina	328	3,799	1,058
S. Carolina	307	3,477	1,033
Tennessee	339	3,671	983
Texas	432	3,991	824
Virginia	466	4,298	822
United States	$595	$4,492	655

Source: U.S., Department of Commerce, *Personal Income by States: A Supplement to the Survey of Current Business*, p. 142; *Survey of Current Business*, 1974, p. 17.

Certain persistent realities accounted for the stubborn economic disparities between the South and the more opulent sections of the country. The South in the 1970s was still less industrialized than the major industrial areas of the Northeast, Midwest, and Pacific Coast. The region's postwar industrial percentage gains were exceptionally high partly because they were measured against exceptionally low initial figures. Nor did the growth of southern industry right its imbalances. It was still primarily extractive, producing minerals, fibers, and fuel for the national industrial machine, while the bulk of the nation's steel, plastics, automobiles, aircraft, radios, televisions, phonographs, and machine tools were made elsewhere. Full diversification of regional industry remained an elusive goal; 38 per cent of all manufacturing jobs in 1970 were still in textiles, apparel, and food processing. In addition to these industries, the most important by volume and value of their products were petroleum and other minerals and lumber. Regional industry was still characterized by relatively low margins of profit, low payrolls, and low capital investment.

The blending of the southern economy into the national economy tended to increase the colonial nature of southern industry. The largest factories built in the South, since World War II as before, were owned by the great nationwide corporations with headquarters, managers, and a disproportionate number of stockholders outside the region. (Despite recent improvement, in 1971 only 9.4 percent of the shares on the New York Stock Exchange—the country's largest—and only 12.2 percent of the shares on all other markets were owned by residents of the former Confederate states.)[9] Inexorably the mineral rights and timber lands of the South were being engrossed by these nonsouthern companies.

For more than a decade after World War II the South lost great numbers of its most energetic, and often best-educated, youth in a steady migration to the more prosperous parts of the nation. While western Europe complained of a "brain drain" to the United States, the South suffered both a "brain drain" and a far heavier "brawn drain" to the North and Far West. But a significant reverse trend began in the mid-1950s and continued throughout the following decade and into the 1970s. The number of outsiders coming into the South began to equal, and then to exceed, the number leaving. Although large numbers of southerners, especially blacks, continued to leave the South, the region between 1955 and 1960 received about 55,000 more migrants than it lost; during the decade of the 1960s it made through migration a net gain of better than 400,000. A large proportion of the newcomers were professionally or technically trained persons coming to work in the area's growing factories, arsenals, or space installations. This change in the flow of population was perhaps the strongest indication of the region's increasing economic vigor.

In agriculture much of the region's soil remained "mediocre in quality, highly erosive under intensive cultivation, and badly damaged by past experience."[10] The South generally produced less per acre of a given crop such as corn, wheat, or soybeans than did other major farming areas. These agricultural shortcomings united with the industrial disadvantages of the region to keep the South relatively poor. But southern spokesmen were optimistic. With their eyes on the rising figures of production and income, they foresaw a South of plenty.

II.

The Challenge to Racial Inequality

The black portion of the southern society during the quarter-century following World War II underwent the most striking changes experienced by the race in America since the Civil War and Reconstruction. They were the principal actors in a second Reconstruction, which, if less dramatic than the first, promised a more lasting result. Through federal authority and coercion, through the exertions of white and black leaders and the resoluteness of the black masses, and finally through the efforts and understanding of a significant minority of the southern white community, southern blacks gained full citizenship, at least in a legal sense. When near the end of this quest the outstanding black leader of the movement became a martyr to his cause, he could die with a vision of its fulfillment before his eyes.

Southern blacks had at first little reason to rejoice over the remarkable postwar developments in the regional economy. They shared but little of the new prosperity; more often than not they were victims rather than beneficiaries of economic and technological advance. This was true throughout the rest of the nation also, but in the South it was more pronounced than elsewhere. Writing in 1951 a black journalist invited American whites to observe how rigidly and shamefully Negroes in the United States were treated economically; he accurately accused the white masters of the business world of restricting blacks to the most menial and the most arduous work.

Such indictments were in harmony with the statistics of the federal census, which showed that in 1949 the median income of southern blacks fourteen years old and older was only about 49 percent as high as that of southern whites. Most of the few prosperous blacks got their earnings from providing segregated communities with funerals, medical care, and insurance. "The color occupational system," reported a black economist, "remains entrenched and unchallenged in the region save in a few outstanding instances."[1] The warborn hopes of black leaders and the inchoate dreams of the black masses seemed idle indeed as the decade of the 1950s began.

Every southern city or town had its black slums, and the region's black sharecroppers and farm hands were in many respects worse off than their slave ancestors had been. Nor did the expanding industries of the region offer a ready escape, for they hired blacks as menials only. During the decade of the 1940s the South lost about 2 million of its blacks as they joined the trek of other southerners seeking a better life through employment in the factories of the North and West.

During the years immediately after World War II the South made a number of token improvements in its treatment of blacks. Tennessee and South Carolina joined North Carolina, Georgia, Florida, and Louisiana in the group of southern states that no longer required a poll tax. North Carolina in 1952 suppressed the activities of the local Ku Klux Klan. Various cities appointed a few blacks to their police forces. The number of black voters increased gradually and the South made significant efforts to improve the black public schools. Yet southern blacks found themselves in virtually the same position they had been in before the war. They were still politically impotent and, except in menial relationships, were totally segregated by law and custom from the white population. The black masses were still a caste marked by ignorance and poverty.

But forces were astir to alter these conditions. This movement began among black leaders and white liberals outside the South, and it received vital support from the federal government. Activated by the fear that racial discrimination in the United States gave an advantage to Communist enemies in the Cold War, by the need to gain black votes in the North, and by a genuine desire to promote equality, the Harry S. Truman administration launched a thoroughgoing assault on southern racial practices.

In 1947 the president appointed the Committee on Civil Rights to survey the conditions of Negro life and recommend measures for improving them. The committee was made up of fifteen persons prominent in the fields of law, labor, education, and industry; Charles E. Wilson, president of General Electric Company, was chairman. The group included two liberal southerners, Mrs. M. E. Tilly of Atlanta, an official in the Women's Society of Christian Service of the Methodist church, and President Frank P. Graham of the University of North Carolina. The report of the committee, published in October of the year of its appointment, was a sweeping denunciation of all governmental and of some private sanctions of racial discrimination or segregation. Among its thirty-five recommendations were federal laws to abolish segregation in the armed services, in public conveyances, in public schools, in housing, and in places of public accommodation; a federal antilynching measure; the establishment of a permanent commission on fair employment practices with the power to penalize employers refusing to hire blacks who were equally qualified with whites; an anti–poll tax law; and a statute protecting the right of all qualified persons to participate in federal primaries and elections.

The committee repudiated the concept of "separate but equal" services, which since the United States Supreme Court decision *Plessy* v. *Ferguson* (1896) had been the legal shibboleth behind regional laws and customs of racial segregation. "No argument or rationalization can alter this basic fact," said the report; "a law which forbids a group of American citizens to associate with other citizens in the ordinary course of daily living creates inequality by imposing a caste status on the minority group." The committee urged the use of coercion, where necessary, to enforce its recommendations. "It is sound policy," said the report, "to use the idealism and prestige of the whole people to check the wayward tendencies of a part of them." To put into effect the objectives of the report, its authors recommended that federal funds be denied to any public or private agency practicing racial discrimination and that appropriate federal commissions be created to search out violations of the civil rights of blacks.[2]

President Truman greeted the report as "an American Charter of human freedom," and in July 1948 he issued an executive order banning racial segregation in all federal agencies, including the armed services. This action brought sharp changes within the South, especially in southern military installations, and it caused widespread grumbling among the white population of the region. But no appreciable opposition arose, because the move did not seriously challenge racial segregation in the everyday life of the area; it hardly touched the color line. In keeping with the committee's recommendations, President Truman in 1948 asked Congress to create the Fair Employment Practice Commission, to enact anti–poll tax and antilynching statutes, and to prohibit the enforcement of segregation on interstate railway and bus lines by the companies themselves. These recommendations genuinely threatened the fundamental racial practices of the South, and they provoked dismay among virtually all of the region's white population. The result was a serious southern political revolt and the formation of a southern opposition in Congress that doomed the measures to defeat. President Truman largely failed in his campaign for civil rights.

But another branch of the federal government was by now beginning to take steps in behalf of the blacks. This was the United States Supreme Court. Even before World War II this tribunal had made an initial move against the "separate but equal" principle as applied to segregation in educational institutions. In 1938 it ruled that in failing to provide a law school for blacks the state of Missouri was in violation of the Fourteenth Amendment to the United States Constitution, in spite of a state provision to pay their tuition in law schools elsewhere. Missouri now opened its law school to blacks, and ten years later by a similar decision of the Court, Oklahoma was obliged to follow suit.

Alarmed by these rulings, the various southern states attempted to circumvent their effect by hastily establishing separate professional schools for black students. These efforts soon collapsed. The schools were usually absurd affairs with virtually no students enrolled and no regular faculties of their own. Kentucky's black law school in 1949 had one student, taught by seven state university professors who made a weekly journey of twenty-five miles to meet his needs. The next year the United States Supreme Court in the case of *Sweatt* v. *Painter* ended this sort of travesty by ordering the state of Texas to admit blacks to the university law school. In grounding this ruling on the argument that a separate school exclusively for blacks was necessarily inferior to the established institution, the Court clearly foreshadowed coming developments in its assault on racial segregation.

Responding to these judicial trends, a number of previously white state universities now opened the doors of their professional schools to black applicants. One by one other southern state universities were forced to do so under specific court orders. In 1950 more than two hundred black students were enrolled in twenty-one graduate and professional schools in eleven of the seventeen states that had once barred them. The border states, where the black population was relatively small, took the lead in this movement. Kentucky altered its laws so as to permit the trustees of its institutions of higher learning to decide whether or not to admit blacks to their undergraduate programs. A number of the state's colleges, including the University of Louisville, the Southern Baptist Theological Seminary in Louisville, and Berea— the only southern college that had admitted black students before the Civil War—now did so. The University of Louisville took the additional step of abolishing its separate branch for blacks. By 1953 only five state universities of the Deep South remained completely white.

Meanwhile, changes began to occur in the lower schools. Spurred by the threat of federal court action, and by a sense of fairness on the part of certain responsible white citizens, the southern states undertook to bring their black public schools up to the level of the white schools in physical plants and teachers' salaries. In other words, southerners belatedly set about to make black schools equal as well as separate. Governor James F. Byrnes of South Carolina spoke for at least a limited number of concerned southern whites when in 1951 he said: "It is our duty to provide for the races substantial equality in school facilities. We should do it because it is right. For me that is sufficient reason."[3] In view of the relative poverty of the southern population, the disproportionately large number of children to be educated, and the high ratio of black to white students in the schools, the states of the region made a truly remarkable effort to equalize the two systems. By 1954 the black schools in the South generally were receiving approximately three-fourths as much money per pupil per year as were the white schools. The pattern varied sharply from state to state; those of more wealth and fewer black pupils presented a better record than their poorer neighbors of heavier black populations. In North Carolina, for example, black pupils were actually being favored somewhat in the distribution of funds, but in Mississippi the expenditure per black pupil was still only about one-fourth that for the white pupils.

Under any circumstances, these efforts to stop the drive for the admission of blacks to the previously white schools were probably doomed to fail. Late and erratic as the efforts were, they had no effect whatever in deterring the advocates of desegregation, who had already begun to take strong measures to accomplish their object. Encouraged by success in opening the state universities to black students, the National Association for the Advancement of Colored People (NAACP) in 1951 brought suit in South Carolina, and the next year in Virginia, to force the admission of black pupils into the white schools of the two states. After the lower federal courts upheld the school segregation laws of the states involved, the cases were appealed to the United States Supreme Court where they were joined with similar cases that had arisen in Kansas and Delaware. The decision, issued in May 1954, was given the title of the first of the suits that had reached the Court—*Oliver Brown et al. v. Board of Education of Topeka, Kansas.*

The *Brown* decision has been called the most momentous judicial decision of the century; it may ultimately be considered the most momentous judicial decision of the nation's entire history. Refusing to "turn the clock back" to the time of the adoption of the Fourteenth Amendment or of the decision *Plessy* v. *Ferguson,* the Court instead addressed itself to the question of public education "in the light of its full development and its present place in American life throughout the Nation." Relying upon evidence offered by sociologists and psychologists, the high tribunal concluded that even where physical facilities and all other tangible factors in the schools were equal, segregation—especially segregation upheld by law—deprives the children of the minority group of equal educational opportunities; that it inflicts upon them an abiding feeling of inferiority. Therefore, said the Court, the doctrine of "separate but equal" facilities is no longer valid, because separate educational facilities are "inherently unequal." Laws requiring the segregation of pupils by race are a deprivation of the equal protection guaranteed by the Fourteenth Amendment.[4]

Regional spokesmen greeted the *Brown* decision with mixed emotions. In view of the furor that was to come, a number of southern political leaders were admirably restrained in their announcements. Governor Thomas B. Stanley of Virginia said he believed the state would be able to find solutions acceptable both to the Court and to the citizens of the state. Governor Leroy Collins of Florida expressed the hope of being able to preserve segregation in the schools of his state, but he asked his constituents to practice Christian tolerance and to observe the law. Other political figures, however, issued ominous statements of disapproval, statements that more accurately reflected the mood of the southern majority. Senator Richard B. Russell of Georgia condemned the Court's decision as "a flagrant abuse of judicial power"; Senator Harry F. Byrd of Virginia called it a serious blow against the "rights of the states." Senator James O. Eastland of Mississippi predicted southern defiance and victory.[5]

The significance of the decision probably was not at once understood by the masses of southern blacks, who initially may have been indifferent to it. But the leaders of the race were jubilant. The black press hailed the ruling as the greatest victory for the Negro people since the Emancipation Proclamation. Mary McLeod Bethune, a famous black educator and pioneer in the struggle for improved conditions of life among her race, said: "Let all the people praise the Lord."[6]

One reason for the measure of restraint at first shown by the southern white population was that the Court's ruling had no immediate effect on the region's schools. They remained segregated. Taking cognizance that the decision marked a reversal of more than half a century of judicial precedent, and that a sudden and wholesale mixing of the races in the schools of the Deep South threatened to create social revolution and possibly violence, the Court was circumspect in offering a formula for carrying out its edict. But in May 1955, after inviting and receiving opinions from the attorney general of the United States and from the attorneys general of the several states where segregation was still upheld by local law, the high court issued such a plan. The plan itself was restrained. It recognized the wide differences in circumstances within the region affected by the decision, and for the purpose of appraising local conditions and putting the ruling into effect it remanded the specific cases to the lower federal courts where they had originated. These courts were to be guided by equitable principles, flexibility, and concern for both public and private interests. They were to require a prompt and reasonable start toward compliance with the *Brown* ruling, and they were to see that progress toward the desegregation of the schools occurred "with all deliberate speed."[7]

The Court's formula of "deliberate speed" drew expressions of relief from a number of southern political leaders and journalists. But even deliberate speed was too fast for most southern whites. Mississippi Congressman John Bell Williams named the day of the *Brown* decision Black Monday. Judge Thomas P. Brady of the circuit court of the fourteenth district, also a Mississippian, used this epithet as the title of a book on the evils of desegregation. The South would not tolerate this attempt to mongrelize its children, he said. A popular resistance movement began to form; the moribund Ku Klux Klan revived.

Far more significant than the upsurge of the Klan was the creation of a new organization called the Citizens' Councils of America. It was founded in Indianola, Mississippi, by Robert D. Patterson, a Delta plantation manager. Patterson was an intense man of thirty-two, who had once been captain of the Mississippi State College football team. His determination to prevent the desegregation of the schools was summed up in the statement: "There won't be any integration in Mississippi. Not now, not 100 years from now, maybe not 6,000 years from now—maybe never."[8] Soon Patterson's zeal was supplemented by the organizational and editorial skill of William J. Simmons of Jackson, who had been educated at Millsaps College in Jackson, at Toule, France, and at the Sorbonne. Simmons became the editor of the Citizens' Councils' monthly publication. By astutely disassociating his organization from the Ku Klux Klan, by renouncing violence, and by promising to abort desegregation through peaceful and lawful means, Simmons appealed to the most respectable element of southern society, including attorneys, bankers, businessmen, and planters. Within a little over a year the Councils' Mississippi membership grew from 14 to an estimated 60,000. Spreading rapidly into all the southern states, the Councils soon claimed a total membership of more than 300,000.[9]

This swelling of popular resentment among the white majority was not ignored by the region's political spokesmen. Led by Senator Harry F. Byrd of Virginia, a group of nineteen United States senators and eighty-one United States representatives from the eleven former Confederate states in March 1956 issued a manifesto against the *Brown* decision. In order to avoid embarrassment, Senate Majority Leader Lyndon B. Johnson and Speaker of the House Sam Rayburn, both of Texas, were not asked to sign the document; the liberal senators from Tennessee, Estes Kefauver and Albert Gore, declined invitations to do so. The manifesto accused the Supreme Court of subverting the Constitution; it pledged the signers to use all lawful means to gain a reversal of the decision and to prevent its enforcement.

The activities of the Citizens' Councils, the rhetoric of southern senators and congressmen, and the enforcement of desegregation in selected places around the borders of the South combined to harden the attitude of southern state political leaders. Moderate governors such as James P. Coleman of Mississippi, who had called for "cool thinking" on racial issues and warned against letting hotheads carry the state "beyond the point of no return," James Folsom of Alabama, and Earl Long of Louisiana were succeeded by such unrestrained critics of the *Brown* decision as Governor Ross Barnett of Mississippi (elected 1956), Governor John Patterson of Alabama (elected 1958), and Governor Jimmie Davis of Louisiana (elected 1960). Segregationist Governor Herman Talmadge of Georgia was followed in office by Marvin Griffin, former state attorney general, who was fully as vehement as Talmadge in racial matters. In other instances, leaders who were at first cautious in their views toward desegregation later turned into bitter opponents of change. Governor Stanley of Virginia, for example, who at first had indicated a qualified endorsement of the Court's decision, now took a stand against it. Governor Orval Faubus of Arkansas at one time expressed acceptance of the ruling, but later he became a symbol of defiance.

Virginia took the lead in designing a program of "massive resistance" to desegregation. Fiery editorials in the *Richmond News Leader* urged abandonment of the public schools in preference to acceptance of racial integration. Senator Harry F. Byrd, acting upon long-held convictions of state rights and white supremacy, dictated the state's policies of opposition. In the winter of 1956 the Virginia General Assembly drew upon the writings of Jefferson, Madison, Calhoun, and other famed political theorists of earlier days in adopting resolutions empowering state authorities to "interpose" themselves between the federal government and the schools in order to preserve racial segregation. Five other states—Alabama, Georgia, South Carolina, Mississippi, and Louisiana—adopted similar resolutions. The Virginia lawmakers supplemented their interposition resolutions with legislation that repealed the state's compulsory education laws, withheld state funds from any school district in which a black pupil was admitted to a white school, created a special commission for the assignment of pupils to specific schools, and provided for state tuition grants to be paid to the parents of children who were obliged to attend private schools because of the closing of their public schools.

Other states adopted programs similar to Virginia's: Florida, Georgia, Louisiana, Mississippi, North Carolina, South Carolina, and Arkansas all enacted legislation that could be used to close integrated schools either by state or local action. Some of the states also approved plans for the ostensible transfer of public schools to private operation in order to avoid desegregation. Liberal thinkers were most disappointed in the actions of North Carolina, which for years had posed as an example of racial harmony, and had been called by V. O. Key the "living answer to the riddle of race." But in the civil rights contest those portions of the state with a heavy black population proved to be quite similar in outlook to other Black Belt areas of the South. Indeed, North Carolina lagged behind various other border states in adopting measures of compliance, and a congressional investigation in the 1960s revealed that North Carolina now had more dues-paying members of the Ku Klux Klan than any other state.

Meanwhile, in the fall of 1956 a few public schools in Kentucky, Tennessee, Arkansas, and Texas moved to admit black pupils under federal court orders. A mob gathered and violence broke out at Clinton, Tennessee, after a segregationist agitator from New Jersey appeared on the scene; similar events occurred at Clay and Sturgis, Kentucky, and at Mansfield, Texas. Governors Frank Clement of Tennessee and Albert B. Chandler of Kentucky suppressed the unruliness in their states and enforced desegregation with state police and national guardsmen, but Governor Allan Shivers of Texas invoked his police power to avoid violence by delaying desegregation for a year. Other disturbances occurred in North Carolina and at Nashville, Tennessee, in the wake of the initial outbreaks. In spite of these episodes, a limited amount of desegregation was now accomplished with a limited amount of trouble.

The next autumn desegregation of Little Rock's public schools brought increased violence and a tense confrontation of state and national authorities. When the city school board attempted to put into effect its court-ordered plan for gradual desegregation, Governor Faubus abandoned his earlier acquiescence and adopted the tactics used successfully the previous year by Governor Shivers of Texas: the prevention of violence by the prevention of desegregation. Faubus stationed Arkansas national guardsmen at the schoolhouse to turn away the nine black enrollees and their escort of federal marshals. Mayor

Woodrow Wilson Mann of Little Rock accused Faubus of calling out the guard to "put down trouble where none existed. If any racial trouble does develop, the trouble rests squarely on the doorstep of the governor's mansion."[10] Mobs now gathered and fighting broke out as the school board undertook to comply with a court order to disregard the troops and admit the black pupils over the governor's objection. Eventually and reluctantly President Dwight D. Eisenhower ordered the Arkansas National Guard into federal service and sent a detachment of federal troops to enforce the court's ruling. The Little Rock imbroglio was an ominous harbinger of the difficulties of desegregation in the Deep South.[11]

Acting under instructions from the Supreme Court, the lower federal courts of the southern districts moved inexorably if often grudgingly to dismantle the barrier of laws and regulations designed to preserve dual school systems in the South. One after another the restrictions were held to be unconstitutional and the local school boards were ordered, under penalty of contempt of court, to admit blacks to previously white schools.

The courts were unable, however, to prevent determined state and local authorities from setting in motion the machinery of opposition. In no case did the entire school system of a state close down, though strong efforts to bring this about were made in the legislatures of Georgia, South Carolina, Florida, Mississippi, and Louisiana. But a number of individual schools and school districts were temporarily closed in keeping with the recently enacted legislation authorizing such procedures.

The first major school closing was at Little Rock. Stung by the federal action of the previous year and by the sight of armed soldiers escorting black pupils into the schools, Governor Faubus in September 1958 issued a proclamation closing the city's four high schools in order to prevent violence, as he said, and to preserve the peace of the community. The schools remained idle throughout the school year 1958–1959. A majority of the white pupils attended schools operated by the hastily chartered Little Rock Private School Corporation in an assortment of buildings, including churches and warehouses; most of the black pupils were without schools. In the summer a special federal court declared invalid the state law authorizing the closing of the schools; the following autumn the Eighth Federal Circuit Court of Appeals issued a restraining order against the Little Rock Private School Corporation on the ground that it was a subterfuge for the circumvention of desegregation. The public schools then reopened with a token number of black pupils enrolled in the previously white institutions.

Individual schools in various southern states were temporarily closed either by executive proclamation or by action of the local authorities. In shutting down the seven high schools of Norfolk in the fall of 1958, Virginia Governor Lindsay Almond called the Supreme Court's rejection of evasive state schemes "the most far-reaching and devastating blow ever to bludgeon the reserved powers of the states of this union." He then announced, "I will never voluntarily yield to that which I am unalterably convinced will destroy our public school system."[12] In most instances the schools were reopened under court order within a few weeks or months, with the black litigants enrolled.[13]

The most notorious episode of school closing occurred in Prince Edward County, Virginia, whose school board had been one of the parties in the original desegregation cases involved in the *Brown* decision. In 1959 the admission of black pupils to the white public schools finally became mandatory, and the county board of supervisors, a six-man governing body, voted to levy no taxes for the public schools, thus obliging them to close. For the next five years the county had no public schools. More than two-thirds of the 1,450 white children of school age were enrolled in private schools established by the Prince Edward Education Foundation. They received county tuition grants until 1961, when the practice was barred by the federal courts. Nearly all the county's 1,750 black children of school age were without schools. In 1964 the United States Supreme Court overruled the Supreme Court of Virginia and a lower federal court and ordered the county to reopen its public schools without delay. Associate Justice Hugo L. Black spoke for the high tribunal in saying that the time for "deliberate speed" had run out; that there had been entirely too much deliberation and not enough speed in enforcing the desegregation decision. A single district may not close its schools to avoid a court order, said the Supreme Court, as long as other public schools are kept in operation by the state. The schools of the intransigent little county were at last reopened. But they were almost as segregated as they had been before they were closed, for most white parents chose to keep their children in the private institutions.[14]

Desegregation made painful progress through the network of measures designed to prevent or delay it. In the absence of state laws requiring desegregation, local authorities were able to set up barriers even after state measures of circumvention were overruled by the courts. Anticipating this strategy, the legislature of Virginia in 1959 again took the lead by enacting a law permitting local school boards to assign pupils to specific schools, subject to the approval of the state board of education. Thus Virginia shifted from a policy of "massive resistance" to one of "local option."

Through passing pupil-placement laws, gerrymandering school districts, and contesting desegregation district by district and case by case, the southern states reduced to a token the amount of actual mixing in the schools during the remaining years of the 1950s. At the end of the decade only an estimated 6.3 percent of the black pupils in the seventeen previously segregated state school systems were attending classes with whites, and most of these were in the border states where the black population was relatively low. In four states of the Deep South—South Carolina, Georgia, Alabama, and Mississippi—not a single public school was desegregated. Observing the snail's pace of desegregation during the first eight years after the *Brown* decision, one cynic estimated that it would be complete only after 7,288 years.[15]

Notwithstanding the celebrated outbursts of violence that required police and military action during the early course of desegregation, on the whole it moved by orderly stages from one legal contest to another. The initiative in the program was primarily in the hands of black and white liberals outside the South, in cooperation with such southern leaders of the NAACP as Mrs. Daisie Bates, chairman of the Arkansas branch, who worked indefatigably to integrate the schools of Little Rock. The preeminent black heroes in the drama were the handful of children who first actually attended the white schools—the "Tender Pioneers," as they were called by a white teacher in the high school at Clinton, Tennessee. Threatened, jeered, ostracized, and abused, they demonstrated remarkable courage and persistence to remain in the schools. Of course, not all of them had the strength to do so. But enough of them remained to make early desegregation a reality, if only a token reality.[16]

III.

The Achievement of Legal Equality

Inevitably the movement for racial equality in the South spread beyond the demand for school desegregation alone and adopted measures less deliberate than those of the courtroom. A prolonged black boycott in 1955–1956 of the city busses in Montgomery, Alabama, ultimately drew a federal court order banning segregated seating on the vehicles. More important, the boycott produced a leader who was to develop a full strategy and an idealistic philosophy of protest, and to rally the black masses to their support. This man was Martin Luther King, Jr. A native of Atlanta, the twenty-six-year-old Baptist minister held a Ph.D. degree in philosophy from Boston University; he was steeped in the teachings of Jesus, Thoreau, and Gandhi. He organized the Southern Christian Leadership Conference (SCLC), and through this body he advocated "nonviolent resistance" against school segregation and other forms of racial discrimination; he announced that the blacks would, if necessary, match the whites' capacity to inflict suffering with the blacks' capacity to endure it. Not only would the blacks win the ultimate victory over injustice, he predicted, but they would so touch the hearts and consciences of the whites as to gain their esteem as well.[1]

The success of the measures employed at Montgomery and King's resourcefulness and steadfastness in applying these measures ultimately spread the resistance movement to other southern cities and made him the recognized leader. In Montgomery he had been arrested, jailed, and bombed, all to no effect. This gave him extraordinary influence over the minds of southern blacks. In February 1960 four black students sat down at a lunch counter in Greensboro, North Carolina, and refused to move when ordered to do so. Quickly similar episodes began to occur throughout the region. Recognizing the "sit-in" as a powerful weapon of protest, King made himself the spokesman and symbol of the movement. Meeting on the campus of Shaw University in Raleigh, North Carolina, with sit-in students from all over the South, he organized the Student Nonviolent Coordinating Committee (SNCC) as an auxiliary of SCLC, and gave his blessing to the new tactics.

Boycotts and sit-ins now became customary practices for exerting pressure upon the white business community to remove color barriers. Other forms of the sit-in were adopted for particular situations: the pray-in, the sing-in, the swim-in, and the march-in for use against discriminatory churches, schools, beaches and pools, and political and administrative offices. The blacks showed a stoic willingness to endure the jailings, fines, and beatings that met these activities. The Southern Regional Council, a liberal organization with headquarters in Atlanta, warned that only through naked force could segregation survive in places of public accommodation.

Although the federal courts took the lead in the protection of civil rights, the aspirations of the blacks were also vitally affected by the attitude and action of the president and Congress. The Eisenhower administration was generally conservative in its handling of the problem. But a rising national impatience with the South's intransigence toward the blacks caused the administration to sponsor and Congress to enact the Civil Rights Acts of 1957 and 1960. Both were primarily concerned with the voting rights of blacks. The most important provision of the first act empowered the attorney general to defend these rights in court; the most important provision of the second act authorized federal judges to appoint referees to register qualified blacks who had been denied registration. The election in 1960 of John F. Kennedy to the presidency on an explicit civil rights pledge marked a new era in federal support of racial justice. Kennedy appointed many blacks to high office, including Robert Weaver as the administrator of the Housing and Home Finance Agency, a position considered to be virtually the equivalent of a cabinet post and one that was especially sensitive to the needs of blacks. The president indicated his determination to support the *Brown* decision and various measures of assistance to blacks.

By the time of President Kennedy's election, the prospects of school desegregation were beginning to brighten in the upper South. A small minority of southerners, holding liberal racial views, had either openly or silently endorsed the *Brown* decision all along. These included the Southern Regional Council, a number of journalists—the most prominent and outspoken of whom was Ralph McGill of the *Atlanta Constitution*—many of the region's university professors, and some of its clergy. McGill believed that to a degree all southerners shared this attitude. "In their secret hearts," he wrote, "the most ardent advocates of the status quo knew that the Constitution of the United States could no longer be interpreted to mean one thing for one citizen and an opposite thing for another."[2]

Stirred perhaps more by practical necessity and common sense than by any deeply held urge for social reform, other voices now joined the liberals in fighting to keep the schools open, even at the cost of admitting some black pupils. Prompted by fear of economic loss and of destruction of the entire school system, various groups of citizens with such names as Mothers' Emergency Committees to Reopen the Schools, Help Our Public Education (HOPE), Save Our Schools (SOS), and Committees for Public Schools began to speak out and to bring pressure on recalcitrant school boards, county boards of supervisors, and state legislatures. As public sentiment changed, so did the mood of the local courts. In January 1959 the Virginia Supreme Court of Appeals overruled the state's entire body of massive-resistance laws as a violation of the state constitution. Governor Lindsay Almond and the state attorney general both now announced that there was no legal way to preserve segregation in the public schools. The following autumn the Little Rock school board defied Governor Faubus and approved the resumption of integrated public high school education in that city.

While desegregation proceeded slowly in the upper South, it made virtually no progress in the lower South. Five years after the *Brown* decision fewer than 350 black pupils in the entire Southeast were attending school with whites. Florida was the only state of the lower South where any integration had occurred. Governor Leroy Collins of this state had prevented the adoption of resistance statutes, and in the fall of 1959 a few blacks had been admitted to the previously white schools of Dade County (Miami).

In 1960 and 1961 the federal courts attacked the segregation of the Deep South by ordering selected white schools in New Orleans and Atlanta to admit blacks. The situation in New Orleans was aggravated by the action of Louisiana Governor Jimmie Davis, who had been elected on a pledge to preserve segregation, and who now fatuously promised to go to jail if necessary in order to do so. But when Davis invoked state law in an effort to take personal control of the threatened schools and was restrained by the Fifth United States Circuit Court of Appeals, he backed down without going to jail. In spite of demonstrations, boycotts, and vandalism by white objectors, four black pupils were then admitted to two schools. Atlanta the next fall proved easier than New Orleans had been. The editorials of Ralph McGill and the work of the Southern Regional Council and of a substantial group of college professors, clergy, and other professional persons had somewhat prepared the citizens for desegregation. Mayor William B. Hartsfield supported it; and Governor Ernest Vandiver's administration did not resist it. Nine black pupils entered the previously white schools of the city without serious opposition. The white schools of Dallas and Memphis also began enrolling a few black pupils in the fall of 1961. By the end of the year the public schools of only three states, Mississippi, Alabama, and South Carolina, remained entirely segregated.

Meanwhile, the desegregation of the state institutions of higher learning continued to go forward slowly but steadily. Popular opposition was less vehement against integration at this level than against the mixing of the lower schools. State after state during the late 1950s yielded to court orders and allowed black students to be enrolled in its colleges and universities, usually without serious mishap. The major exception to peaceful desegregation in higher education during the 1950s occurred at the University of Alabama, when protesters in 1956 temporarily prevented the admission of a young black woman named Autherine Lucy. Admitted later under court order, she was promptly expelled for alleging that the board of the university had been in collusion with the rioters who had driven her away. The admission of two blacks to the University of Georgia in

1961 touched off a week of disorder that caused the state legislature to attempt to close the school. The legislators were restrained by a court order, and the black students then returned to the campus without further significant opposition. This episode doubtless influenced the state government in its decision not to interfere with the desegregation of the Atlanta public schools a short time later. By the fall of 1962 only the state universities of Mississippi, Alabama, and South Carolina remained entirely white.

As anticipated, the most violent stage in the course of desegregation came in Mississippi. With blacks comprising about 42 percent of its population, the state was the citadel of white supremacy. Although a few of its prominent citizens counseled moderation, including the novelist William Faulkner and the newspaper editor Hodding Carter, the great majority of the white population was implacably opposed to any degree of racial integration. Governor Ross Barnett, who had been elected with Citizens' Councils support, promised "to rot in jail" rather than admit a single black to a white school. This spirit of defiance was tested in the fall of 1962 when the officials of the University of Mississippi were ordered by the United States Fifth Circuit Court of Appeals to enroll the black applicant James Meredith. Governor Barnett and Lieutenant Governor Paul B. Johnson now resorted to interposition by physically preventing Meredith from registering. After a futile exchange of telephone calls between President Kennedy and Governor Barnett, a force of more than 300 federal marshals supported by troops escorted Meredith to the campus, where they were met by a mob of about 2,500 aroused students and segregationist sympathizers. Only after a clash in which two persons died was Meredith enrolled. Protected by marshals and soldiers, he remained until he graduated.

The example of the outcome of defiance in Mississippi was not lost on the officials of other southern states. Although South Carolina had previously been as strongly committed to resistance as any other state, Governor Ernest F. Hollings in January 1963 said pointedly, "We of today must realize the lesson of one hundred years ago, and move on for the good of South Carolina and the United States."[3] Two weeks later the newly inaugurated administration of Governor Donald S. Russell offered no opposition when Clemson College admitted a black student under court order. Soon the state university and then the public schools were enrolling small numbers of blacks without serious hindrance.

School desegregation in Alabama, the last state to yield, was anti-climactic after the violence at the University of Mississippi and the disorders arising out of the blacks' campaign to desegregate places of public accommodation. No serious opposition arose when in the summer of 1963 two black students were enrolled by court order at the University of Alabama. Instead, Governor George C. Wallace staged a symbolic resistance by personally blocking the entrance of the black enrollees and their escorting marshals until he was ordered by the commanding officer of the federalized Alabama National Guard to stand aside. That fall the public schools of various Alabama cities, including those of Birmingham, Mobile, Huntsville, and Tuskegee, successfully admitted token numbers of black pupils over the governor's objections and in spite of his use of state police to close a number of schools temporarily.

As desegregation moved slowly into the Deep South it gained momentum in the border areas. By the close of 1962 the state of Texas had admitted almost 7,000 blacks to previously white schools, and the upper South had desegregated an estimated 5,517 black pupils. Under the pressure of sit-ins and boycotts, lunch counters in hundreds of southern department and variety stores were now serving black customers along with the whites.

The decline of overt resistance to school desegregation in the lower South was not accompanied by a decrease in violent opposition to the desegregation of places of public accommodation. Indeed, except for the confrontation on the University of Mississippi campus, the major battleground of the civil rights movement during the early 1960s was in the stores, hotels, lunch counters, and swimming pools of the region. In the spring of 1961 an Alabama mob fell upon a busload of "Freedom Riders" who were being sponsored by the Congress of Racial Equality (CORE) to test local segregation laws. Mississippi state police solved the problem to their taste by jailing the Freedom Riders who entered that state. Blacks who were engaged in sit-ins in Jackson, Mississippi, and other places were beaten by angry whites.

The southern racial friction reached its peak in the spring of 1963 in Birmingham. Tensions had long run high in the Alabama industrial center; it had the reputation of being the toughest of all the "segregation nuts" to crack. For more than a year the blacks had maintained a partially successful boycott of white businesses in an effort to desegregate public accommodations and force white employers to hire blacks equally with whites. The commissioner of public safety, T. Eugene "Bull" Connor, was notoriously harsh in enforcing the city's racial ordinances. When in May Dr. Martin Luther King, Jr., and the Reverend Fred Shuttlesworth challenged the city authorities with a protest demonstration, Connor arrested hundreds of blacks. After the residence of Dr. King's brother and the motel headquarters of the demonstration were dynamited, presumably by the Ku Klux Klan, thousands of enraged blacks rioted in the streets with bricks, knives, and firebrands. The police fought them with clubs, guns, fire hoses, and police dogs. Miraculously no one was killed, but thousands of blacks were arrested before Connor was able, with the support of state troopers sent in by Governor Wallace, to impose an uneasy peace. The newly elected city administration and a committee of anxious business leaders now made concessions by agreeing to desegregate lunch counters and public facilities and to cease discriminating against blacks in hiring employees.

The increasing tempo of racial unrest and violence brought a widespread demand for civil rights legislation of greater effectiveness than the laws then in force. Televised scenes of the events in Birmingham and elsewhere in the South kindled sympathy for the blacks throughout the rest of the country. In the summer of 1963 Medgar Evers, field secretary of the NAACP in Mississippi, fell mortally wounded by sniper fire as he entered his front door; a few weeks later four young black girls died in the bombing of a Birmingham church. White Americans, including many southern believers in white supremacy, were appalled and indignant over these atrocities.

Black Americans made their own response to the rising violence in the South. In late August 1963 they staged a peaceful demonstration of more than 200,000 persons, mostly blacks, in Washington, D.C. The high point of the occasion was an address by Dr. Martin Luther King, Jr., from the steps of the Lincoln Memorial. Warning of a "whirlwind of revolt" that would sweep the land if the rights of the blacks continued to be ignored, he said he had a vision of better things to come. "I have a dream that one day this nation will rise up and live out the true meaning of its creed [of equality]." Even Mississippi, he predicted, would one day be transformed into "an oasis of freedom and justice."[4]

Alarmed by the prospect of widespread violence and moved by sympathy for the blacks, Congress enacted the Civil Rights Act of 1964, a measure thought by some to be as important as the *Brown* decision itself. Indeed, one prominent black leader, Whitney M. Young, Jr., executive director of the National Urban League, called the act the greatest single triumph for human rights in the United States since the Emancipation Proclamation. The act prohibited discrimination in the application of voter registration tests and procedures; it barred discrimination in hotels, restaurants, places of amusement, and the like; it authorized the attorney general to intervene in private suits where denial of equal protection of the law under the Fourteenth Amendment was alleged; and it forbade discrimination in hiring by establishments with 100 or more employees, and by 1968 with as few as 25 employees.

Sponsored by President Kennedy and, after his assassination in 1963, strongly supported by President Johnson, the civil rights legislation was eventually passed as a bipartisan measure. The great majority of the southern congressmen fought it unshakably; even Senator Albert Gore of Tennessee, who had refused to sign the southern manifesto against the school desegregation ruling and who was usually considered to be a southern liberal, opposed the bill. Led by Richard Russell of Georgia, who was assisted by James O. Eastland of Mississippi and Sam Ervin of North Carolina, the southern senators resorted to every parliamentary trick at their disposal to kill or cripple it. After a debate that lasted for more than three months, the Senate for the first time in history imposed cloture to cut off a southern filibuster. On July 2 President Johnson signed the bill into law with an expression of hope that it would "close the springs of racial poison."[5]

At the very moment of this legislative victory, the state of Mississippi was serving as a battleground in the civil rights struggle. During the summer of 1964 hundreds of white and black northern college students were recruited and trained by the Council of Federated Organizations (COFO), whose chief members were SNCC and CORE. These students poured into Mississippi to participate in a Summer Freedom Project. Whites derisively called the movement a children's crusade, but unlike its medieval namesake the modern crusade could point to solid accomplishments. Using the black churches as bases of operations and black ministers as a cadre of local leadership, the idealistic and adventurous COFO youths established schools for black illiterates, set up black community centers, and encouraged and assisted blacks in registering to vote.

The Freedom Workers paid dearly for their efforts, for the local white population looked upon them as a new breed of carpetbaggers. Although the majority of Mississippians abstained from actual participation in violence, they showed little concern about the activities of the Ku Klux Klan and other terrorists. The COFO list of casualties included at least three killed (some counts went as high as fifteen), scores beaten, and more than a thousand arrested. The most appalling incident of violence was the slaying of three of the civil rights workers, one black and two white, in Neshoba County. They disappeared on June 21, and not until almost two months later, after a search involving FBI agents and hundreds of servicemen from the Meridian Naval Air Station, were the bodies of the slain men discovered, with the help of an informer's tip, under an earthen dam near the town of Philadelphia. Thirty black homes and thirty-five black churches burned under circumstances indicating arson by angry whites. Yet the freedom movement was a success, for it provided an incalculable stimulus to the aspirations and hopes of the hitherto passive black masses, and it riveted the attention of the nation on their plight. In the opinion of one of the Freedom Workers, "For the first time in a century, [Mississippi] became a part of the national consciousness."[6]

Despite the voter registration measures of the various civil rights acts and the efforts during the early 1960s of the many civil rights workers, vast numbers of blacks in the lower South remained disfranchised because they could not meet the required literacy and understanding tests, or because of discrimination in the administration of the tests, or because of fear or apathy on the part of the blacks. A rule of southern politics said that the larger the proportion of blacks in a community, the smaller the proportion that voted. In 1964 less than 45 percent of the adult blacks of Louisiana, Mississippi, Alabama, Georgia, and South Carolina were registered to vote. In Alabama only about 30 percent were on the rolls; many counties in the Black Belt of the region did not have a single black voter.

To remedy this imbalance, Dr. Martin Luther King, Jr., lent his presence to an intensified voter registration drive in the state. He was now at the peak of his prestige, having just returned from Oslo where he had received the Nobel Peace Prize. He supported the voter registration campaign rhetorically by calling it "a march on the ballot boxes throughout Alabama." To focus the nation's attention on the movement, and also to protest the recent killing of a black civil rights worker, he planned a demonstration to move on the highway from Selma, in the heart of the Black Belt, to Montgomery, the state capital. Refused a permit to march by Governor Wallace, who said that the demonstration would incite violence beyond control, King and his advisers chose to defy the state authorities. On Sunday, March 7, 1965, a group of several hundred blacks began the trek. State troopers and a sheriff's posse met them with clubs, tear gas, and mounted charges at the Alabama River bridge in Selma, wounding fifty of them, seventeen severely enough to require hospital care.

Selma now became the scene of moral outrage and frenzied activity as thousands of white and black sympathizers rushed to the city from all quarters. Public anger and horror reached a new height when three visiting white Unitarian ministers were assaulted on the city street. One of them, the Reverend James J. Reeb of Boston, died of his wounds. Ultimately, Federal District Judge Frank M. Johnson of Montgomery ordered the state officials to permit and protect a demonstration of three hundred marchers. Escorted by units of the federalized Alabama National Guard, the column moved out of Selma on March 21 and reached its destination four days later. Standing on the steps of the state capitol where Jefferson Davis was inaugurated provisional president of the Confederacy, King addressed a great rally to proclaim the triumph of nonviolent resistance. But that night a white woman from Detroit was shot to death while riding back from Montgomery to Selma with a black civil rights worker.

The march on the ballot boxes and the recalcitrance of Governor Wallace brought the result that King and other civil rights leaders had anticipated: a nationwide demand for legislation to protect black voters. On the night of March 15 President Johnson addressed a televised joint session of Congress to call for immediate passage of such a law. "Their [the blacks'] cause must be our cause too," he said. "Because it's not just Negroes, but really it's all of us who must overcome the crippling legacy of bigotry and injustice." Then to emphasize his point he drew upon the blacks' freedom hymn to say, "And we . . . shall . . . overcome."[7] The Voting Rights Act was promptly passed. Carefully written to encroach upon as few states as possible, especially nonsouthern states, the statute provided for the appointment of federal examiners to work in the registrars' offices and prohibit discrimination in the registration of voters in those states and political subdivisions where fewer than 50 percent of the population had voted or been registered to vote in the 1964 presidential election. Literacy tests and comparable screening measures were banned in places subject to federal examiners.

Seven southern states, or parts of states, were affected by the Voting Rights Act. These were Virginia, North Carolina, South Carolina, Georgia, Alabama, Mississippi, and Louisiana. Examiners were at work within a week after the signing of the act by the president. Other measures supported the voting rights of the blacks. The ratification in 1964 of the Twenty-fourth Amendment to the Constitution outlawed the poll tax as a requirement for voting in federal elections; a few months after the Alabama protest march the United States Supreme Court banned the poll tax as a requirement for voting in state and local elections. All of these developments, aided by the Voter Education Project of the Southern Regional Council and an awakening of political awareness on the part of the blacks, brought a great upsurge in black registration. During the first year after the passage of the Voting Rights Act more than 400,000 blacks were added to the rolls.

Meanwhile, the blacks felt the effects of the federal program of desegregation and support set in motion by the previous civil rights acts, especially the act of 1964. The public accommodations legislation caused southern hotels, restaurants, and places of business and amusement to open their doors to the few blacks who had the money and the desire to patronize them. This of course did not come about without many incidents of violence and intimidation, the most notorious of which was the attempt by the proprietor of an Atlanta chicken restaurant, Lester Maddox, to exclude blacks by issuing ax handles to be used as clubs by his white customers. The Equal Employment Opportunity legislation brought a slow but steady rise in the number of blacks hired in other than menial jobs. The policy adopted by the United States commissioner of education to withhold federal money from segregated school districts increased the pace of school desegregation. Gradually the state governments yielded to the pressure for "local option," and the local school boards admitted token numbers of blacks to the previously white schools. By the fall of 1966 better than 10 percent of the black pupils of the lower South were in school with whites.

The federal program to eradicate poverty and ignorance among the black masses also began to bear fruit. The Office of Economic Opportunity (OEO), created by Congress in 1964, was the major organization devoted to this task. Among its subsidiaries was the Community Action Program, which strove to improve the skills and motivations and the living and working conditions of the poor. By distributing a substantial portion of its staff among the poor themselves, the OEO sought to enhance their dignity and self-confidence along with their incomes. Hundreds of agents of the Volunteers in Service to America (VISTA), the so-called domestic Peace Corps, were active in the effort to assist black communities. The Job Corps provided subsistence and training for thousands of unemployed youths, many of them black, who had dropped out of school. The Head Start Program sought to help the children of needy and poorly educated families to overcome their cultural handicap through preschool instruction.

The federal judiciary and the Johnson administration also made some progress in securing justice for blacks and civil rights workers in southern courts. As a rule, local police who beat or killed blacks or their supporters were cleared without trial. Whites of no official capacity who slew or practiced violence upon blacks were usually acquitted by white juries, or, at the most, were given nominal sentences. The alleged assassin of Medgar Evers in 1963 was released on bail after two trials in which the juries were split. No one was brought to trial for the Birmingham church bombing that killed four black girls. In 1966 President Johnson sponsored a bill that contained a prohibition against the exclusion of blacks from juries, but southern congressmen drew enough support from northern colleagues who feared other measures in the bill to enable them to kill it.

Gradually, however, by declaring mistrials in cases involving black litigants or whites accused of crimes against blacks, the federal courts forced the acceptance of black jurors. Still, in the surroundings of the rural South the conviction of such whites was rare, even with blacks on the juries. One of the men tried for participating in the murder of the white woman after the Alabama march in 1965 was acquitted by a jury containing eight blacks. Social and economic intimidation were said to sway black jurymen, if they no longer feared physical harm. The situation nevertheless did improve. In the fall of 1967 a federal jury of white Mississippians brought a verdict of guilty against seven white men accused of conspiring to murder the three civil rights workers in Neshoba County three years before. A segregationist judge, Harold Cox, pronounced sentence, the most severe being ten years' imprisonment.

By the late 1960s the focus of the civil rights movement among blacks had broadened to include the cities of the North and West. Successful in their crusade against legal segregation and discrimination in the South, they now began to concentrate their energies upon the massive "de facto" segregation and discrimination elsewhere. The target of the first and second Reconstructions was the South; presumably the target of the final Reconstruction was to be the entire nation. But the legal attack upon de facto segregation provoked northern and western opposition in Congress. A major cause for the failure of the civil rights bill of 1966 was the inclusion of a measure prohibiting discrimination in the sale or rental of residential property. In the words of Senator Sam Ervin of North Carolina, the act would have "gored someone else's oxen." Nor was Dr. Martin Luther King, Jr., able that same year to break the residential segregation of Chicago by the protest march he led there.

Frustrated at every turn in their search for redress, many blacks of the northern and western ghettos resorted to violence. A series of summer riots convulsed New York City, Rochester, Jersey City, Philadelphia, Los Angeles, Detroit, and other nonsouthern cities. Militant black leaders such as Stokely Carmichael of SNCC and Floyd McKissick of CORE coined the slogan Black Power, and openly advocated force as a means of attaining racial justice. "To hell with the laws of the United States," cried Carmichael.[8] An armed black organization with the suggestive name Black Panthers came into existence, presumably to serve as the shock troops of the black revolution. Racial violence reached a climax during the "long, hot summer" of 1967 with outbreaks in 75 communities at a cost of 130 deaths, more than 3,500 injuries, and more than $7 billion in damages. Detroit, with 43 killed and more than 2,000 hurt, was the scene of the most serious uprising. Thousands of national guardsmen supported by contingents of regular army troops eventually restored order to the stricken city.[9]

No major eruptions occurred in the South. Possibly the relative calm of the region was the product of a modus vivendi that had prevented massive racial conflagrations since the days of Reconstruction. Perhaps both races shunned the holocaust they sensed would be the result of an absolute showdown. Yet there were moments as the champions of Black Power tested the determination of the Deep South when the region seemed on the brink of disaster. During the summer of 1966 both James Meredith and Dr. Martin Luther King, Jr., accompanied by Carmichael and McKissick, made appearances in Mississippi for the purpose of revealing to the nation the dangers besetting their people in the state. They were not disappointed in their expectations. In his first attempt, Meredith was wounded by a shotgun blast; King's group, marching in Neshoba County, was set upon with rocks and clubs. Both movements were rescued by state troopers acting under the orders of Governor Paul Johnson.

President Johnson responded to the spreading racial violence by appointing a special National Advisory Commission on Civil Disorders to investigate the causes of the riots and recommend remedies. In March 1968 the commission reported its findings, which warned of the rapidly growing estrangement of the races and placed the entire blame on white racism. The commission recommended vastly increased federal expenditures to improve black living conditions and education, and it called for a complete change of heart toward blacks on the part of the nation's white population.

Meanwhile, Dr. Martin Luther King, Jr., sought to develop an effective strategy for attacking racial discrimination and inequality throughout the country. He was aware of the growing alienation from the civil rights movement of whites outside the South—the threatened "white backlash" against black militancy. He was also convinced that the war in Vietnam was diverting resources and a national sense of purpose that might otherwise be used to support black uplift. Moreover, he saw his leadership of the blacks eroding under the challenge of the militants. He still refused to advocate violence; instead, he declared to a Chicago audience, "Our power does not reside in Molotov cocktails, knives, and bricks. . . . Our power is in our unity."[10] Nevertheless, by the epochal summer of 1967 King appeared to be more sympathetic to violence than observers of his past behavior had ever thought he would be. His rhetoric became grimmer with the course of events.

In December 1967 Dr. King began organizing a Poor People's Campaign designed to bring thousands of blacks, Puerto Ricans, poor whites, and members of other disadvantaged groups to the nation's capital, where they would camp at the doorstep of the government in an effort to induce Congress to pass a multibillion-dollar program of relief and rehabilitation. During the following February he returned to many of the memorable southern scenes of his career as a civil rights leader. He spoke in Birmingham and Selma, and he revisited Montgomery, where it had all begun. Then he and his wife flew to Jamaica for a brief vacation.

In March, King returned to the United States with a decision to stage a protest demonstration on behalf of the Memphis garbage workers, who were in the midst of a grim boycott and strike for higher wages. To King's dismay he was unable to control the militants on the march, who broke into vandalism and looting. Halting the demonstration, King flew to Atlanta in a state of depression. But after a staff meeting in which he was told, "The Holy Spirit is in this room," he decided to return to Memphis, reschedule and lead the demonstration there, and then go on to Washington to launch the Poor People's Campaign.[11]

Back in Memphis, King found himself under a federal judge's restraining order that temporarily prohibited the resumption of the demonstration. Denouncing the ruling as illegal and unconstitutional, King appealed it to the United States Court of Appeals. What would he do if the appeal should be denied? He implied that he intended to ignore the restraining order and continue the demonstration. "Beyond that," he said, "it is a matter of conscience. It will be on the basis of my conscience saying that we have a moral right and responsibility to march." That night, April 3, he told an audience of 2,000 in Mason Temple: "We've got some difficult days ahead. But it really doesn't matter with me now. Because I've been to the mountaintop. I won't mind. Like anybody, I would like to live a long life. . . . But I'm not concerned about that now. I just want to do God's will. And He's allowed me to go up to the mountain. And I've looked over, and I've seen the Promised Land. I may not get there with you, but I want you to know tonight that we as a people will get to the Promised Land. So I'm happy to-night. I'm not fearing any man. Mine eyes have seen the glory of the coming of the Lord!"[12]

King's premonition of martyrdom was uncannily accurate. The next evening as he came out of his motel room to go to dinner he was mortally wounded by an assassin's bullet.

The sequel of King's death was one of grief and rage, followed by an act of atonement by the United States Congress. Schools and places of business closed on the day of the dead leader's funeral; countless millions of Americans watched the televised services conducted in the Ebenezer Baptist Church of Atlanta and the burial procession of the bier on a humble mule train. A tense quiet lay over most communi-ties, but burning and looting by angry blacks occurred in many. Troops were required to stop the rioting in Washington, D.C. The Civil Rights Act of 1968, enacted by Congress a few days later, was a memorial to the fallen champion of the cause. Its most important provision was the banning of discrimination in the sale or rental of residences where the transaction was conducted through a real estate agency. This was esti-mated to include 80 percent of the nation's residential property. Soon the United States Supreme Court applied the principle of open housing to the remaining 20 percent.

Dr. King's death marked the close of a remarkable epoch in civil rights for blacks. They now held complete legal equality with whites throughout the nation. Whether for want of his leadership, or, more likely, because of the alarm kindled among the white population by the recent ghetto riots, most of the crusading zeal of the sort that had inspired the Freedom Workers quickly disappeared. When King's successor as head of SCLC, Dr. Ralph Abernathy, attempted to carry out the Poor People's Campaign in Washington, he failed to accom-plish anything of significance. In late June a pathetic remnant of the movement—about 300 persons, including Dr. Abernathy—yielded to arrest for trespassing on the mall. The nation as a whole turned to other interests. But race was still the most acute social, economic, and political concern of the South.

IV.

The Politics of Transition

Southern politics after World War II was as much concerned as ever with protecting the region's traditional economic and social interests against both external and internal pressures. In spite of the vast economic changes and the significant legal and social developments of the 1940s and 1950s, the foundations of regional politics long remained intact. For more than a decade after World War II the Democratic party continued to dominate southern politics at all levels; blacks were excluded from party leadership and their interests largely ignored in party policy. The turbulent 1960s gave a new quality to the politics of the region. At the close of this period coalitions of white and black voters elected liberal administrations in a number of southern states. But the forces of change were balanced by the forces of continuity. In the 1970s these ancient regional impulses placed the South in the vanguard of a national move to the political center.

The civil rights contest combined with regional economic interests to present the earliest and most persistent challenge to the traditional supremacy of the Democratic party in the South. President Truman's advocacy of civil rights for blacks alienated the masses of southern voters and aroused a number of regional political leaders to the point of overt rebellion against the party. In successfully opposing most of Truman's civil rights proposals in 1948, southern congressmen denounced them as sounding "like the program of the Communists"; southerners accused the northern wing of the Democratic party of being controlled by "an organized mongrel minority." Senator John J. Sparkman of Alabama said, "The people of the South are so bitter that they will never accept Truman as a candidate" for president in the forthcoming campaign.[1]

Sparkman's warning was partly borne out by subsequent events. Unable to prevent the nomination of Truman and Alben W. Barkley by the 1948 Democratic convention, some of the southern delegates walked out, while the remainder sat in angry silence. A southern journalist wrote: "The South has been kicked in the pants, turned around, and kicked in the stomach."[2] Dissenting southerners promptly decided to place in the field their own candidates for president and vice president in an attempt to draw away enough electoral votes to force the election into Congress, where they hoped to seize the balance of power and win concessions in return for support. The situation appeared to be especially favorable for this strategy because the regular Democrats were further weakened by the defection of the Progressives, a liberal group endorsing the candidacy of Henry Wallace of Iowa for president and Glen Taylor of Idaho for vice president.

Three days after Truman's nomination, delegates from thirteen southern and border states answered the call of Governor Fielding Wright of Mississippi to meet in Birmingham to carry out their purposes. Organizing themselves into the States' Rights party, popularly known as the Dixiecrat party, they adopted a platform denouncing the Democratic program and explicitly endorsing racial segregation. Governor J. Strom Thurmond of South Carolina and Governor Wright of Mississippi were nominated for the top two offices of the United States. The Dixiecrats failed to achieve their goal; they carried only those southern states—South Carolina, Mississippi, Alabama, and Louisiana—where they were able to get the local Democratic organizations to list them on the ballot under the Democratic emblem. There were several reasons for this weak showing. The candidates were not major southern political figures. Opponents made telling accusations that the new party actually stood for the interests of millowners, oil magnates, bankers, and other members of the southern Bourbon class and their corporation allies in New York City. Finally, in splitting the Democratic party the Dixiecrats were guilty of heresy against southern political orthodoxy. Except for the four states carried by Thurmond and Wright, the South remained solid behind the triumphant Democrats.

The failure of the Dixiecrats to win the South was hailed as an indication of profound change in the region's political thinking. "The States' Rights campaign did one good thing," wrote the *New York Times*. "It showed how a great majority of Southern voters disagree with the antediluvian attitude that it represents."[3] A rising southern journalist, Harry S. Ashmore of the *Arkansas Gazette*, offered the opinion that the outcome of the election proved southern voters were no longer chiefly moved by racial prejudice. *Time* expressed similar views, but added the prophetic warning that if organized labor and northern liberals should continue to dominate the Democratic party, the southern revolt might kindle into a permanent political realignment.

Actually, much of the southern vote for Truman and Barkley signified no preference for the candidates themselves or for their announced principles. It simply represented traditional southern party loyalty. Perhaps the then attorney general of Virginia, J. Lindsay Almond, voiced the sentiments of most southern voters when in endorsing the Truman candidacy he said: "The only sane and constructive course to follow is to remain in the house of our fathers—even though the roof leaks, and there be bats in the belfry, rats in the pantry, a cockroach waltz in the kitchen and skunks in the parlor."[4] Certainly the southern vote indicated no change of heart on the issues of civil rights and federal authority. Rather than forfeit their rank and prestige, the region's elder political leaders such as Harry F. Byrd, James F. Byrnes, and Richard Russell preferred to wage the battle as Democrats and with weapons of their own choice. When the next year President Truman placed his program before Congress, the southern senators opposed it successfully with a panoply of devices that gave practical effect to John C. Calhoun's doctrine of the Concurrent Majority, an arrangement that if adopted would have granted the minority South a veto over unwelcome legislation. They employed the advantages of seniority and the Senate privilege of unlimited debate; when administration forces asked for a simplified form of cloture to break the filibuster, the southern opposition was reinforced by Republican senators who were jealous of the safeguards of their own minority position. This informal coalition of southern Democrats and northern Republicans carried the day.

In subsequent elections southern voters demonstrated convincingly their approval of the antiadministration stand taken by most of their representatives. Only in Arkansas did they indicate a tentative sympathy with Truman's policies by electing an administration supporter, Sid McMath, to the governorship. McMath's defeats for reelection as governor in 1952 and for the United States Senate two years later illustrated the weakness of his hold on the Arkansas electorate. Virginia showed its continued faith in Byrd, the sharpest senatorial critic of Truman's measures, by electing John S. Battle, a member of the Byrd organization, to the governorship. Byrd campaigned personally for Battle, denouncing the rival candidate in the Democratic primary as the choice of organized labor. South Carolina in 1950 overwhelmingly elected James F. Byrnes to its highest office. This veteran statesman had served the New Deal in positions as high as secretary of state; he had been an associate justice of the Supreme Court of the United States; as director of war mobilization during World War II he had been virtually an assistant president of the United States. Disillusioned with the recent course of his party, he now returned to his native heath convinced that the South Carolina way was best. Though most southern governors stuck to the Democratic party, none of them endorsed the civil rights proposals of the national leadership.

The defeat of two prominent southern candidates who supported the Truman program—Senators Claude Pepper of Florida and Frank Graham of North Carolina—was a warning to those who believed regional convictions had changed fundamentally. Pepper made racial statements in New York not shared by a majority of his constituents. Graham, or "Dr. Frank," as he was affectionately known by thousands of Carolinians, was a former president of the state university. He had been a member of Truman's Commission on Civil Rights, a service that now worked against him. Desperately but futilely he sought to escape the taint of radicalism by declaring he opposed compulsory FEPC legislation and forced school desegregation. Both of these men were victims of their faith in southern liberalism.

Yet the conservative trend of southern politics did not indicate a revival of the Dixiecrat party as a political entity. After the 1948 election the leaders of the faction found themselves out of popular favor because of having bolted the Democratic party. The 1950 senatorial race in South Carolina was in a sense a test of the wisdom of their course. Governor Thurmond challenged Senator Olin D. Johnston in a bitter campaign in which each candidate tried to outdo the other in denouncing the national administration. At one point the two men almost came to blows in the heat of a face-to-face debate on this issue. Thurmond accused Johnston of having failed to protest the racial desegregation of the armed forces. Johnston responded, "Liar!" Only the intervention of an aide prevented fisticuffs.[5] But Johnston's record of loyalty to the Democratic party in contrast to Thurmond's recent bolt helped to bring about Thurmond's defeat. Governor Wright of Mississippi faded into political obscurity after the expiration of his term; he retired to private life in 1952 and died four years later.

The South approached the presidential election of 1952 under the leadership of experienced Democratic party regulars who were nevertheless unshakably opposed to the major points in Truman's domestic program. The most prominent members of this group were Senator Byrd of Virginia, Senator Russell of Georgia, and Governor Byrnes of South Carolina. Byrd was especially vocal in his dissent and implacable in his conservatism. "The South is not impotent," he warned. "True, it is a minority in the Democratic party, but no Democratic President can be elected without the vote of the Southern states."[6] He demanded the restoration of the two-thirds rule for the nomination of presidential candidates, an ancient party requirement that had been dropped in 1936, and he urged the adoption of a platform opposing the heavy costs of the federal establishment and the president's social and economic programs. Even Senator Russell's views were sometimes too liberal for Byrd, who initially favored the Georgian for the Democratic nomination but withdrew his support because of Russell's acquiescence in altering the Taft-Hartley labor law to make it less stringent in its regulation of strikes and union practices.

Meanwhile, a cadre of former Dixiecrats held annual meetings in Jackson, Mississippi, where they formed a National States' Rights Committee that seemed likely to be the nucleus for a resurgence of the party in the forthcoming election. Six southern state Democratic organizations, those of Texas, Louisiana, Mississippi, Georgia, South Carolina, and Virginia, decided to withhold commitments to the party pending the national convention. All these pronouncements and moves suggested the possibility of a southern bolt more serious than that of the preceding election.

Despite the signs of regional discontent with the Democratic party, no southern walkout occurred at the 1952 nominating convention. The bolt was prevented by the action of moderates who sought to heal the party wounds by seating the Dixiecrat defectors of the previous convention. Members supporting the candidacy of Averell Harriman of New York and Senator Estes Kefauver of Tennessee wished to impose a strongly phrased loyalty oath, one that they doubtless hoped would purge the opposition, but they were overruled by the majority. Instead, the delegates were asked to pledge themselves to "exert every honorable means" to have the party's nominees placed on the state ballot under the Democratic label.

Most of the southern delegations signed this equivocal pledge, but those of Virginia and South Carolina refused on principle to do so. The Louisiana delegation split, with Governor Robert Kennon and his followers refusing and Senator Russell Long and his supporters agreeing. Eventually, the delegations from the three southern states were seated, but only after Governor Battle of Virginia had made a conciliatory address assuring the convention that state law was sufficient to cause the party nominees to be listed on the ballot as Democrats. The majority of the region's political leaders supported the Democratic party even though its nominees, Governor Adlai Stevenson of Illinois and Senator John Sparkman of Alabama, forthrightly endorsed its civil rights and social welfare programs and the plan for federal ownership of the offshore Gulf of Mexico oil reserves.

Although southern political leaders chose not to revive the Dixiecrat movement in the presidential election of 1952, they were by no means united or enthusiastic in their backing of the Democratic ticket. Two of the most influential of the region's spokesmen, Senator Byrd and Governor Byrnes, refused to support Stevenson. Byrd adopted a position of neutrality in the campaign, thus in effect releasing his followers to support the ticket of their choice; Byrnes explicitly endorsed the Republican candidates, General Dwight D. Eisenhower and Senator Richard M. Nixon. Governors Shivers of Texas and Kennon of Louisiana also supported the Republican cause; and it was obvious that many other southern Democrats gave only half-hearted loyalty to the national ticket. The region's ancestral practice of voting for Democrats enabled Stevenson and Sparkman to carry most of the southern states in the election, including those that had gone to the Dixiecrats in the preceding canvass. But Eisenhower and Nixon received the electoral votes of four border states of the South—Virginia, Florida, Texas, and Tennessee—and in every other southern state except Alabama and Mississippi they drew more than 40 percent of the popular vote. The erosion of Democratic ascendancy in southern presidential politics was unmistakable.

This growth of Republican strength in the South came from a combination of personal, economic, and social attitudes and interests. General Eisenhower's immense popularity as a brave, genial, and reverent hero of World War II overreached the bounds of region or party; it held a special appeal for a people whose fondest traditions were those of military renown and whose allegiance to the Almighty was still strong. In announcing his decision to support the Republican candidate, Governor Byrnes touched both of these chords by calling Eisenhower "a man of decision and courage. . . . [He was in] supreme command of our armed forces in Europe. He had to decide on the invasion of North Africa and Italy. In his book he has told us how he prayed for Divine guidance in making the fateful decision as to the timing of the Normandy invasion."[7] Eisenhower's Texas birth and his Virginia-born mother gave him at least indirect ties with the region. He astutely claimed two "home states," Kansas and Texas.

Opposition to the growing welfare programs of the Democratic administration also caused many southern voters to abandon the party in the presidential election of 1952. In urging Texas Democrats to vote for the Republican candidates, Governor Shivers warned them against "statism and socialism" in the federal government, against the infiltration of high offices by Communists, and against policies of increased taxing and spending. Both Shivers and Governor Kennon of Louisiana, speaking as representatives of heavy oil-producing states of the Gulf Coast, attacked the Democratic candidates' stand in favor of federal ownership of the oil-bearing tidelands as being an unconstitutional invasion of private and state property rights.

Finally, the Republican position on civil rights was more acceptable to most southern voters than that of its opponents. The party platform condemned the Democratic administration for hypocrisy and false promises to minorities. It pledged federal action against lynching, the poll tax, and discrimination in employment, but it endorsed as a general principle the primary responsibility of each state to control its domestic institutions. General Eisenhower explained that in his opinion a compulsory FEPC would aggravate rather than ease racial tensions, and the federal government ought not to invade areas of authority reserved by the Constitution to the states. The Republican party was beginning to move into the political vacuum being left in the South behind its withdrawing rival.

The Democratic party's continuing support of civil rights and the Eisenhower administration's relatively inactive role in the controversy gave the Republican party reason to hope for the emergence of a genuine two-party South. Other developments of the 1950s favored the growth of permanent Republican strength in the customary stronghold of the Democrats. The actual and prospective growth of southern industry and business kindled sympathy for the party that traditionally pictured itself as the friend, and was traditionally caricatured by its opponents as the toady, of these interests. A rising southern desire for tariff protection, especially among the textile manufacturers and laborers of the Piedmont, helped the Republican cause in the region. The suburban middle class of the growing southern cities veered away from the taxing and spending policies of the Democrats. The movement of population to urban areas was eating away the old foundations of Democratic strength in the rural South.

During Eisenhower's first administration the South weighed his performance against his campaign pledges. Understandably, many of the region's elder statesmen were critical. In a comment that could hardly have come from any Democrat except a southern Democrat, Senator Russell denounced the president's 1956 State of the Union message as "a medley of New Deal platitudes and shibboleths." By the time of the presidential nominating convention of 1956 the South was in agitation over the Supreme Court's *Brown* decision, which it attributed primarily to the malign influence of Chief Justice Earl Warren, an Eisenhower appointee. The region's course in the forthcoming election was uncertain. Former Governor Byrnes of South Carolina warned his hearers that the threat of competition between the major contestants for the support of minority groups might yet force the South to create a third political party.

But the time was not ripe for such a move as Byrnes suggested. In the South the 1956 presidential election was virtually a repetition of the previous canvass. Almost without a murmur, the southern delegates to the Republican convention supported the unanimous renomination of Eisenhower and Nixon on a platform that included a guarded acceptance of the Supreme Court's ruling against racial discrimination in public schools. The Democratic convention placated the southern wing of the party and eliminated any likelihood of a walkout by discarding its loyalty oath and by seating the regular delegations from such former Dixiecrat states as Mississippi and South Carolina. Over nominal southern opposition and a scattering of southern votes for Byrd, Russell, and others, the convention renominated Stevenson for president and placed Senator Estes Kefauver of Tennessee on the ticket for vice president. A compromise statement on civil rights said that Supreme Court decisions were a "part of the law of the land."

Again the defeated Democratic candidates received the electoral votes of most of the southern states, though President Eisenhower was able to hold those states that he had carried four years earlier and gained the state of Louisiana, drawing a slightly increased popular vote throughout the entire region. This election clarified the nature of the emerging southern Republicanism. Although Eisenhower received support among all areas and classes of the South, his major strength came from two sources. The first of these was traditional: the mountainous region that had been Republican since the Civil War. The second and far more significant source of Republican influence was the growing urban and suburban white population that represented the South's postwar industrial and business prosperity. The rural South generally was still in the Democratic party.

Eisenhower continued to please his southern supporters with the general conduct of foreign and domestic affairs. But in the realm of civil rights his second administration was increasingly subject to southern disapproval. His action in sending troops to Little Rock to enforce federal court desegregation orders angered many southern voters. James F. Byrnes and Senator Russell were two of the most influential figures to give public utterance to this regional feeling. Neither man challenged the president's authority to use troops to preserve the peace or questioned his personal motives or integrity in doing so. Byrnes accused him of being misled by his attorney general, Herbert Brownell, who, said the South Carolinian, acted out of political considerations. "He can safely say that the Democrats cannot beat that." Senator Russell protested what he believed to be an excessive use of force accompanied by illegal arrests and detentions—"tactics," he said, "which must have been copied from the manual issued the officers of Hitler's storm troopers."[8] A Georgia political spokesman doubted that any Republican could get that state's vote after "the Little Rock debacle."

The Little Rock episode was followed by the enactment of the Civil Rights Acts of 1957 and 1960, legislation that challenged the barriers to the black franchise in the South. Both acts were supported by the administration, and both were opposed by most southern voters. However timid the moves of President Eisenhower may have seemed to the champions of civil rights, they caused the white South to approach the presidential election of 1960 with alarm and confusion.

Southern Democrats pinned their forlorn hope on the presidential nomination of Lyndon B. Johnson of Texas, majority leader of the United States Senate. Johnson was a southern moderate whose pragmatic political philosophy, unusual parliamentary skill, and strong force of personality had enabled him to bridge the gap between the conservative southern and the liberal northern and western wings of the United States Senate. He had not been a signer of the southern manifesto of 1956 against the *Brown* decision, and he had steered the recent civil rights bills through the mine fields of senatorial debate and passage. But in sponsoring this legislation he had worked out compromises that reduced its effectiveness and pleased his southern colleagues. He seemed to offer the South its best protection against civil rights radicalism.

This southern hope was quickly dashed by the first-ballot nomination of the youthful Senator John F. Kennedy of Massachusetts. Kennedy was by the usual standards a moderate in all of his views, but his nomination represented a threat to southern intransigence in racial matters. He was pledged to work for equal voting rights, for compliance with the school desegregation decision, for the banning of discrimination in employment, and for enlarging the powers of the Justice Department to deal with such problems. His platform implied approval of the sit-ins that protested segregation at lunch counters. Southern members of the platform committee repudiated the civil rights plank with the biting accusation that it was part of a calculated effort to drive the South out of the Democratic party.

Besides his position on civil rights, Kennedy bore another severe handicap in competing for the affections of the militantly Protestant South. He was a Roman Catholic. Bitter memories of the South's treatment of presidential candidate Al Smith in 1928 haunted Kennedy's

supporters. Nor were these misgivings entirely groundless; many southerners, especially among the clergy, seriously considered the Massachusetts politician to be under the shadow of the Vatican; some of
them preached a virtual crusade against him. Wisely refusing to dodge
the issue, Kennedy went so far as to hold a question-and-answer meeting with 150 members of the Greater Houston Ministerial Association.
He emphatically denied that he was in any sense obligated to consult
with or get the approval of any ecclesiastical source in matters per-
taining to the office of the president of the United States. He would
resign the presidency, he said, rather than be subject to outside religious
pressure on any decision of national interest. Unquestionably Kennedy's religion cost him votes in the southern hinterland, but it probably
was not decisive in any state.

To offset Kennedy's disadvantages in the South, the Democratic
convention nominated Lyndon Johnson for vice president. It was a
superbly astute move. Johnson's name on the ticket, along with his
convincing oratory, reassured southern party stalwarts and great numbers of the southern rank and file that the region would be protected
in a Democratic administration. Johnson campaigned personally in
the South, traveling on a chartered train that announced his presence
with loudspeakers blaring "The Yellow Rose of Texas." Reporters
called his train the "Cornpone Special." Johnson's southern drawl grew
increasingly southern the farther south he went. He was said to be
talking about "Mah grandpappy" and "Mah great-grandpappy," and
to have expressed the wish at one community that he could "stay and
do a little sippin' and whittlin' with you."[9]

Johnson of course transacted his real business in private conversations, "eyeball to eyeball" with the leading political figures of the
region, discussing the possibilities of acceptable compromises on civil
rights and bargaining over the location of air bases, training camps,
shipyards, and other federal installations. The favorable responses of
such men as Governors Ernest Hollings of South Carolina and John
Patterson of Alabama and Senators Herman Talmadge of Georgia,
James Eastland of Mississippi, and Russell Long and Allen Ellender of
Louisiana were good omens for the Democrats in the forthcoming
canvass. Of the South's major active spokesmen, only Byrd remained
aloof.

The Republicans lacked the advantages in the South that they had enjoyed during the two previous presidential elections. Not only had the racial events and legislation of the second Eisenhower administration disenchanted many of the region's voters, but the Republican platform and candidates in 1960 were as threatening as the Democratic platform and candidates. The Republicans promised new legislation and vigorous enforcement of all existing laws against racial discrimination in voting, education, housing, and employment. The Republican candidates, Vice President Nixon for the presidency and Senator Henry Cabot Lodge, Jr., for the vice presidency, were perhaps more explicit than their Democratic opponents in offering strong action in these fields. Finally, the Republicans no longer had a man of Eisenhower's personal appeal among southerners. Only in religion did Nixon as a Protestant hold an edge over his rival in the minds of southern voters, and he refused to exploit this issue.

The Democratic strategy in the South worked. Nixon got a somewhat smaller proportion of the popular vote throughout the region than Eisenhower had drawn four years earlier, and the distribution of these votes was less favorable to the Republicans than it had been in the preceding election. Texas and Louisiana by slight margins returned to the Democratic ranks, leaving the Republicans only the three habitual southern bolters, Virginia, Tennessee, and Florida. In holding the bulk of the South, if by a hair, Kennedy won the presidency.

In spite of the rising defection of southern voters in presidential elections, the Democratic party during the 1950s retained a firm control over the congressional, state, and local politics of the region. Southerners increasingly "split their tickets" at the polls by voting for a Republican presidential candidate while they continued to support Democrats at all other levels. The strength of local Democratic organizations combined with the obvious advantages of congressional seniority to keep every United States senatorial seat of the old Confederate South in Democratic hands. Out of 105 United States representatives from the region in 1960, only 7 were Republican; these came chiefly from the traditional mountain Republican enclaves. All southern governors and the overwhelming majority of southern state legislators and local officials were Democrats. In many instances the Republicans still did not put up candidates for office. As late as 1960 only 39 percent of the southern seats in the United States House of Representatives were contested. A far higher proportion of such minor positions as magistrate, sheriff, and membership on the local school board went by default to Democrats.

Once in Congress, southern Democrats sought to protect what they considered the vital interests of the region by voting together, by voting with northern Republicans on special issues, and by the exercise of the privileges of seniority in office. The growing emphasis of the national Democratic party on civil rights added cohesion to the southern congressional caucuses, especially the Senate caucus, which became the major instrument of regional political strategy. The growing emphasis of the party on increased taxation, welfare spending, and sympathetic labor legislation strengthened the incipient "conservative coalition" of southern Democrats and northern Republicans. Seniority kept southerners in the chairmanships of a disproportionate number of the most important committees in Congress, and therefore in position to exert a disproportionate influence on national legislation. Southerners in 1960 were at the head of more than 60 percent of the standing committees of each house in Congress.

Among the most powerful figures in the House of Representatives were Speaker Sam Rayburn of Texas; Carl Vinson of Georgia, chairman of the Armed Services Committee; and Wilbur Mills of Arkansas, chairman of the Ways and Means Committee. Among the most powerful members of the Senate were Lyndon Johnson of Texas, majority leader; Richard Russell of Georgia, chairman of the Armed Services Committee; Harry Byrd of Virginia, chairman of the Finance Committee; James Eastland of Mississippi, chairman of the Judiciary Committee; and Lister Hill of Alabama, chairman of the Labor and Public Welfare Committee. Every piece of legislation that passed the Congress bore the imprint of southern Democratic unity and seniority. This was especially true of laws dealing with military-patriotic or regional issues. For example, southerners played top roles in supporting American diplomacy and arms in the cold war and in the American intervention in Korea.

The most striking illustration of how southern political power operated out of proportion to the region's population was the effectiveness of the southern opposition to the civil rights measures of the Truman and Eisenhower administrations. Regional congressmen killed Truman's program. Unable later to prevent the enactment of the civil rights legislation of 1957 and 1960, they nevertheless stripped both acts of much of their force. From the first act they deleted an article authorizing the Department of Justice to initiate school desegregation suits; from the second they excised a provision authorizing the elimination of racial discrimination in hiring by firms under government contract. One student of American politics has called the United States Congress "the southern-most of our national institutions," a jibe that in 1960 would have been remarkably apt.[10]

During the decades of the 1940s and 1950s state and local politics in the South did not change essentially from its prewar nature. As has already been pointed out, it remained predominantly Democratic and almost exclusively white. And because of a combination of ancient gerrymanders and the refusal of state legislatures to reapportion themselves according to recent population changes, it continued to be disproportionately influenced by the rural counties, many of which through loss of residents to the cities had come to resemble the "rotten boroughs" of early nineteenth-century England. Georgia perpetuated an extreme form of this imbalance by retaining its county-unit system of primaries whereby each county was allotted a given number of unit votes based roughly on its population in the late nineteenth century. In 1960 the smallest county in the state, with a population of 1,876, had two unit votes while Fulton County (Atlanta), population 556,326, had only six unit votes, a ratio of 98.1 to 1 in representation.[11]

Southern state governments in the 1940s and 1950s still operated in familiar ways. Virginia remained firmly under the Byrd machine with its efficiency, financial integrity, and frugality. Louisiana lived in and out of the shadow of Huey Long as Earl Long, Huey's younger brother and self-declared political heir, twice occupied the governor's mansion. Earl sponsored programs similar to Huey's of taxing and spending for social services; in his own manner Earl was as colorful as Huey, if not as imaginative or dynamic. In Georgia the Talmadge regime extended through the postwar era with Herman Talmadge, Eugene's son, twice serving as governor before rising to the United States Senate in the mid-1950s.

A majority of the states had no clearly established political machines, or no dynastic families comparable to the Byrds, Longs, or Talmadges. Vigorous factional rivalry prevailed within the Democratic party in all of them. North Carolina's political system generally represented a pragmatic combination of government and business in support of improved schools, roads, and other state institutions and services. South Carolina maintained its traditional social, political, and economic conservatism. Tennessee witnessed the decline of the Ed Crump machine in Memphis and retained a strong emphasis on localism and on the personality of individual candidates. Florida was a state of moderate conservatism. Texas with its immense oil, industrial, and agricultural interests was the most consistently Bourbon of the southern states.

The political factions of Mississippi, Alabama, and Arkansas coincided loosely with the states' geographic divisions: hill-country farmers and townsmen against low-country planters and their city machine and businessmen allies. The dominant figures to emerge out of this rivalry were Governor Folsom of Alabama and Governor Faubus of Arkansas. Both stood for a resurgent agrarianism or Populism in southern affairs. Both supported programs of improved roads, schools, hospitals, and social services. Folsom was a man of Rabelaisian stature and appetites; he was sometimes called "Big Jim" because of his size, sometimes "Kissing Jim" because of his taste for embracing pretty girls. He was enough of a racial liberal to entertain black Congressman Adam Clayton Powell in the Alabama governor's residence; he vetoed the interposition bills passed by the segregationist state legislature. Eventually he drank himself into political oblivion. Faubus was initially a racial moderate but when he became a champion of segregation in the Little Rock crisis, the action made him a state hero, even if a national villain. Invincible at the polls, he was reelected for four additional terms until in 1966 he announced he was no longer a candidate.

Southern politics in 1960 was remarkably similar to southern politics in 1940. But the forces generated during the intervening decades were moving the region toward a serious challenge of the political status quo.

V.

The Politics of Accommodation

The year 1960 may be considered a landmark in recent southern political history. The election of John F. Kennedy and Lyndon B. Johnson as president and vice president opened a series of events that brought about the most profound changes in southern politics since Reconstruction. During the decade of the 1960s the economic, legal, and social developments of the times began to make themselves felt in the public policies and practices of the region. By the mid-1970s the two most distinguishing observable characteristics of the old politics—Democratic solidarity and white exclusiveness—were gone.

Yet in a deeper sense southern political distinctiveness remained. Behind a new political rhetoric lay many traditional attitudes; behind the decline of Democratic control lay a form of political cohesiveness grounded upon ancient economic and social interests. Class and race continued to play dominant roles in the new politics. In reviewing the last quarter-century of southern political experience William C. Havard says: "The contemporary South, in brief, is both more heterodox and more subject to change than it has usually been pictured. It also continues to have identifiable social and political features that both tie it to the nation and yet keep it distinctive in its regional identity."[1]

A majority of the southern voters looked with dismay and anger upon President Kennedy's actions in supporting civil rights for blacks. His use of troops to enforce the desegregation of the University of Mississippi in the fall of 1962 brought unrestrained denunciation from Governor Barnett and various other state officials in the South. Senator Byrd called it "offensive to our form of government"; Senator Ervin of North Carolina criticized the government for resorting to force before the United States Supreme Court had ruled on an appeal in the case. The role of the Kennedy administration the following year in the Birmingham crisis and in the desegregation of the University of Alabama also provoked the resentment of great numbers of the region's citizens. So bitter was this hostility that some groups of school children in the Deep South were reported to have applauded the announcement of Kennedy's assassination.

The accession in November 1963 of Vice President Johnson to the presidency marked an ironic turn of events for the South. Three years earlier the region had yearned to see Johnson, a southerner, in the White House. But in his capacity as vice president he had grown progressively more liberal on civil rights. He had served as chairman of President Kennedy's Committee on Equal Employment Opportunities, and, notwithstanding a certain amount of criticism about his apparent efforts to avoid ruffling the feelings of southern congressmen, he had toured the country promoting civil rights and had exerted considerable pressure on national corporations to hire more blacks. His record was strong enough to cause the editor of *Ebony* to express faith in his determination to press the issue to its conclusion. "What does history tell us about Southerners in power? It suggests . . . that total national power changes them totally." Then, citing the example of Supreme Court Associate Justice Hugo Black of Alabama, "There is no Southerner like a reconstructed Southerner."[2]

Johnson's unwavering sponsorship of the epochal Civil Rights Act of 1964 confirmed great numbers of southern voters in their hostility to him. This emotion found its outlet in the support of Governor Wallace of Alabama, whose show of opposition to desegregation of the state university, whose course in temporarily closing a number of public schools in the face of desegregation, and whose fiery rhetoric against the pending civil rights bill had made him the champion of the state rights cause. During the spring of 1964 Wallace entered the Democratic presidential primaries of a number of southern and nonsouthern states, with the announced purpose of attempting to draw enough uncommitted electoral votes in the forthcoming election to prevent either principal candidate from gaining a majority, thus forcing the election into the House of Representatives. Denying that he was a racist, though acknowledging his belief in segregation, he laid major emphasis on preserving the constitutional rights of the states and liberties of individuals. These expressions were generally accepted to be "code words" meaning he would halt, if not reverse, the entire civil rights movement. That Wallace's views should be popular with southern voters caused no surprise, but his strength in the three outside states whose primaries he entered was astounding. He drew 34 percent of the primary vote in Wisconsin, 30 percent in Indiana, and 43 percent in Maryland. He now appeared to be a serious threat in the election.

But President Johnson's strength throughout the Democratic party was too great to be denied. Governor John B. Connally of Texas placed his name in nomination at the Democratic national convention, and southern delegates had no choice but to accept him and his chosen running mate, Senator Hubert Humphrey of Minnesota, a civil rights spokesman of long standing. The Democratic platform included a statement pledging full enforcement of the recently enacted civil rights legislation.

Although no walkout of southern delegates comparable to that of 1948 occurred, the convention was the scene of a bitter contest over the recognition and seating of the delegations from Alabama and Mississippi. Because of a recently adopted Alabama law barring the national Democratic ticket from the state ballot, the Alabama delegation was required to sign a pledge to support the ticket. The delegation as a whole rejected the pledge, but thirteen of thirty-six individual members eventually signed it and were seated. The problem of seating the Mississippi delegation was more serious. A racially mixed group of delegates calling themselves Freedom Democrats challenged the all-white regular delegation on the ground that it systematically excluded blacks. The convention adopted a compromise that seated the regulars but required a pledge to support the party ticket, seated two members of the Freedom Democrats as "delegates at large," and stipulated that no future convention would recognize delegations that excluded persons because of race or color. Both competing groups denounced the compromise, but it paved the way for sweeping changes in the nature of southern delegations to come. The voters of Mississippi and Alabama in 1964 probably would have turned away from the Democratic party under any circumstances short of the repudiation of the recent civil rights legislation; the fracas over the seating of their delegations made this outcome certain. In the view of the Mississippi regulars, Mississippi did not leave the Democratic party; the party left Mississippi.

The Republican presidential cause in the South in 1964 enjoyed formidable advantages. The party presidential candidate, Senator Barry Goldwater of Arizona, had voted against the Civil Rights Act of 1964; he now proposed to slow desegregation by giving the states a freer hand in the process. On the eve of the Democratic national convention Governor Wallace withdrew from the campaign, thus presumably releasing his supporters to vote for the Republican ticket. Wallace announced over national television that he had fulfilled his hopes of "conservatizing" the high councils of both major political parties. During the campaign Senator J. Strom Thurmond formally switched from the Democratic party to the Republican. Originally a Johnson admirer, Thurmond had grown more and more unhappy with his support of civil rights and with what Thurmond called his "no-win" foreign policy. Johnson's selection of Humphrey as the vice presidential candidate was the last straw for Thurmond. Against the advice of most of his political friends, including the elder statesman James F. Byrnes, Thurmond made the party leap.

But if the Republicans enjoyed advantages in the South arising out of their position on civil rights, they suffered insurmountable disadvantages in most of the southern states from the nature of their candidates themselves. Goldwater turned out to be perhaps the most inept campaigner up to that point in American history. He made impulsive and ambiguous pronouncements that could be, and were, interpreted to indicate an intention to escalate a minor American military involvement in remote Vietnam into a major war, to sell TVA to private power companies, to move lucrative southern war industries elsewhere in the interest of efficiency and economy, and to jettison the farm subsidy and social security programs. Ironically, even some of his statements on civil rights were capable of being twisted to mean that he was more zealous here than his opponent. The Republican vice presidential candidate, Congressman William E. Miller of New York, was a political nonentity. Johnson shrewdly countered Goldwater's overtures to the South by keeping his own running mate, Humphrey, out of the region, and by sending instead the First Lady on a train called the Ladybird Special to appeal to southern ties and to southern sentimentality about women. In the national avalanche of electoral votes for Johnson and Humphrey, only five southern states joined with Goldwater's own state of Arizona in voting the Republican ticket.

The elections revealed a number of significant things about the kaleidoscopic nature of recent southern politics. For the first time since Reconstruction the black vote had an impact in a number of states. A black was elected to the Tennessee state legislature, and a second black went to the Georgia legislature, the first having won a seat two years earlier. Blacks were elected to minor offices in a number of counties scattered throughout the region. More important, in the presidential race the black vote tipped the balance in four states (Arkansas, Tennessee, Virginia, and Florida) in favor of the Democrats. Because of the increased black vote, the Republicans drew a smaller proportion of the South's popular vote than Nixon had received four years before. Still these statistics did not conceal a rising southern discontent with the Democratic party. Goldwater captured the four old Dixiecrat states, South Carolina, Alabama, Mississippi, and Louisiana, plus the state of Georgia; of these, only Louisiana had ever voted Republican since Reconstruction. Mississippi gave him over 87 percent of its popular vote. Every state of the border South except Texas gave him more than 40 percent of the popular vote; Texas gave him better than 36 percent. In the light of southern history, the very dependence of the Democratic victory on black votes made it extremely precarious.

By the mid-1960s the movement of population from country to city, the growth of southern industry and prosperity, the increase in southern literacy along with the spread of formal education, and the appearance of an influential black vote all united to reshape the organic structure of the southern body politic. In 1962 the United States Supreme Court in the case *Baker* v. *Carr* began to give political effect to these recent developments by ruling that state legislative district lines must be drawn to result in equal representation for all districts. Two years later, in the case *Reynolds* v. *Sims*, the Court extended this principle to the apportionment of the upper houses of state legislatures; and two years later yet, in the case *Drum* v. *Seawell*, the principle was applied to congressional districts. Already, in 1963, the Court in the case *Gray* v. *Sanders* had ruled Georgia's county-unit system of primaries unconstitutional. The purpose of these "one man, one vote" decisions was to break the grip on the state governments of the over-represented rural counties and shift the political center of gravity to the growing cities. Many observers hailed the advent of a new, two-party politics in the South.

The most striking new development in southern politics was the rise of the black vote and the consequent election of blacks to public office. In 1947 fewer than 600,000 blacks in the eleven old Confederate states, about 12 percent of the black population of voting age, were registered to vote. Stimulated by a gradual improvement in economic status and education, by the civil rights movement in general, and particularly by the efforts of the Voter Education Project, the number and proportion of black registrants climbed steadily during the 1950s and 1960s; by 1964 the number stood above 1.9 million, representing about 38 percent of the black population of voting age. A substantial number of southern blacks supported Eisenhower in the 1950s, but they moved swiftly into Democratic ranks after he left the political scene. Understandably, virtually all of them voted for Johnson against Goldwater in 1964. As we have seen, their votes decided the outcome of the election in four southern states.

By 1966 more than 2.3 million blacks of the former Confederate states were registered, or about 46 percent of the total number of voting age, as compared with a registration of about 70 percent among the white population of the region. In that year's elections, black voters provided the margin of victory in the gubernatorial contest of Arkansas and probably in that of South Carolina. Southern blacks were also credited with casting the decisive votes in the election of one United States senator and two members of the House of Representatives. Nine additional blacks won seats in southern state legislatures, bringing the total to twenty. The Georgia legislature now had eleven blacks; the Tennessee legislature had six. Almost 300 blacks held elective offices in the region.[3]

Southern officeholders now began to alter their appeals and programs to meet the new economic and political conditions. They muted the stridency of their rhetoric on race, avoiding derogatory comments about blacks and shunning explicit appeals to prejudice. A group of governors came into power who were known as racial moderates and economic progressives; in other instances, men previously identified as racial or economic traditionalists, or both, moderated their decisions, if not their convictions, once they were in office and faced with the responsibility of keeping order and promoting prosperity. Whether neo-Populist, neo-Progressive, or neo-Bourbon, all still represented to a considerable degree a pragmatic blend of the three philosophies. All were dedicated to progress through governmental paternalism toward business, industry, and agriculture, as well as through expenditures for a wide range of public facilities and benefits, including highways, schools, hospitals, and welfare. All were aware of the necessity of racial tranquillity to the pursuit of this goal.

Perhaps the most obvious examples of these new trends in southern politics occurred in the decline of the Byrd machine in Virginia and the retreat from overt radicalism of Governor Lester Maddox of Georgia. Virginia in 1965 elected Mills Godwin governor; he was a product of the Byrd organization but was not shackled to its traditional thinking. In 1964 he had supported Johnson for president while Byrd himself had kept a "golden silence" and had retired from office soon after Godwin's election. Under the new governor the state abandoned both Byrd's hallowed pay-as-you-go principle in public finance and the vestiges of massive resistance to desegregation. Governor Maddox was the former segregationist restaurateur who had suggested the use of ax handles in ousting blacks from his premises. Maddox in office was anything but liberal; yet he practiced restraint in not trying to prevent court-ordered desegregation, and he appointed some blacks to state office and treated them with personal respect.

Even Governor Wallace of Alabama, who in the national mind was now the arch-racist, exercised sufficient moderation in his racial policies not to challenge federal authority except symbolically and rhetorically. Also, there was another side to Wallace. As a former legislative leader and campaign manager of "Big Jim" Folsom, he was a latter-day Populist. He lost the 1958 Democratic gubernatorial primary to John Patterson because he was not so vehement as Patterson on the racial issue. As Wallace inelegantly put it, "John Patterson out-nigguhed me. And boys, I'm not goin' to be out-nigguhed again." He wasn't. In 1962 he concentrated on race to defeat his old chief, Folsom, for the governorship. In office Wallace built fourteen new junior colleges and fifteen new trade schools, vastly increased state expenditures for schools and textbooks, inaugurated the greatest highway program in the state's history, and planned additional nursing homes and medical clinics for the aged and the poor. So effective along these lines was his administration that a Folsom supporter admitted, "His economic programs surpassed the fondest dreams of every liberal in the state. He did what all the Populists have always dreamed of doing."[4]

At the same time, Wallace favored business and industry by keeping corporate taxes low and by raising most of his revenue through levies on tobacco, beer, sports events, automobile licenses, and gasoline, the chief burdens of which fell upon the "common folk." Yet an outspoken critic of Wallace has said that aside from race he would have been one of the "most beneficial stewards ever to preside over Alabama."[5] In addition to his actual programs, Wallace's energy, truculence, and flamboyant personality captured the imagination of many supporters who might otherwise have been indifferent. Except for his emphasis on white supremacy, he has been aptly compared with the Louisiana potentate Huey P. Long.

Republican strength continued its erratic but persistent growth in the region. Besides retaining its traditional base in the mountainous areas, the party gained through the migration of newcomers into the South and through the appeal of its generally conservative economic and social outlook to a growing body of voters in the thousands of small towns and cities and in the spreading middle-class suburbs. Republican influence in the suburbs was especially significant. Fed by streams of professional employees and skilled workers from afar who were drawn to the region's expanding industries, and by the exodus of middle-class whites from the inner cities, the suburbs experienced the South's most rapid population growth. As a result of their expansion, under the United States Supreme Court's reapportionment rulings the suburbs came increasingly to hold the South's political balance of power. The Republican party also enjoyed a heavy windfall of votes from "mad Democrats" in all areas of the South because of the distaste among the white population for the civil rights programs of the Johnson administrations. Ironically, the party of emancipation and Reconstruction was now considered the white man's party.

For the first time since Reconstruction the Republicans began seriously to challenge the Democrats for state and local offices in the South. In 1966 the Republicans captured the governorships of Florida and Arkansas. The Republican victor in Florida was Claude Kirk, a businessman turned politician. Making a strong appeal to the state's widespread preference for racial segregation, Kirk gathered enough votes to win despite his loss of populous Dade County (Miami). The successful Republican candidate in Arkansas was Winthrop Rocke-feller, multimillionaire grandson of John D. Rockefeller, who drew enough urban, black, and affluent white votes to capitalize on a reaction against Faubus and oust the Democrats.

In 1964 the Republican gubernatorial candidate in Louisiana, Charlton Lyons, a Shreveport businessman, drew approximately 38 percent of the state's vote against Democrat John McKeithen, an exceptionally skilled political tactician who was able to present himself at once as a Longite, a reformer, and a segregationist. In 1966 the Georgia Republican candidate, Howard "Bo" Callaway, won 47 per-cent of the vote against the winner, Maddox. Mississippi Republican leader Reubel Phillips got more than 30 percent of the vote in the 1966 election against John Bell Williams. Two years later the Repub-lican nominee in North Carolina, James Gardner, took better than 48 percent of the vote against Robert Scott, who was the popular son of a popular former governor. That same year in Texas the Republican candidate, Paul Egger, got 49 percent of the vote in opposing the suc-cessful Democratic nominee, Preston Smith.

In 1969 Republican Linwood Holton capitalized upon the disarray of the old Byrd organization to win the governorship of Virginia; a year later Republican Winfield Dunn captured the top office in Ten-nessee; and in 1972 Republican James Holshouser was elected gov-ernor of North Carolina. These Republican gains were partly offset, however, by the loss of the governorships of two states, Arkansas and Florida.

The Republicans also made telling southern gains in Congress and in the state legislatures. In 1961 Republican John Tower of Texas won a special senatorial election to fill the place left vacant when Lyndon Johnson resigned to assume the vice presidency. In 1964 Senator Thurmond of South Carolina made his switch from the Demo-cratic to the Republican party. In 1966 Republican Howard Baker of Tennessee captured the senatorial seat formerly held by Estes Kefauver, who had died three years before. In 1968 Republican Edward Gurney defeated Senator Leroy Collins to take one of Florida's sena-torial positions. Two years later, in one of the most celebrated sena-torial contests of recent years, the veteran liberal Democratic senator from Tennessee, Albert Gore, lost his place to the Republican chal-lenger, W. E. Brock III. In 1972 Republicans Jesse Helms from North

Carolina and William Scott from Virginia captured seats in the Senate. Republicans now held seven of the twenty-two senatorial seats of the South.

Republican gains in the lower house of Congress were almost as impressive as in the Senate. In 1948 there were only two Republican representatives from the old Confederate states; they hailed from traditionally Republican districts of East Tennessee. By 1960 the number had risen to seven, and in 1972 Republicans held thirty-four southern seats, almost one-third of the region's strength in the lower house. Two southern states were represented by Republican majorities: Virginia, by six Republicans to four Democrats; and Tennessee, by five Republicans to three Democrats.

Although the rise of Republican membership in southern state legislatures was not so sharp as that in the United States Congress, it was nevertheless significant. In 1948, of a total of more than 1,300 seats in the lower houses of southern legislatures only 43 were held by Republicans; of 450 seats in the upper houses only 10 were held by Republicans. Little change occurred during the 1950s; in 1960 the Republicans still had only 48 seats in southern lower houses and 12 seats in upper houses. But the following decade, with its rapid industrialization and urbanization, its widespread racial unrest, and its reapportionment rulings, brought a gradual but steady growth of Republican strength at the state level, particularly in the border states of Tennessee, North Carolina, Virginia, and Florida, which provided most of the increase in Republican legislators. In 1970 Republicans filled 178 seats in southern lower houses and 58 seats in upper houses, about 13 percent in both cases. At one point, in 1968, the lower house of the Tennessee legislature was evenly divided between the two parties. Georgia was the one state of the core South that showed a sizable growth in the number of Republican legislators. In 1948 Georgia had a lone Republican in each house; in 1970 it had 22 Republican representatives and 6 Republican senators.

In spite of the countless recent changes in the life of the South, the traditional forces of race and "state rights" continued to exert a decisive influence on the politics of the region. The idea of a third party to bring southern pressure upon the candidates of the major parties and upon the administrations in power remained dormant but not dead. The man who picked it up and gave it new purpose and energy was Governor Wallace of Alabama. Wallace demonstrated his audacity, determination, and political resourcefulness in the manner in which he kept himself politically afloat until the 1968 presidential election. Prevented by the state constitution from serving consecutive terms as governor, Wallace in 1966 had his wife, Lurleen, run for the office, making clear his intention to direct her administration if she should be elected.

The outcome of the election made unmistakable the strength of the Wallace appeal. In the Democratic primary Mrs. Wallace won a stunning victory by taking a clear majority (52 percent) of the votes over a field of nine other candidates, including State Attorney General Richmond Flowers, who as a racial moderate got most of the black vote, and ex-Governors Folsom and Patterson. In the general election Mrs. Wallace defeated a highly respected Republican opponent, James D. Martin, by a two-to-one margin. The people of Alabama had spoken. Wallace served as "de facto" governor until his wife's death of cancer in 1968, when Lieutenant Governor Albert Brewer succeeded to the position. By now Wallace was well established as the leader of the strongest political force in the Deep South and of the major third-party threat in the nation.

The presidential election of 1968, along with the accompanying congressional and state elections, brought together the many divergent strains of recent southern politics. A majority of the southern Democrats found themselves hopelessly alienated from the national party by the decisions taken in the ill-fated Chicago nominating convention. Again there were bitter controversies over the recognition and seating of delegations from such states as Mississippi, Alabama, and Georgia.

Acting under the antibias mandate of the preceding convention, these states included token numbers of blacks in their regular delegations. For example, of sixty-eight positions in the Mississippi delegation four were originally held by blacks, but three of these four seats were vacated when delegates resigned in protest against alleged discrimination and were not replaced. Governor John Bell Williams, a known Wallace supporter, led the delegation with its lone black member. A rival group of blacks and white liberals calling themselves the Loyal National Democrats of Mississippi, led by such prominent blacks as Dr. Aaron Henry and Charles Evers, brother of the slain NAACP official, and by Hodding Carter III, son of the Greenville editor and author, challenged the regulars on the usual grounds of racial bias in the method by which their members were selected. Carter privately admitted that real improvement had occurred in the state party since the previous convention, but he contended the improvement was not enough to justify recognition. As he pungently phrased it, the party could not be "half pregnant." Evers ended his appeal to the convention credentials committee with the emotional plea, "If you close the door in our face this day, God help us."[6]

The Georgia regulars were led by Governor Maddox, who with the state party chairman had handpicked the members. This delegation also contained a token number of blacks. The young black Georgia legislator Julian Bond, leader of the challenging delegation, pointed out that the regulars had only a 2.01 percent black membership, while blacks comprised 23 percent of the state's population. The Alabama delegation, dominated by Governor Wallace, was similar in makeup to the Mississippi and Georgia groups. It was contested by a delegation under the leadership of the Birmingham attorney David J. Vann, calling itself the Alabama Independent Democratic party.

The convention voted to recognize many of the challengers. The Georgia and Alabama votes were split between the regulars and the contenders; the Mississippi regulars were unseated and replaced by their rivals, who were equally divided between whites and blacks. By discarding the unit rule in voting, by nominating Hubert Humphrey and Edmund Muskie for president and vice president, and by pledging vigorous enforcement of the existing civil rights acts, along with enactment of additional laws if the present statutes should "fail to serve their purposes," the convention virtually forfeited southern support in the forthcoming election.

At the opening of the Republican nominating convention in Miami the former vice president and former presidential candidate Richard M. Nixon was the choice of most southern delegates. They doubtless preferred the views of another candidate, Governor Ronald Reagan of California, who now represented the right wing of the party. But sobered by the Goldwater fiasco of four years before, the southerners were determined to throw their support to a man with a chance of winning, and they sensed that Nixon was that man. In an early caucus of party chairmen from the South, Nixon drew 259 votes to Governor Reagan's 57 and New York Governor Nelson Rockefeller's 18.

Nixon was nevertheless anxious about Reagan's appeal to conservatism, and the southerners played upon this anxiety. Influenced by his foremost southern champion, Senator Strom Thurmond, Nixon adopted what came to be called a southern strategy, designed to hold the region in line without alienating the nonsouthern delegates. The exact nature of his commitments to Thurmond are not known, but they satisfied the old Dixiecrat, a man not easily appeased, and through him they satisfied the bulk of the southern delegates. Their vote was critical in giving Nixon the nomination on the first ballot and in placing Governor Spiro Agnew of Maryland, a practitioner of stern measures against civil disorder, on the ticket for the vice presidency.

Meanwhile, Governor Wallace was already in the field under the banner of a third party, the American Independent party. In announcing his candidacy, Wallace promised to try to get Congress to repeal the "so-called civil rights acts," which he condemned as violations of constitutional property rights, free enterprise, and local government. He later called for a return of the public schools to absolute state control. Denouncing the legion of "briefcase totin'" HEW bureaucrats, he promised to throw all of their briefcases into the Potomac River. He advocated attempting to negotiate peace in Vietnam, but if this should fail, then he would bring a quick end to the war through increased military action. His central theme was "law and order," an appeal to white southerners generally and to the increasing number of white nonsoutherners who were angry over the rioting of blacks in the cities. Wallace promised to suppress the violence even if he had to patrol the streets with soldiers wielding bayonets.

Wallace first approached former Governor and former Senator Albert B. Chandler of Kentucky as a possible vice presidential running mate. Chandler withdrew, accusing Wallace's aides of attempting to persuade him to drop his liberal attitude toward the blacks. He alleged also that Wallace was pressed to drop him by "Mr. Big," the oil interests of the Southwest, to which Wallace retorted, "Mr. Big are the people of the country, and they are very big." Wallace then selected retired Air Force General Curtis LeMay. LeMay was an unequivocal spokesman of peace through military victory in Vietnam. Although Wallace largely shared this view, he sometimes found LeMay's blunt pronouncements politically embarrassing. For example, he was obliged to "reinterpret" the general's statement that, if essential for victory in Vietnam, he would resort to nuclear arms.[7]

Wallace campaigned with his usual vigor throughout the country, arousing demonstrations of protest wherever he appeared outside the South. In many northern places he was saved from mobs only by the determined intervention of the police. Nevertheless, many observers predicted for him a heavy northern vote because of the "white back-lash" against black militancy. Public opinion polls taken in the early fall indicated he was favored by 21 percent of all American voters and was drawing more votes away from Nixon than from Humphrey. The polls also showed that a major source of Wallace's strength out-side the South was among the laboring classes. Wallace was aware that he could not win the election. His appeal was aimed primarily at southerners in the hope he could carry out the Dixiecrat scheme of attracting enough of the region's total electoral votes to prevent either major candidate from receiving a majority, thereby forcing the elec-tion into the House of Representatives where southerners might hold the balance and gain desired concessions.

But Nixon carried all the states of the border South except Texas and Arkansas, plus Thurmond's South Carolina. Wallace carried only five states: Georgia, Alabama, Mississippi, Louisiana, and Arkansas. He won only 13 percent of the national vote. This was scarcely bet-ter than the Dixiecrats had done twenty years before. Yet the election vividly illustrated the durability of the old perceptions in southern politics. In the lower South Wallace drew a proportion of the popular vote ranging from 43 percent in Georgia to 65 percent in Alabama. In the border South his support was understandably weaker; it varied from 20 percent in Texas and Florida to 40 percent in Arkansas.

But Wallace's presence exerted a powerful influence in those south-ern states he did not win. It caused the victorious Republican candidate to trim his strategy ever closer to the southern pattern by emphasizing the need for improved "law and order," denouncing the "liberal cast" of the United States Supreme Court, and promising to review HEW guidelines on public school desegregation. Had Nixon followed a dif-ferent course, Wallace probably would have won the great majority, possibly all, of the southern states. Humphrey carried only one southern state, Texas. Ironically, those traditional forces that once created a solid Democratic South had now brought into being a virtually solid non-Democratic South in presidential politics.

Still the long ascendancy of the Democratic party in the South prevailed in all but presidential contests. So redoubtable was this form of Democratic strength that as late as 1972 more than one-third of the region's congressional seats were uncontested by the Republicans.[8] Many southerners who voted for Republican presidential candidates were actually Democrats in protest against the men and measures of the national party. On the other hand, many southern Democrats were crypto-Republicans; they were Republican in sentiment but were registered as Democrats in order to strengthen their hands in local politics. In the presidential elections they voted the Republican ticket, and some of them did so in the elections for Congress and the governorship. But as registered Democrats they voted in the Democratic primaries, thereby giving southern support to the "soundest" (that is, to the most conservative) Democratic presidential candidates, and assuring that in the general elections for state and local offices the candidates of both parties would be "acceptable." For whatever reasons and in whatever guise, a strong majority of the electorate officially remained Democrats. This kept the bulk of the region's congressional representation, state administrations, and county and municipal offices securely in Democratic hands.

In spite of ultimate defeat in the civil rights acts and other social and economic legislation of the 1960s, the South with its high degree of solidarity among congressional spokesmen continued to exert a disproportionate influence over the nation's policies. Southern senators and representatives were customarily reelected for such long periods that they appeared to serve by divine right, and through a combination of seniority, experience, and native political astuteness they retained an imposing share of the most powerful offices in Congress: as late as 1972, the chairmanships of eight of seventeen Senate standing committees and eight of twenty-one House standing committees.

Nor was this the full measure of their strength, for they also held other positions of great consequence, and many of the committees they chaired were especially strategic ones. For example, Senator Russell, dean of the southern group, was until his death in 1971 president pro tempore of the Senate and chairman of its Appropriations Committee; he was perhaps the most influential figure in the upper house.[9] Until his defeat for reelection in 1974 Senator William Fulbright of Arkansas was chairman of the Committee on Foreign Relations. Senator John Stennis of Mississippi was chairman of the Armed Services Committee. Senator Russell Long of Louisiana until 1969 was majority whip of the Senate, and after losing this post he remained chairman of the important Finance Committee; Congressman Hale Boggs, also of Louisiana, was until his accidental death in 1972 the majority whip of the lower house. And until Congressman Wilbur Mills of Arkansas succumbed in 1975 to a mental and emotional upset involving excessive drinking and a series of escapades with an exotic female dancer, he ran the most powerful committee in the House of Representatives, Ways and Means.

From these vantage points the southern leaders employed a host of parliamentary devices such as bottling up bills in committee, offering crippling amendments, resorting to unlimited debate (filibustering), bargaining collectively with Democrats from other regions, and, in extremity, joining forces with Republican colleagues to kill or modify legislation they and their constituents opposed or to introduce or support legislation they favored. This "conservative coalition" of Republicans and southern Democrats was an old one, though V. O. Key found that its importance in the 1940s was exaggerated in the minds of political thinkers. But his conclusion was no longer valid in the postwar decades, for the incidence of roll call votes in which Republicans and southern Democrats in the House of Representatives voted together against northern Democrats more than doubled between the 1940s and the 1970s. In one session (1967) this alliance occurred in better than a third of all the votes taken on controversial issues.[10]

Regional political cohesiveness, whether represented by southern Democrats or southern Republicans, was at its height in the civil rights contest, but it made itself felt also in many other fields of domestic legislation. It continued to assert a traditional southern conservativeness in its general opposition to increased federal spending for welfare and urban development, the growth of the federal bureaucracy, federal control over local educational and welfare agencies, federal support of civil liberties, and all attempts to curb the func-

tions of the House Un-American Activities Committee or the Sub-
versive Activities Control Board. Southern spokesmen were the largest
and most vehement group against those ambitious programs for
economic and social uplift that President Kennedy called the New
Frontier and President Johnson called the Great Society.

Southern influence was as strong in national foreign affairs as it
was in domestic policy. It was particularly notable when there was a
question of military operations, for at the end of World War II the
southern people held perhaps the least isolationist outlook of all
American regions. Their political leaders gave virtually unbroken support to the creation of the United Nations Organization, tariff reduction, foreign aid through the Marshall Plan, and the containment of
Communism through the Truman Doctrine, the North Atlantic Treaty
Organization (NATO), and American military preparedness. Perhaps
it was not accidental that American armed intervention in Korea occurred under a president of Confederate ancestry and the action in
Vietnam took place under a president of southern birth and rearing
as well as southern forebears.

But southern spokesmen reflected also the shifting moods and
rising uncertainties of their constituents in response both to domestic
and overseas developments. Industrial growth at home further cooled
the historic regional antagonism against tariffs, as representatives of
the textile, oil, and other manufacturing and extractive interests
sought protective import duties or quotas. Disillusioned over the ques-
tionable effects of foreign aid, particularly in non-European areas, and
bitter over the stalemate in Korea, southern leaders in the 1950s and
1960s showed a loss of faith in cooperative foreign undertakings.
The debacle in Vietnam eroded their faith even in the most pronounced form of southern internationalism, belief in the effectuality
of military power. Senator Russell privately warned against American
entry into Vietnam; Senator Fulbright initially supported the action
but ultimately became one of its most vehement critics. Yet southerners and their political leaders remained into the 1970s perhaps the most
dedicated of all American advocates of the unilateral employment of
arms, keeping alive a vestigial spirit of "going it alone" to police the
world.

By the 1970s all regional political processes and decisions were
showing the effects of the mounting black vote. In 1972 more than

3.5 million southern blacks were on the voting rolls, approximately 62 percent of all who were eligible to vote. As a result of this increased strength the number of blacks elected to office in the former Confederate states rose to 1,148. There were now two southern blacks in the United States House of Representatives—one from Texas and one from Georgia. Southern state legislatures contained sixty-one blacks. In local elections the blacks won control of a number of city, town, and county administrations. In some of the most celebrated of these victories Charles Evers in 1969 became mayor of Fayette, Mississippi; Clarence E. Lightner in 1974 became mayor of Raleigh, North Carolina; and Maynard Jackson the same year captured the mayoralty of Atlanta, the most symbolically important city of the South, as well as one of the region's largest and most progressive metropolises.[11] The administration of New Orleans rested upon a coalition of whites and blacks; a similar coalition, but with Chicanos included also, had hopes of taking control of Houston.

These were striking black gains. They unquestionably were forerunners of more black political advances to come. But the outcome of the recent elections also pointed up the persistence of the color line in southern politics. Here and there black candidates were able to draw sizable numbers of white votes. Jackson got the votes of a liberal white minority in Atlanta; more significant, Lightner won in Raleigh with substantial support from the city's white majority. But these were rare exceptions. In general, the blacks could prevail only in localities of heavy black concentration; on statewide racial issues they lacked the numbers to win. Also, the economic dependency and traditional deference of many blacks caused them to continue voting for white candidates. Some of them were reported to say with an inverted pride, "I ain't votin' for no nigger."[12] The higher posts—governor and United States senator—remained exclusively white. The total number of southern blacks in elective offices in 1972 represented only about 1.3 percent of the number of positions.

The best example of the limits of black political power appeared in the 1971 Mississippi governor's election, where Charles Evers challenged tradition directly by running against the leading white Democratic candidate, William Waller, a racial moderate by local standards. Evers campaigned vigorously. He appealed to the small white farmers and poor white laborers as well as to the blacks; he received financial support from friends and liberals in the North. Still he lost disastrously. Although blacks comprised 30 percent of the registered voters, Evers got only 22 percent of the total number of votes. A Mississippi editor hit close to the mark in writing: "The election . . . proves that an historic relationship of paternalism of the whites for the blacks still exists in Mississippi; that the blacks look upon the whites for leadership, for guidance, for favors, for loans, for friendship." Another "historic relationship" also caused many blacks to vote for the white candidate, that of fear and economic pressure. Four racial killings occurred in the months preceding the election. Reportedly, some blacks asking for bank loans were told, "Go see Charles Evers." But the decisive reason for Evers's failure lay in the determination and cohesiveness of the whites, who went to the polls in unprecedented numbers, and who, almost to a man, voted for Waller.[13]

President Nixon in his first administration responded to the white dominance of southern politics with a vigorous promotion of his so-called southern strategy. He encouraged a slowdown in the pressing of school desegregation suits by the Justice Department; he made futile efforts to place strong southern conservatives, Judge Clement F. Haynsworth of South Carolina and Judge G. Harrold Carswell of Florida, on the United States Supreme Court; and he issued statements disapproving the widespread bussing of pupils in order to meet a racial formula for the schools. After the outlawing by the courts of the freedom-of-choice plans of desegregation, the Justice Department entered suits to compel the creation of unitary school systems in the rural and small-town South, where the remaining dual systems were interpreted to represent an extension of the earlier legal segregation; but the administration shrewdly forbore stern measures against the actual, or "de facto," segregation in the suburban schools of both North and South.

The Alabama Democratic gubernatorial primaries in the spring and summer of 1970 offered a test of the vitality of the inchoate political coalition of southern liberals, businessmen, suburbanites, and blacks as against the continuing strength of George C. Wallace. In the runoff election Wallace faced Governor Albert Brewer, winner in the initial canvass, who because of his relative moderation on race had received the bulk of the state's almost 300,000 black votes. Wallace's appeal was explicit. He denounced the recent federal court decisions, the HEW guidelines, and the bussing of pupils in order to desegregate the schools; he urged whites to vote for their "own kind"; and he warned that his defeat would doom the state to fifty years of "black bloc voting." Wallace carried the state by about 32,000 ballots out of a total of better than 1 million. This was his narrowest victory. In addition to the black voters, roughly one-third of the whites opposed him. But he remained secure among the white farmers and laborers, traditionally his stanchest supporters. Moreover, he was running against a conservative white Alabamian. There could be no doubt of Wallace's ability to score heavily among southern voters if he should again be a contender for the presidency.

Wallace's continued success in Alabama and the defeats of Gore in Tennessee and Evers in Mississippi did not fully measure the effect of increased black voting and the disillusionment of many whites with the incumbent administrations. In the 1970 elections liberal candidates swept into the governorship of a number of southern states: Reubin Askew in Florida, Jimmy Carter in Georgia, John C. West in South Carolina, Dale Bumpers in Arkansas, and Edwin Edwards in Louisiana. Georgia's Governor Carter was hailed as a spokesman for a genuinely "new" South when he proclaimed: "The time for racial discrimination is over." All of the victorious liberal governors stood for increased taxes on industries and corporations and for progressive social legislation. Also, sixteen new southern congressmen elected in 1972 tended to be more liberal than their senior regional colleagues in voting on current issues.

Governor Askew of Florida took the lead in actual liberal accomplishments. He was an abstemious north Floridian, who served apple juice at press conferences in the governor's mansion. But he showed remarkable determination and adroitness in pushing his reforms through the state legislature. He was said to have beaten the lobbyists at their own game. The base of his legislative support came from urban south Florida, which was the chief beneficiary of the Supreme Court's reapportionment rulings. Dade County (Miami) alone now had twenty-eight representatives, whereas it had previously been entitled only to four. Askew promptly got a tax on corporation profits that increased the levy on General Motors from $1,500 a year to an estimated $2.2 million. The new tax brought an aggregate increase of an estimated $120 million in the state's annual revenue. Askew also sponsored laws for improvement of the schools, reform of the penal system, authorization of no-fault automobile insurance and no-fault divorce, increased workmen's compensation, and environmental protection. Finally, he appointed blacks to many responsible positions in the state government.[14]

Obviously, new forces were astir in the South. But new forces, such as Populism and Progressivism, had stirred in the region before, only to be absorbed and adapted to traditional ends. The presidential election of 1972 and subsequent political developments in both region and nation indicated that the old southern fires were not quenched. The bitter southern opposition to the bussing of pupils to desegregate the schools was perhaps the chief factor in keeping these emotions alive. Also, recent federal court rulings against de facto segregation in schools outside the South spread the civil rights antipathy throughout the nation. The growing malaise over inflation, the activities of the federal bureaucracy, alleged tax favors to business and industry and tax loopholes for the rich, abuses of the welfare system, and continued crime in the streets contributed to the likelihood of revolts; and controversies over the Vietnam war and over measures for environmental protection and the conservation of resources united with the other sources of discord to provide an expanded base for a political protest movement.

Governor Wallace moved decisively to seize this opportunity. Entering a number of Democratic primaries, he quickly established that he was still an effective candidate by condemning both the Nixon administration and the programs of such Democratic rivals as Senators Edmund Muskie of Maine, Hubert Humphrey of Minnesota, and George McGovern of South Dakota. Bussing was Wallace's major theme, but he appealed to the nation's rural and middle classes by denouncing inequities in the tax system and fraud and waste in the welfare and social security programs; and he invoked American patriotism by demanding an "honorable" solution in Vietnam, and by opposing any agreement on arms control that denied nuclear supremacy to the United States.

Wallace stunned his opponents by winning a plurality in the Florida primary, in spite of Governor Askew's opposition, with 42 percent of the vote. He won in Tennessee and then in North Carolina, where the popular ex-Governor Terry Sanford entered his own name presumably in an attempt to draw Wallace's fire away from the other Democratic candidates. Incredibly, Wallace won the Democratic primary in Michigan by a clear majority over the combined counts for McGovern and Humphrey. On May 15, while campaigning successfully in Maryland, he was shot and left permanently disabled in a nearly successful assassination attempt.

Wallace quite probably would have carried the entire South if he had been able to remain in the campaign. The popular response to his appeals gave pause to liberal politicians of the region, most of whom began to equivocate on racial matters. Governor Carter of Georgia made a series of antibussing statements that sounded suspiciously like those of Wallace. Only Governor Askew of Florida stood firm on the issue.[15]

More significant than the retreat of southern politicians was the attitude of President Nixon, who now adopted opposition to bussing as an official part of his campaign for reelection, while his Democratic rival, Senator McGovern, was committed to bussing as an acceptable means of school desegregation. McGovern was also handicapped in the South by his liberal views on taxation and welfare and his advocacy of unconditional withdrawal from Vietnam. With Wallace out of the contest, Nixon carried every southern state overwhelmingly in his landslide victory. Louisiana with 66 percent of its vote gave him his lowest southern majority; Mississippi with 79 percent, his highest. Thus, for the first time the South voted solidly for a Republican. Yet, ironically, perhaps never, not even at the height of Reconstruction, was the color line so distinct in southern politics; the great majority of the whites voted for Nixon while most of the blacks supported his opponent.

Southern gubernatorial primaries and elections in 1973 and 1974 also indicated that the earlier victories of the liberal governors and congressmen had not paved the way for a liberal sweep of the region. For example, Wallace again won convincingly in Alabama. But the situation in Virginia was perhaps the clearest local sign of the persistence of traditional forces in spite of sharp realignments. Mills Godwin, who as a Democratic governor in the 1960s had abandoned the principles of the Byrd leadership, now won the top state office as a Republican. The most telling points in his campaign were opposition to bussing and endorsement of the state's right-to-work law. Many of his pronouncements sounded like a voice from the tomb of the elder

Byrd. For example, "Continuity and predictability have been [Virginia's] prime assets."[16]

In national politics the South was deeply involved with the second Nixon administration. The South was the most patient region of the nation with the president's deliberate withdrawal from Vietnam, and it was generally the region most reluctant to impute guilt to him in the Watergate and related scandals which now came to the fore. Though Senators Ervin of North Carolina and Baker of Tennessee drew upon ancient regional concepts of strict construction of the Constitution and fears of executive power to probe Nixon's role in these affairs, his main hope of escaping conviction and removal from office lay in the deep-rooted conservatism of the southern bloc in the United States Senate. The ultimate erosion of this support helped to bring on his resignation.

A wave of congressional reform following the collapse of the Nixon administration crippled and threatened to destroy one of the South's most cherished means of political influence, the congressional seniority system. In early 1975 a revolt of liberal young Democrats in the House of Representatives ousted Louisiana's F. Edward Hebert from the chairmanship of the Armed Services Committee and Texas's W. R. Poague from that of the Agriculture Committee; the same revolt played a significant part in the forced resignation of Wilbur Mills as chairman of Ways and Means. Possibly the long southern exercise of the Concurrent Majority was coming to an end.

But no realistic consideration of the South and national politics could ignore the presence of George C. Wallace. Paralysis of his legs confined him largely to a wheelchair, and he lived in constant pain; but he nevertheless remained a formidable figure in regional and national politics as well as in Alabama affairs. He had moved closer than before to the middle of the political road, for he now accepted legal desegregation as a fact of life. Still he was implacably opposed to bussing school children to achieve desegregation; also, he spoke for those Americans who were resentful that Vietnam had been "lost" because of an unwillingness to make a more decisive military effort in the 1960s. A significant number of southern blacks, disenchanted with bussing and attracted to his Populist measures, now joined with the white masses in supporting him. Charles Evers was reported to have said he might vote for Wallace for vice president if he should run on a ticket with Senator Edward Kennedy for president.[17] National public opinion surveys in the spring of 1975 showed Wallace leading the field of active contenders for the Democratic presidential nomination.

Events of the 1970s appeared to place the South nearer than ever to the mainstream of American politics. Unquestionably the region had experienced vast political changes in the preceding decade. But one might ask whether the American political mainstream had not made as great an accommodation to southern politics as southern politics had made to the American mainstream.

VI.

Turbulent Progress in Education

Southern faith in formal education reached new heights in the post–World War II years. The unparalleled prosperity of the times seemed to be partly the result of the great educational efforts made by the southern people during the first half of the century, and thus it appeared to fulfill the prophecies of earlier generations who had looked to the schools as the cure for the ills of the region. Every prominent public figure—whether Democrat, Dixiecrat, or Republican, whether liberal, moderate, or conservative in social and political outlook—gave unflagging support to the expansion and improvement of the schools. The region made strides toward excellence in education, but in the early 1970s it still had not attained its goal of parity with the rest of the country.

The increased birth rate of the war years and immediately thereafter created unprecedented demands for teachers, classrooms, and educational equipment in an area where the proportion of children of school age within the population was already well above the national ratio. Between 1940 and 1972 the number of pupils in elementary and secondary schools of the former Confederate states increased almost 60 percent, and there was a dramatic shift in the major centers of the school population. For example, during this period the number of pupils in Mississippi actually declined slightly, while the number in Texas more than doubled and the number in Florida more than quadrupled. Fortunately, the rising productivity and income of the region made possible an immense program of educational expansion. State legislatures, local authorities, and taxpayers all cooperated in providing

Table 5

SOUTHERN SCHOOL ENROLLMENTS 1940, 1971

	Public elementary and high schools		Colleges and universities	
	1971 (thousands)	% change since 1940	1971 (thousands)	% change since 1940
Alabama	821	+ 21	112	+460
Arkansas	460	− 1	53	+382
Florida	1,570	+325	252	+191
Georgia	1,136	+ 54	136	+491
Louisiana	874	+ 85	130	+400
Mississippi	545	− 8	77	+450
N. Carolina	1,198	+ 35	185	+478
S. Carolina	649	+ 35	76	+375
Tennessee	936	+ 44	142	+468
Texas	2,812	+112	463	+517
Virginia	1,110	+ 95	164	+531
Total South	12,110	+ 67	1,790	+542

Source: U.S., Bureau of the Census, *Statistical Abstract of the United States*, 1943, p. 213; Department of Health, Education and Welfare, *Digest of Educational Statistics*, 1974, p. 32.

ever-increasing sums for the construction of new public schools and the enlargement and improvement of those already established. By 1973 the yearly appropriations for capital outlay were approximately equal to the total value of school property at the end of World War II. A majority of the new institutions were located in the booming cities and suburbs, but new facilities were required for the rural areas as well. Not only were the prewar country school plants often outworn and dilapidated; they were considered archaic in design and ill-suited to the spirit of economic and social progress now astir in the region.

Also, the rural school consolidation movement, which was well under way before the war, came into its final stage with the paving of country roads and the use of fleets of busses to bring the scattered pupils to central locations. During the 1950s and 1960s the yellow school bus became a symbol of educational advance in the region, while the disappearing one-, two-, and three-teacher schools came to be looked upon as relics of a backward and indigent past. Bigness was considered a virtue by most school authorities; it made possible the concentration of funds for hiring a more adequate faculty and staff, for the erection of superior buildings, and for the purchase of more and better teaching and recreational equipment. It also assembled enough husky boys and girls to enable the country schools to develop competitive athletic teams. Many of the consolidated rural schools became as large as those of the smaller cities.

Within a decade after the war most of the region's schools were in newly constructed, streamlined buildings of concrete, steel, and glass. Their libraries and laboratories often were as extensive as those of the smaller colleges before the war. They were heated with automatically controlled central furnaces, and by the 1960s many of them were air-conditioned against the heat of the spring and fall. In addition to the usual classrooms, auditoriums, and gymnasiums, they had modern cafeterias and, often, modish lounges for faculty and students. As this school architecture in turn grew dated in the late 1960s and early 1970s it began to be replaced with construction of more advanced design, sometimes including clusters of round buildings somewhat resembling oil storage tanks, but purporting to promote better space utilization and a less inhibited flow of learning experiences.

Legislators and local officials were usually more generous with money for physical plants than for other educational needs. But they did not neglect measures to improve the quality of administrators and teachers. Salaries rose sharply in the postwar years, with extra financial inducements to faculty and staff members holding advanced degrees or comparable postgraduate training. Statistics on teacher qualifications showed the results of these efforts. Before the war few high school teachers had degrees beyond the bachelor's; many had not finished college. By the early 1970s better than one-fourth of the high school teachers in the southern states held the master's degree or beyond, while scarcely any lacked the bachelor's.

Between 1940 and 1950 teachers' salaries rose to two-and-a-half times what they had been at the beginning of the decade. Black teachers, who were initially paid much less than the whites, got raises of greater proportion. By mid-century a number of states of the upper South were paying black and white instructors equally, while various states in the lower South were approaching equality. Salaries for all teachers more than doubled again during the decades of the 1950s and 1960s.

The determination of the southern people to maintain an effective school system showed in their willingness to bear an unusually heavy financial burden, for the region still suffered an unfavorable ratio in the number of pupils to be educated in relation to the wealth of its citizens. During the 1950s and 1960s most of the eleven former Confederate states customarily spent more money than the nation as a whole for this purpose in proportion to their personal income. In 1968, for example, Mississippi with the nation's lowest per capita income spent approximately 6.3 percent of it on the public schools. At the same time, Connecticut with the nation's highest per capita personal income spent only about 4.6 percent of it on schools. By the early 1970s, however, the South had fallen behind the national average in this respect. Only one southern state, Louisiana, spending a sum equal to about 6.1 percent of its aggregate personal income, now came up to the national average.

In addition to state and local revenues, the southern schools enjoyed an advantage in the receipt of federal funds for education. The Federal Aid to Education Acts passed by Congress in the mid-1960s provided extra money for school districts that were under the financial burden of racial desegregation. In 1970, for example, the eleven former Confederate states received a total of more than $502 million in federal grants for elementary and secondary education; this was better than one-third of all annual federal support for such schools. That year the state of Mississippi got from the HEW Office of Education approximately $66 per pupil enrolled in its public schools, while the states in the nation as a whole got only about $32 per pupil.

The effects of increased financial support showed in the enlarged libraries, expanded curricula, special enrichment programs, and instructional developments in the southern schools. By the early 1970s the better high schools offered several foreign languages, as well as a number of courses such as sociology, economics, and black studies that formerly were reserved for college. Like their northern counterparts they offered honors courses, independent studies, and "advanced placement" programs that enabled the brighter and more ambitious pupils to skip comparable freshman courses when they got to college and, in selected cases, to receive college credit for such work done in high school. All progressive school systems had staffs of counselors to help pupils overcome personal difficulties and guide them into courses appropriate to their college and professional interests. For those pupils interested in vocational training the southern school systems offered a variety of specialized courses, including such subjects as automobile mechanics, carpentry, masonry, metalwork, plumbing, cosmetology, and practical nursing. In 1971 more than 2.5 million pupils in the South were enrolled in vocational programs.

The most difficult problem encountered by the public schools of the South during the postwar years was racial desegregation. In spite of repeated court orders in support of integration, the rate of change was glacially slow. As the pupil placement measures employed in the 1950s to maintain racially separate schools were ruled illegal by the federal courts, they were replaced by "freedom-of-choice" programs that retained the dual system but permitted individuals to attend the schools of their preference. At the same time a number of states began to issue tuition grants to subsidize pupils who entered private segregated schools.

Both of these devices were quickly challenged in the courts as subterfuges to evade desegregation. In the mid-1960s the federal courts began to invalidate the tuition grants. In outlawing the practice in Louisiana in 1967 the United States Fifth Circuit Court of Appeals called it "the fruits of the state's traditional policy of providing segregated schools for white pupils. . . . The state is so financially involved in the discrimination practiced by private schools in Louisiana that any financial aid from the state to these schools . . . in the form of tuition grants or similar benefits violates the equal protection clause of the 14th Amendment."[1] Similar rulings occurred throughout the region, and by the end of the year tuition grants were dead.

The Johnson administration supplemented the work of the courts by withholding HEW funds from school districts that refused to submit positive desegregation plans. By the fall of 1965 a substantial proportion of the South's school districts had turned in such plans, and the following autumn an estimated 15.9 percent of the region's black pupils were in previously white schools. But the filing of plans did not of itself end segregation. States of the lower South, with heavy black populations, failed to put their plans into immediate effect. Most of the integration took place in the upper South, in areas of relatively thin black population. As late as the summer of 1969 dual systems still prevailed in most of the school districts of the Deep South. Approximately 80 percent of the black pupils in the entire region remained in racially separate schools.[2]

Again the federal courts supplied the critical pressure in favor of integration. By the late 1960s it was clear that the freedom-of-choice method would bring about only a limited desegregation. It placed the full burden of change upon the blacks; virtually no white pupils chose to enter black schools. For a variety of reasons, including economic and social duress, inconvenience, apathy, fear of school violence, dread of academic competition with the whites, and a genuine desire to preserve the integrity of their own schools, most black pupils and parents did not make the transfer. But in the spring of 1969 the Supreme Court ruled that the freedom-of-choice plans were no longer acceptable if they failed to desegregate the schools as effectively as other plans would. The climactic judicial move came in October of that year when the high court in *Alexander* v. *Holmes,* a case arising in Mississippi, declared that the "all deliberate speed" formula was now exhausted. In keeping with this ruling the lower federal courts promptly began to dismantle the remaining freedom-of-choice plans in other states.

As the courts took this action, HEW initiated moves to replace the remaining dual school systems with unitary systems embracing the pupils and teachers of both races. A favorite method of accomplishing this goal was the "pairing" of schools, with certain entire grades from the black schools being bussed out to previously white schools, and an equal number of grades from the white schools being bussed in to the previously black schools. These developments again brought the lower South into a school crisis. Hoping to arouse a northern reaction against forced school integration, United States Senator John Stennis of Mississippi introduced to an education appropriations bill an amendment calling for uniform federal action against racial segregation in all parts of the country, whatever the causes of such segregation. Supported by a majority of the southern senators and by many northern liberals, most notably Senator Abraham Ribicoff of Connecticut, the measure passed the Senate. But the final version was modified to apply only to "de jure" segregation, thus leaving the "de facto" segregation of the North untouched.

Various southern governors, including John McKeithen of Louisiana, Lester Maddox of Georgia, and Claude Kirk of Florida, vehemently denounced the federal actions, especially the requiring of bussing to achieve an arbitrary degree of integration. George Wallace of Alabama again urged defiance. A flurry of new laws based upon similar statutes in northern states provided for nondiscriminatory school systems but prohibited the transfer of pupils for the purpose of attaining a racial balance. Violence broke out in a number of places. Widespread white boycotts were threatened; some black boycotts were staged; and many schools temporarily closed down as the new plans began to go into effect during the winter of 1970. Governor Kirk reenacted a scene from the previous decade by physically occupying a county school administration building in order to prevent the bussing of pupils. He yielded only after he was ruled in contempt of court and fined $10,000 a day. Private schools sprang up overnight throughout the region; by February 1970 an estimated 400 to 700 of these "segregation academies" were in operation; the Southern Regional Council reported that some 300,000 white pupils were attending them.

In spite of the furor, most public schools remained open, and after a few days of absence most of the missing pupils returned to their classes. Formal opposition to desegregation yielded significantly before the combined pressures of the federal courts and HEW. By 1970 the great majority of the region's black public school pupils were in school with some whites. The proportion of blacks still completely segregated varied from 8.6 percent in Arkansas to 25.9 percent in Tennessee. This compared quite favorably with nonsouthern states of heavy black population. For example, 30.2 percent of the black pupils in Missouri and 36.2 percent of those in Illinois were in all-black schools. By 1975 more than 90 percent of all black pupils in the South were attending integrated schools.

But general statistics on school integration did not tell the whole story; the desegregation of individual black pupils was far from complete. Resistance to integration in the South now began to take forms that were particularly difficult for the courts to control. There was evidence of segregation and discrimination within the desegregated schools themselves. One way this showed was in the dismissal or demotion of black administrators and teachers. In addition, the introduction of the "track system" whereby pupils were assigned to classes according to scores on aptitude or achievement tests usually resulted in concentrating the more poorly trained and less confident black pupils in the slower groups. The adoption of dress codes could often be considered discriminatory against the blacks. And extracurricular and social activities were often simply canceled to avoid interracial contact.[3] A candid liberal observer of the mixed schools in a Black Belt county of South Carolina wrote in 1971 that they were failing the black pupils miserably. "The impact of cognitive learning is largely ineffective. White parents move from these areas and send their children to private schools. Black children leave school in great numbers."[4]

By far the most effective means of resistance to integration was white mobility. Resegregation through the exodus of whites from the cities into the suburbs and countryside threatened to undo the recent gains. As early as 1968 the superintendent of schools in Atlanta, where the process of desegregation was thought to be a model, pointed out that within the preceding eight years twelve or fifteen of the city's schools had changed from completely white to completely black. He predicted that within ten years the Atlanta enrollment would be 80 percent black. Actually, only six years after this prediction the city's schools were more than 80 percent black, and were losing white pupils at an incredible rate. In 1972 approximately 5,000 white pupils withdrew, a figure that represented almost 18 percent of the total white enrollment.[5] But the supreme example of this phenomenon was Washington, D.C., where the public schools were now 94 percent black.

This trend prevailed throughout the cities of the South. The public schools of such places as New Orleans, Memphis, and Richmond were two-thirds or more black and growing blacker every year. While the increasing outward surge of white population caused much of the change, the private school movement also continued to expand, removing still more white children from the public schools. The "segregation academies" were still in operation, and in addition many churches now began to open private schools supported by tuition payments and donations. For tax exemption, if not for idealistic reasons, they usually admitted qualified black pupils. But because of economic or academic demands, or social pressures, these institutions were largely white. By 1972 an estimated 700,000 pupils of the region were in private schools, and the number was climbing. Whether right or wrong, most white parents identified heavy school integration with violence and deterioration of quality. In the end the vast majority of them, including many who on principle opposed racial discrimination, surrendered to the seemingly inexorable laws of separation and tokenism. A journal sponsored by the Southern Regional Council lamented, "Resegregation is an alarming fact of life."[6]

Seeking to reverse the outflow of whites, groups of black parents brought suits in the federal courts to compel sufficient increases in the bussing of both white and black pupils to maintain the desired racial balance. A celebrated case occurred in the Charlotte-Mecklenburg County, North Carolina, schools. In 1970 a federal district court ordered such a plan into effect there; the next year the United States Supreme Court upheld this decision on the ground that bussing was necessary to break up the traditional pattern of segregation that had been established by the earlier dual system of schools.

Throughout the years 1971 and 1972 every southern city was involved in expanded programs of bussing to achieve greater school integration. But in 1971 a federal district court in Atlanta rejected such a plan with the argument that it would merely accelerate the flight of the whites. Instead of increased bussing, the court approved a compromise worked out by the school board and the local chapter of the NAACP whereby blacks would secure the position of superintendent of schools and half the administrative jobs in the system, but bussing would be held to a bare minimum. The national hierarchy of the NAACP challenged this decision in court and suspended the local leaders for approving it. But the president of the Atlanta chapter defended his action with the explanation: "Times have changed since 1954, and the leadership of the civil rights movement is going to have to rethink the whole question of how you educate to the maximum extent the inner city kids." In the spring of 1973 the new plan was ordered into effect.[7] Both white and black leaders in the city believed the "Atlanta Compromise" was an important step toward racial accommodation.[8]

Meanwhile, a court suit in Richmond, Virginia, sought to impose an even greater expansion of bussing to achieve school integration. In 1972 a federal district judge there ruled that the city's predominantly black system must be merged with the predominantly white districts of two adjoining counties. The order kindled vehement protest and the threat of civil disorder. But the Fourth United States Circuit Court of Appeals reversed the decision on the ground that it deprived the states of rights reserved to them by the Tenth Amendment of the United States Constitution. Bussing soon became a critical issue in the 1972 presidential campaign. Various cities outside the South were under court orders to integrate their schools through this method; President Nixon explicitly denounced it; a great majority of the electorate opposed it. In May 1973 the United States Supreme Court ruled on the Richmond school situation. By a four-to-four count, with Associate Justice Lewis F. Powell of Virginia recusing himself because of prior involvement in the case, the high tribunal sustained the decision of the Court of Appeals against the merger. For the moment, urban school desegregation seemed to be approaching its legal and demographic limits.

Rural and small-town schools were now pretty thoroughly integrated. But here the traditional caste system kept a large measure of social segregation. Moreover, the proportion of black pupils in these schools was dwindling, for the trend among rural blacks was to move into the cities, where, despite the actual segregation, they enjoyed economic, social, and political advantages over the restrictions of country life.

Notwithstanding the grave social and academic problems of the post–World War II years, the region's elementary and secondary schools during this period made the greatest progress of their entire history. Southerners in the early 1970s could with justifiable pride feel that the South at last had a truly modern school system.

Southern support of higher education in the postwar years was comparable to the region's efforts to improve the elementary and secondary schools. Colleges and universities grew rapidly in the late 1940s to meet the demands of the multitude of discharged World War II servicemen who took advantage of veterans' benefits to continue their education. Economic prosperity, a rising awareness of the importance of formal education, subsidies to veterans of the Korean and Vietnam wars, and the booming population increase of the times all contributed to sustain this growth. The capacity of the higher educational system expanded both through an immense enlargement of the established institutions and through the addition of new colleges and branches of the universities. The total number of institutions of higher learning in the former Confederate states rose from 430 in 1948 to 649 in 1971. By the early 1970s southern college and university enrollments were almost seven times as high as they had been on the eve of World War II.

Public colleges and universities were slightly more numerous in the South than private institutions; and because of the greater diversity of their programs and their lower tuition fees, the state-supported schools were on the average much larger than the private ones. Almost 80 percent of the region's college students were enrolled in public institutions. Among the nonpublic institutions, more than two-thirds of which were affiliated with religious denominations, were many of the region's most distinguished universities and liberal arts colleges, as well as many of its most obscure schools. The nonpublic institutions faced severe financial problems in the postwar decades. Rising costs reduced the adequacy of fixed endowments and forced an ever heavier reliance upon increased tuition fees, thus obliging many students who might ordinarily have attended them to turn to the public colleges instead. Nevertheless, most of the nonpublic institutions remained in full operation in the early 1970s, a vital ingredient of higher education in the South.

The growth in college enrollments required unprecedented sums of money from southern taxpayers, from donors, and ultimately from the federal government. The total value of southern college and university physical plants in 1973 was more than ten times what it had been thirty years before. In the early 1970s a typical southern state university spent more funds annually than all of the region's state universities together spent at the end of World War II. The southern states in the late 1960s were spending on higher education about 10 percent more money in proportion to their aggregate per capita income than were the American people as a whole.

In an attempt to improve regional professional and graduate education and at the same time to prevent a bankrupting duplication of facilities, the governors of fourteen southern states (the old Confederate states along with Kentucky, Maryland, and West Virginia) in 1948 created the Southern Regional Education Board. This body consists of the governors of the member states plus four other persons from each state appointed by the governor. In addition to conducting studies, making reports, and providing consultations on the educational needs of the region, the board serves as fiscal agent for interstate educational arrangements, the most successful of which has been the subsidization by various individual states of their students enrolling elsewhere in programs not available in the home state. The fields of medicine, veterinary medicine, dentistry, architecture, forestry, social work, and nuclear studies have so far been included in such agreements. Kentucky, for example, sends its students of veterinary medicine to Auburn University in Alabama; Tennessee sends its students of architecture and forestry to other southern state institutions. In 1974 plans for similar cooperation in certain fields of graduate work were authorized.[9]

These efforts in higher education brought positive results. Southern universities and colleges advanced markedly in the qualifications of their faculties, scope and diversity of curricula, and strength of libraries and laboratory facilities. The professional schools (especially the colleges of medicine, law, engineering, architecture, and social work) of the state and privately endowed universities expanded their staffs and facilities, and upgraded their programs of teaching, research, and service. Among the professional schools of national distinction in the old Confederate states were the medical schools of Duke, Vanderbilt, and Tulane; the engineering schools of Rice University and the Georgia Institute of Technology (Georgia Tech); the law schools of Duke, Vanderbilt, the University of Virginia, and the University of Texas; and the school of social work of Tulane.

Perhaps the major development in the universities was the growth of the graduate schools. All of these institutions offered some postgraduate work before World War II; most of them had programs for the master's degree in a number of fields and for the Ph.D. in a few. But the graduate schools were generally small and undistinguished. In 1947 the total graduate enrollment in the region was approximately 17,500. A combination of state, federal, and private financial support in the 1950s and 1960s caused unprecedented growth. Among the major sources of funds were the National Institutes of Health, the National Science Foundation, the National Endowment for the Humanities, and the Ford Foundation. Also, during the years 1959 to 1971 the federal government through the National Defense Education Act provided fellowships for the training of more than 6,000 graduate students in the South. By the 1960s all the state universities and the leading private institutions were offering the Ph.D. degree in numerous fields, some of them in more than forty. By the early 1970s seventy-two institutions in the region were granting the doctorate in one or more subjects; the total graduate enrollment was approximately 152,000.

Though the southern graduate programs were behind those of the older, better equipped and staffed, and more prestigious graduate schools outside the region, they nevertheless earned a deserved reputation for soundness. The demand for southern-trained Ph.D.'s was strong throughout the nation; more than half of those produced by the larger and more distinguished southern universities found employment beyond the borders of the South. In recognition of their achievements in all aspects of higher education, six of the region's leading institutions—North Carolina, Virginia, Texas, Duke, Vanderbilt, and Tulane—gained admission into the selective Association of American Universities.

While the established southern universities grew in size and quality, many additional institutions acquired both the title of university and some of the programs associated with the title. During the 1950s most of the former teachers' colleges were renamed state colleges, and during the following decade most of them were redesignated universities of certain geographic portions of their states, with names such as the University of Southwestern Louisiana, the University of South Florida, or East Carolina University. All of them received authorization to establish limited programs of graduate and professional work. Some inaugurated doctoral programs in selected fields.

There were comparable developments in southern undergraduate education. The outstanding liberal arts colleges of the region, including such schools as Davidson in North Carolina, the University of the South (Sewanee) in Tennessee, and Washington and Lee and Hollins in Virginia, increased their endowments and strengthened their staffs and programs. A major undertaking in public undergraduate training was the establishment of state systems of community junior colleges that greatly increased the opportunities of the less affluent and less mobile high school graduates to obtain at least some higher education; they served, too, as screeners and feeders for the state and regional universities. Through enlarged extension, correspondence, and evening programs, the institutions of higher learning offered both credit and noncredit college work to hundreds of thousands of part-time students who were obliged to hold regular jobs while they sought to prepare themselves for better jobs or to broaden their intellectual horizons. By 1969 there were almost 300,000 part-time and extension students enrolled in southern colleges and universities.

During the late 1960s and early 1970s, as a result of student demands for "student power," both graduate and undergraduate students obtained representation in most faculty governing bodies and boards of trustees. Also, at least partly because of student demands, college curricula and teaching methods underwent significant changes. New courses in black studies, women's studies, and environmentalism were inaugurated, and honors work, independent studies, and colloquia supplanted the lecture hall for many undergraduates. Students gained more freedom than formerly to plan their programs to suit individual needs, tastes, and capacities. Classes often tended to become general discussions with such free exchange of ideas that the instructors were hardly distinguishable from the students, especially those young teachers who took on the protective coloration of student dress and hair styles. Many of the students and faculty believed the new modes created superior "learning situations"; traditionalists scorned them as being nothing more than bull sessions under sophisticated names.

Although southern institutions of higher learning were on the whole more conservative than those elsewhere, they were beehives of liberal thought and practice in comparison with the deeply conservative society about them. This was especially true of the major universities, many of whose faculty members were from other sections of the country. Southern campus life reflected the various social and political movements of the times, including the diligence and seriousness of purpose of the immediate post–World War II years and the calculated slovenliness, drug use, sexual license, and anger toward the military that marked the students of the Vietnam war period. During the late 1960s many schools experienced protest demonstrations over the issues of the war, conscription, classified military research, and the Reserve Officers Training Corps.

In the spring of 1970 the spread of American military action into Cambodia and the killing by national guardsmen of four students in a demonstration at Kent State University (Ohio) caused sympathy riots and the burning of buildings on some southern campuses. In a few instances school and civil authorities used state troopers and contingents of the National Guard to restore order. The most serious disturbances occurred at the black schools, where occasional boycotts, demonstrations, and outbreaks of vandalism grew out of the broader movement for racial equality and recognition. The slaying by Mississippi police of two black students and the wounding of nine others in a melee at Jackson State University heightened the revulsion and re-crimination caused by the Kent State tragedy. Two years later a similar killing of black students by police occurred at Southern University in Baton Rouge, Louisiana.

Yet compared with the universities of the North and Far West the southern schools were models of decorum and stability. Often the core of dissidents on the southern campuses was composed of students and instructors whose origins were outside the region. Such radical organizations as the Students for a Democratic Society (SDS) made little gain against the deep-rooted conservatism and respect for authority among southern youth. Indeed, in a number of instances the school administrators had to restrain these students from organizing groups to oppose the demonstrators with force.

Despite the official desegregation of the South's colleges and universities, the majority of the region's black college students continued to attend institutions that were predominantly black. Whether because of higher costs, social discrimination, inability to compete with the better-trained whites, or a simple preference for black companionship, most blacks stayed away from the traditionally white campuses. Although integration remained the ultimate goal of many black educators, most of them acknowledged that temporarily the largely black colleges served an essential need. Attempts in the late 1960s by local HEW officials to force the adoption of actual unitary systems of higher education collapsed in the face of determined opposition from both black and white administrators and faculties. In 1971 the Carnegie Foundation on Higher Education endorsed this de facto segregation as a pragmatic solution to the increasing black demand for college training.[10]

Of the 104 predominantly black colleges and universities, 35 were public and 69 private, most of the latter affiliated with religious denominations. Twenty-one of these institutions offered graduate and professional training as high as the master's degree; Atlanta University offered the Ph.D. degree, Meharry Medical School in Nashville offered the degrees of Doctor of Medicine and Doctor of Dentistry, and Tuskegee Institute in Alabama offered a degree in veterinary medicine.

Traditionally poorer and weaker in almost every sense than the predominantly white colleges and universities, the black institutions, ironically, found themselves the victims of desegregation at the very moment when they were being called upon to play a decisive role in the training of the black youth.[11] The more affluent white schools, under duress by the federal government and impelled by their own announced ideals to desegregate their faculties and staffs, now raided the black schools of many of their best black teachers and administrators. At the same time a growing racial pride caused many black students to demand that preference in the hiring of instructors for black colleges be given to blacks. Efforts to relieve this strain through temporary exchanges of instructors between the principally white and principally black schools brought only meager results. Higher education for a majority of the blacks remained for the time largely separate and unequal.

The South's strenuous educational efforts of the postwar years brought marked improvements at all school levels, but they were not sufficient to bring equality with other sections of the country. A comprehensive study made in the early 1960s by the George Peabody College of the 4,776 public high schools operating in eleven southern states, including Kentucky but not Texas, revealed serious shortcomings in comparison with national standards. The southern schools on the average were still too scattered and too small to afford truly excellent facilities, curricula, and equipment; only about 13 percent of them had senior classes of as many as 100 pupils, the minimum considered by educational experts to be capable of supporting a first-rate program. Southern teachers were relatively underpaid, and a smaller proportion of them held the master's degree or beyond. Southern libraries were less adequate, and southern course offerings less complete. Less than 70 percent of the regional institutions offered any foreign language; in Mississippi, the lowest state in this respect, less than half offered any.

Many of these shortcomings were remedied during the late 1960s and the early 1970s. The final consolidation of rural schools and the creation of large institutions in the growing cities and suburbs tended to eliminate the deficiencies associated with small schools, though unfortunately these problems were replaced with the perhaps more serious ones of anonymity, depersonalization, and unruliness that came to be associated with such large establishments. Also, the South's public schools still lagged behind those elsewhere. The southern states in 1974 remained significantly below the national average in the estimated yearly amount of money spent on each pupil. The highest southern state in this expenditure, Florida, was almost $100 under the national average, while the lowest state in the region and in the nation, Alabama, was less than 70 percent of the national average. The gap in annual expenditure per pupil between Alabama and New York, the nation's highest, was more than $1,000. Southern schools were still relatively deficient in teacher qualifications, libraries, laboratories, and curricula.

Nor did the admirable accomplishments in higher education eradicate the South's weakness in this field or fundamentally alter its standing. In spite of the generosity of state legislatures, private foundations, and the federal government, southern colleges and universities continued to be poor in comparison with others. Ironically, much of the

Table 6

CURRENT EXPENDITURES PER SOUTHERN
PUBLIC SCHOOL PUPIL 1940, 1974

	1940	1974	% change
Alabama	$31	$ 716	2,210
Arkansas	27	773	2,763
Florida	58	1,041	1,695
Georgia	34	869	2,456
Louisiana	51	978	1,818
Mississippi	25	787	3,048
N. Carolina	40	900	2,150
S. Carolina	34	856	2,418
Tennessee	38	759	1,897
Texas	60	809	1,248
Virginia	44	983	2,134
United States	$82	$1,120	1,266

Source: U.S., Bureau of the Census, *Statistical Abstract of the United States,* 1943 and 1974, pp. 215, 130.
Note: All figures rounded to nearest dollar.

largess of the major foundations and the federal government tended to widen the gap, because the grants were dispensed either to match funds already available or to take advantage of superior scholarship, research, and equipment. In any case, the southern institutions usually got the jackal's share while those of the North and Far West got the lion's share. The region's universities were further embarrassed by stretching their meager resources in the 1950s and early 1960s to add new programs in the bid for foundation and federal grants. As these grants dwindled and often disappeared in the late 1960s the southern schools found themselves severely pressed to maintain all their programs; in some instances they were obliged to cancel certain of the recently established ones.

The shortcomings of the southern institutions of higher learning were obvious. On the average, faculty salaries and research funds were lower than those elsewhere; library and laboratory resources were less adequate. In the academic year 1973–1974 only two southern universities, Duke and Virginia, were in the top professorial salary scale of the American Association of University Professors. Of sixty American university libraries that in 1971 held as many as 1 million volumes each, sixteen were in the South. But most of the truly great collections were elsewhere. For example, the Harvard University library alone had a million more books than the collective holdings of the three largest southern university libraries. The libraries of four major eastern universities possessed approximately as many volumes as all the leading southern university libraries together.[12]

Virginius Dabney in the mid-1960s noted the advances in the quality of southern universities, but conceded the "stubborn fact" that the region still did not possess a single one of the top ten universities of the country, probably not one of the top twenty. Surveys in the late 1960s and early 1970s among thousands of scholars throughout the nation confirmed the persistence of this condition.[13] Despite the presence of many excellent scholars in the southern institutions, too often when one of these men began to show great promise he was lured away by the higher salary, superior research facilities, and stronger prestige of a northern or western school. Many of the most outstanding teachers of southern birth ended their careers at a Harvard, Yale, or Stanford, rather than at a southern university.

Table 7

CURRENT EXPENDITURES FOR SOUTHERN INSTITUTIONS
OF HIGHER EDUCATION 1940, 1970
(In millions)

	1940	1970[a]	% change
Alabama	$ 6.7	$254	3,691
Arkansas	3.5	. . .	. . .
Florida	4.3	497	11,476
Georgia	7.1	350	4,830
Louisiana	8.9	. . .	. . .
Mississippi	4.5	163	3,522
N. Carolina	12.6	528	4,090
S. Carolina	5.0	185	3,600
Tennessee	9.0	345	3,733
Texas	19.4	803	4,039
Virginia	11.1	353	3,080
U.S. state average	$10.8	$420	3,789

Source: U.S., Bureau of the Census, *Statistical Abstract of the United States,*
1943 and 1973, pp. 224, 135.
[a]Rounded to nearest million.

Want of money was the most visible handicap in southern higher learning. But this deficiency was aggravated by the proliferation of graduate programs in competition for the region's precious funds. Lewis B. Mayhew believes that if the South is to produce major centers of excellence in graduate training, it must do so within what he calls the "developed institutions," that is, the leading private and state universities. Warning that doctoral work is expensive, he questions whether the South's "developing institutions," among which he names such schools as Florida State University, Virginia Polytechnic Institute and State University, and the University of Houston, can become full universities.[14] Perhaps what the South most needs in higher education is an extension of the Southern Regional Education Board's idea of concentrating financial resources upon a few selected universities to create truly distinguished centers of research and scholarship, while the majority of the universities scale down their ambitions for graduate work and the rest of the institutions strive for excellence in undergraduate education.

The region's need in the 1970s for superior schools, elementary through the university, was still as keen as ever. Despite postwar efforts to gain educational equality with the rest of the nation, and despite countless examples of success in these attempts, southerners on the average were still behind. Statistics for the years 1958 to 1965 on the results of armed services preinduction mental tests showed that the proportion of white southerners who failed was more than one-third higher than that of white Americans generally. The proportion of black southerners who failed was more than three times that of southern whites, and was over 12 percent higher than that of American blacks generally.[15]

The 1970 census revealed that illiteracy remained more persistent in the South than elsewhere. Almost 68 percent of the nation's adult illiterates now were southerners, about equally divided between whites and blacks. During the preceding decade the region lowered its number of these persons by only one-fourth, while the rest of the country cut its number in half. Efforts to combat illiteracy in the South often encountered suspicions of federal meddling and sometimes met with a certain proud defiance among the illiterates themselves. One of them, at age eighty-three, rebuffed his questioner by saying, "I guess I made it O. K. didn't I? . . . After all, a man's got a right not to read, ain't that right?"[16] Also, the southern population was nearly a year below the general American population in the median number of school years completed. Much of this deficiency could be attributed to the lag in the education of blacks, but southern whites, too, were substantially under the level of the white population in other regions.[17]

In the mid-1970s southern schools like those elsewhere felt the adverse effects of the new social and economic trends. A declining birthrate had now stopped or slowed the expansion of the region's schools at all levels; southerners either were unable or unwilling to continue spending a higher proportion of their incomes than nonsoutherners on their schools; recession and inflation threatened to cancel many of the recent gains. Regional education, at least for the time being, seemed to have reached a plateau.

During the quarter-century following World War II southern schools consistently made progress. Almost without exception, southerners continued to adhere to the national faith in universal education

as a means to prosperity and well-being. Schools received unprecedented moral and financial support from the people of the region, and
they made strenuous and successful efforts to upgrade their physical
facilities, faculties, and programs. Despite these gains, the South still
lagged behind the rest of the nation in the quality of its schools and in
the academic attainments of its population.

VII.

Religion & Controversy

Southern religion like the rest of southern life felt the effects of postwar change, as those forces that challenged traditional political, economic, and social practices challenged also the conservative regional theology with its relative indifference to schemes for earthly betterment. Liberal stirrings among a minority of church members threatened the tranquillity of every denomination and caused rifts in some. Yet religious orthodoxy remained largely triumphant; the South in the 1970s was perhaps as much as ever the nation's Bible Belt.

Observers agreed that southerners continued to practice their religion in distinctive ways and with an intensity that exceeded that of other regions. The South remained the most Protestant section of the country. Nine out of ten of the church members of such states as Tennessee, Alabama, Georgia, and South Carolina were Protestant. Three out of four were Baptist, Methodist, or Presbyterian. According to Samuel S. Hill, Jr., the regional society was the only one in history dominated by low-church Protestantism.[1]

Almost half the southern church members were in the "ultra-Baptist" Southern Baptist church, a denomination so embracing and influential in the region that it was aptly called "the folk church of the South." With some 35,000 congregations in 1973 and a membership of better than 12.4 million, it was the largest Protestant group in the United States. Refusing to confine its activities to the South, it made significant gains in other parts, especially where southerners settled in the great migrations of the war years and afterward. It remained unshakable in rejecting overtures of reconciliation with the American (Northern) Baptist church or of union with other denominations. Liberal members who in 1951 sought merger with the Federal Council of Churches soon gave up and became Episcopalians. So apparently settled among the bulk of the members was the question of merger that it has not been seriously mentioned again in the Baptists' general convention.

Not surprisingly, the most spectacular evangelist of the postwar era, Billy Graham, was an affiliate of the Southern Baptist church. A native of North Carolina, Graham began his religious career as a Presbyterian but later became a Baptist preacher of impressive appearance and forceful address. Tall, slender, handsome in an ecclesiastical way, he captivated his hearers with his piercing stare, a long index finger that he brandished in the manner of "a two-gun sheriff in Dodge City," and a sincere and compelling style of southern pulpit oratory. Combining homilies on "Christ and Him crucified" with exhortations against "sin, sex, and Communism," he became nationally famous in 1949 when he caught the eye of the journalist William Randolph Hearst in a Los Angeles revival that converted a number of prominent figures, including one former gangster. Soon Graham was attracting audiences so large that they could be accommodated in nothing smaller than athletic stadiums. Linking religion with patriotism, calling for a penitent and redeemed America to sanctify its role of world leadership, Graham became virtually the White House chaplain during President Nixon's first administration.[2]

Almost 4.5 million southerners in 1970 were members of the United Methodist church. The long regional Methodist schism that began in the 1840s over slavery had ended in 1939. But formal reconciliation did not bring an end to differences; the Southeastern Methodist Jurisdiction continued to resist further national assimilation and guarded its remaining autonomy among the five major jurisdictions of the church. Strong reactions to the controversial social issues of the post–World War II years combined with the theological conservatism of most southern communicants to distinguish the regional branch from the rest of the body in all but form. Southern delegates to the General Convention usually represented the most vehement group of dissenting voices against the adoption of liberal measures.

The regionally oriented Churches of Christ claimed an even faster rate of growth than that of the Southern Baptists. In 1970 they had a membership of about 2.5 million, with their major concentrations in Tennessee and Texas. Their strength, like that of the Southern Baptists, resulted from their refusal to compromise with the liberal tendencies of other religious groups and their emphasis upon congregational structure, a point that appealed to the ingrained southern preference for local autonomy. Whereas Baptist congregational purity was somewhat compromised, at least in form, by the centralizing policies of the regional and state conventions and the Sunday School Board, the deep conservatism of the local churches was strong enough to deter their ministers from following other Protestant clergymen into unrestrained modernism. The Churches of Christ, on the other hand, practiced a virtually absolute congregationalism that precluded conventions or churchwide boards, gave local elders control over ministers, church property, funds, and programs, and rendered impossible or meaningless all efforts to merge with other religious groups, whether denominational or regional.

Related by origin to the Churches of Christ were the Disciples of Christ with more than 1.3 million members and the Christian Church with slightly more than a million members. Theologically more liberal than the Churches of Christ, they were more heavily concentrated in the upper South and border states.

The southern branch of the Presbyterian church (Presbyterian Church in the U.S.), with a membership in 1970 of slightly less than a million, followed a course similar to that of the Southern Baptists in refusing to merge with the northern wing of the body. Reunification efforts that were initiated with optimism in the 1940s collapsed amid the social and doctrinal disputes of the following decade. In the late 1960s the General Assembly voted to study a plan looking to reunification, but this decision aroused bitter controversy and threats of schism. In the mid-1970s reunification was not yet a reality. Instead, some eighty congregations had now withdrawn to form new presbyteries, and the General Assembly was obliged to adopt an "escape clause" permitting any group to withdraw with its property if it saw fit to do so as a result of reunification, when and if reunification should occur.

The Episcopal church in the South remained numerically small, with fewer than 800,000 communicants in 1970, though it attracted many individuals of social ambition, wealth, or intellectual stature who had been reared in the evangelical faiths. Numbers of southerners continued inadvertently to imitate the historic religious example of Jefferson Davis, who was born a Baptist but crowned his rise to the gentry by becoming an Episcopalian shortly after his inauguration as president of the Confederacy. Except for the Atlantic seaboard, where low-church Episcopalianism had always been strong among all classes, the Episcopal church was largely confined to the cities. Perhaps, however, it exerted an influence beyond its numbers, for it played a traditional role as exemplar of moderation and good taste in the life of the region.

Although the South as a whole remained overwhelmingly Protestant, the Roman Catholic church continued to be predominant in South Louisiana and in scattered areas of Florida and Texas—places where the descendants of the original French or Spanish settlers were still the majority. Catholicism also made gains elsewhere in the South through conversion, intermarriage, and the immigration of nonsoutherners. Yet in most parts of the region the Church of Rome was considered an exotic, confined to cities, and having little or no influence on private mores or public policy. Hundreds of southern counties and thousands of towns contained not a single Catholic church.

In addition to sustaining its major denominations, the South continued to be the home of various predominantly white sects and branches of the traditional churches. Among these were the Primitive Baptists, membership 72,000; the National Association of Free Will Baptists, membership 197,957; the Regular Baptists, membership 204,357; the Cumberland Presbyterians, membership 86,340; and the Southern Methodists, membership 4,025. All these bodies represented conservative vestiges or outgrowths of the larger denominations of similar name.

The South also continued to provide fertile ground for the proliferation of the Pentecostal and Holiness bodies, which comprised almost a score of different groups, and which collectively were said to be making the deepest inroads in the statistical ranks of the traditional southern churches. The four largest of these were: the Pentecostal Holiness church, membership 67,000; the Pentecostal Church of God of America, Incorporated, membership 115,000; the Church of God, membership 258,000; the Assemblies of God, membership 625,000. According to recent scholarship, these four sects by the early 1970s had become both "sedate and respectable" and were about to achieve "maximum efficiency" (which is to say they were about to join the mainstream of southern denominationalism).[3] The most obvious sign of this rise in status, along with the increased prosperity of the members, was the improved appearance of their meeting houses, in the 1940s mostly frame or cinder block, but now modishly designed buildings of brick or stone, steel, and glass.

The steady growth of the South's major denominations, along with that of the Pentecostals, indicated a continuing vitality of biblical faith in spite of the secularizing forces of modern American life. In 1962 the Southern Baptist General Convention reaffirmed its belief in the unique inspiration, divine authorship, and "inerrancy" of the Scriptures, and enjoined the church's seminaries against teaching any doctrines not consistent with this position. Six years later the president of the convention, Dr. W. A. Criswell, pastor of the First Baptist Church of Dallas, unequivocally set forth fundamentalist beliefs in a book entitled *Why I Preach That the Bible Is Literally True*. Emphasizing at once the "spiritual efficacy, self-attestation, and historical accuracy" of the Bible, this work rejected all implications of error of any kind, whether moral, theological, or factual. A liberal minority of Baptist ministers were critical of the book, but a former professor of theology at the Baptist Theological Seminary in New Orleans perceptively summed up the attitude of most of his fellow churchmen when he defended it and said: "The vast majority of Southern Baptists hold that Scripture is the very Word of God and constitutes the one and only source of divine truth, the sole epistemological foundation of faith."[4]

Other religious bodies primarily identified with the South held biblical views similar to those of the Southern Baptists. So ingrained was this faith in the Churches of Christ that their leading periodicals scarcely bothered to address themselves to the issue. They sometimes offered refutations of scientific accounts of creation that did not support the biblical version; or for a similar reason they challenged the radioactive method of dating prehistoric objects. On rare occasions an author did discuss the evil results of questioning the inspiration of Holy Writ. The conclusion was: "To reject the Lord's message is to reject the Lord. We must make the same choice men have always had to make. Will we follow the wisdom of God or the wisdom of men?"[5] Most of the writings and sermons produced by this religious group were grounded upon a conviction of biblical inspiration that was strong enough to make explicit affirmations of it seem unnecessary.

The leading spokesmen of the southern Presbyterians held stead-fastly to the position that the Bible is "God's divinely inspired and infallible revelation." Preachers and teachers were cautioned not to stray from the Bible in their sermons and lessons. Warning against the recent overemphasis on relevance, one influential scholar wrote: "Relevance in preaching, like consistency, is a jewel . . . but preaching that becomes so contemporary as to be divorced from the infallible and inerrant Word is so bad that it must be anathema."[6]

The Pentecostal and Holiness bodies were the most thoroughly fundamentalist among the southern religious groups. Lacking a formal common creed, they relied upon an interpretation of the Bible that was sufficiently literal to embrace a belief in present-day miracles and physical manifestations of God's power at work among the faithful. Emphasizing "spiritual baptism" and an "outpouring of gifts" by the Holy Spirit, they practiced emotional singing and shouting, faith heal-ing, and "speaking in tongues," which was an eruption of apparently meaningless sounds and syllables. Some of the remote Pentecostal and Holiness sects continued to display a faith that impelled them to handle live rattlesnakes or copperheads, and to drink "salvation cock-tails" of strychnine mixed with water. "They start with the faithful —mostly low-income whites with low-status jobs—singing and shouting to get the spirit," wrote a shocked observer from Boston. "The praying and music then start in earnest and it gets frantic as they speak in tongues, sway and jerk." He then described the manner in which the snakes were finally brought out and draped wriggling over the arms and necks of the worshipers.[7] Neither laws to the contrary nor occasional fatalities by snakebite or poisonous drink deterred these primitive rites. Did not the Scripture say: "And they shall take up serpents, and if they drink any deadly thing, it shall not hurt them"?

The fundamentalism of the Pentecostals was more directed to the Book of Revelation than to the Book of Genesis. They interpreted lit-erally the apocalyptic prophecies that were treated symbolically if not ignored by the major denominations. Hence the Pentecostals were premillennialists; they believed that Jesus soon would return to earth, where he would establish a kingdom of righteousness over which he and his saints would reign for a thousand years.

All these signs indicated that orthodox Protestant Christianity remained at the core of the region's ethos. Most southerners who had no formal denominational affiliation shared in the general convictions, if not in all the conventions, of the prevailing orthodoxy, as did those southern church members who had dropped the tenets of fundamentalism. Not even the skeptics were immune to these forces. What Hodding Carter said of southerners in the 1940s was still true of them thirty years later: that if some of them scoffed at things religious, they did so uneasily and with a hollow laughter.

Southern religious orthodoxy may have waned in the postwar years, but only in an absolute sense; in comparison with nonsouthern theological views it was probably as strong as ever. A series of opinion polls taken from the late 1940s to the early 1970s indicated significant differences between the collective religious outlook of southerners and nonsoutherners. Southern Protestants were more inclined than Protestants elsewhere to believe the biblical teachings about a God who keeps watch over the affairs of the world, a God "whose eye is on the sparrow," as well as a devil whose eye is on the transgressor. "The people [of the Deep South] believe strongly in an anthropomorphic Satan," wrote an Episcopal bishop in 1950. Then he added hyperbolically, or perhaps whimsically, "They believe more in the reality of Satan than in the reality of God."[8] Southerners were likelier than nonsoutherners to believe in the immortality of the soul and the promise of reward and the threat of punishment after death. Southern ministers were more given to the use of biblical expressions in discussing everyday issues.

Southern Protestants more consistently than Protestants elsewhere defined sin as a violation of God's will rather than as "antisocial conduct" produced by ignorance or an unfavorable environment. A larger proportion of southern Protestants expressed the belief that regular church attendance is necessary in order to be a good Christian. Relatively more southerners reported that they attended church one time or more each week, that they listened or watched religious services on radio or television, and that they read parts of the Bible from time to time.

Southerners were more prone than nonsoutherners to believe that religion holds the answer to the great problems of the world, but they also tended to believe that religion is losing its influence in American affairs. A larger fraction of students in southern colleges than in other colleges considered religion a relevant part of their lives.

Psychologists even detected in southerners a greater tendency to depend upon prayer rather than technology for protection against tornadoes. Southern Protestants were likelier than nonsouthern Protestants to abstain from drinking alcohol, to blame drinking for their family problems, and to favor laws prohibiting or restricting the sale of alcohol. Southern Protestants were also more inclined to be offended at the sight of women drinking or wearing shorts in public.[9]

Belief in the suffering, death, and resurrection of Jesus remained the foundation stone of southern faith. A liberal critic in the late 1960s described the religion of the Southern Baptists as a kind of romance that was peculiarly attuned to the tragic sentimentality of the region, in which Christ himself came to resemble a thin-faced, bearded, doomed, and melancholy young Confederate officer. Other critics said the philosophy of the Southern Baptists was, "Hang on, there's a better life coming." The targets of these gibes were not shaken. Some of them proudly displayed bumper stickers bearing the affirmation: "God said it. I believe it. That settles it." Evangelist Billy Graham accurately represented his native region when he declared, "We can't get away from the Bible, or we're doomed."[10]

Long accused of being so preoccupied with the hereafter that they were blind to the ills of society here and now, most of the major southern denominations after World War II undertook programs to increase social concern among their members. Actually, they had never been so indifferent in such matters as their more severe critics had pictured them. Even before World War I the regional Methodist, Presbyterian, and Baptist churches had created social service commissions and had officially approved objectives of broad social reform such as prohibition, regulation of working conditions for women and children, and improved hours, wages, and safety for laborers generally. The churches also endorsed the progressive measures of Presidents Woodrow Wilson and Franklin D. Roosevelt and supported liberally the establishment and maintenance of orphanages, hospitals, schools, and other humanitarian enterprises. In the late 1940s the churches began to expand the staffs and programs of their social service commissions, with instructions that they produce suitable literature and proposals to stimulate interest in the relationship of the churches to social and economic problems.

Lockheed-Georgia airplane factory, Marietta, Georgia
Courtesy of Lockheed-Georgia Company

Mechanical cotton picker in action
Courtesy of the Allis-Chalmers Company

Dr. Martin Luther King, Jr., speaking from the Lincoln Memorial
United Press International Photo

Birmingham firemen and black protest demonstrators in 1963
Wide World Photos

Mayor Maynard Jackson of Atlanta
Courtesy of the Mayor's Office,
City of Atlanta

Governor George C. Wallace of Alabama greeting the public
during the 1972 presidential campaign
Courtesy of the Governor's Office, State of Alabama

Evangelist Billy Graham
Courtesy of the Billy Graham Evangelistic Association

Colonel Robert Scruton addressing a campus protest demonstration
Courtesy of the Department of University Relations, Tulane University

Peachtree Center, Atlanta, Georgia, including the
Hyatt Regency hotel in the background
Courtesy of Atlanta Chamber of Commerce

Davenport House, a restoration by Historic Savannah Foundation, Savannah, Georgia
Courtesy of Frederick Baldwin and Historic Savannah Foundation

Crucified Sun 'A' by Lamar Dodd of the
University of Georgia
Photograph by W. Robert Nix

Country music star Loretta Lynn
Courtesy of the Mike Douglas Show

Alabama's Wilbur Jackson sprinting for a touchdown against Tennessee, 1973
Courtesy of the Sports Publicity Director, University of Alabama

Effects of these efforts became visible during the 1950s and 1960s in the form of annual reports favoring the United Nations as a hope for world peace and urging support of armaments reduction agreements, nuclear weapons controls, and government financial assistance to disadvantaged nations. By the late 1960s there were scattered instances of direct involvement of urban southern churches in such programs as the sponsoring of day-care nurseries for working mothers and health centers for the children of the poor, the administration of federal loans to construct low-income housing, participation in black voter registration drives, the organization of politically oriented minority community centers, assistance to projects in black capitalism, and the formation of "experimental ministries" in collaboration with psychiatrists, black militant leaders, and city planning experts.

Yet these manifestations of an awakening social consciousness did not reflect a fundamental shift of southern religious emphasis from the salvation of souls to the reform of society any more than the earlier support of hospitals or child labor laws had portended such a turn. The recommendations of commissions and the activities of the special agencies of a few urban groups largely represented an elitist movement within the churches that was far removed from the religious interests of the great masses of the membership.

The course of church development in recent years suggested that social as well as theological conservatism was the major reason for a remarkable expansion of the southern groups. The nationwide social turmoil of the late 1960s, including the race riots in the cities, protest demonstrations against the Vietnam war, and the drug, sex, and hair counterculture all provoked a reaction that stimulated the growth of the nation's conservative churches, most of which were either of southern origin or were chiefly concentrated in the South. By the early 1970s the South appeared to be outpacing the rest of the nation in the proportion of its population who were church members. Meanwhile, those national religious bodies that were most liberal in their theology and most active in their programs of social uplift either slowed down or stopped growing. The United Presbyterian Church in the United States of America (northern Presbyterian) actually lost over 100,000 members in 1972. "[The most rapidly growing churches] are not 'reasonable,' " plaintively concluded one student of the phenomenon. "They are not 'tolerant,' they are not ecumenical, they are not 'relevant.' " Instead, he said, they represented the very opposite of all these acclaimed characteristics.[11]

Outweighing all affirmations of social purpose was the continued emphasis of the vast majority of southern church members upon the regeneration of the individual both for better service in this life and for an eternity of bliss. So persistent was this theme that in the late 1960s Samuel S. Hill, Jr., wrote: "It has rarely occurred to the churches of the South that there is a Christian social ethic. In their eyes the New Testament does not contain one."[12] He exaggerated; but although the South's attitude did not eliminate social concern, it did relegate it to a secondary position in the religious scale of values. The official journal of the southern Presbyterians forcefully explained that love and compassion are merely by-products of faith; one might engage in all kinds of social action without them, in which case, it said, the action would be to the detriment of the recipients. "Christian love and compassion are an integral part of Christian faith," was the reasoning. But "humanitarianism as an end in itself is a denial of faith."[13]

This subordination of social objectives was reflected in the position taken by southern churches on the major secular issues of the postwar years. Thus it was consistent with regional theology to condemn all proposals of a guaranteed annual income as a violation of Paul's injunction: "If any would not work, neither should he eat." Or to denounce the alleged tendency of northern churches to convert their Sunday school curricula into studies of urban renewal, economic boycotts, open housing, family planning, and the like. Should this happen, said a southern critic, then true religious education would doubtless disappear.

Southern churchmen tended to oppose a condemnation of American involvement in Vietnam. At the height of the conflict the Southern Baptist General Convention issued the statement: "We assure our duly elected leaders in government that we support them in developing strong and wise policies, in pursuing a just peace in Vietnam, and in helping to maintain order in the world. . . . We uphold in prayer men who are engaged in restrictive measures against destructive forces of invasion so that law and order may obtain."[14] Four years later in passing a resolution commending President Nixon for the gradual withdrawal of American troops, the General Convention deleted a proposed clause concerning the "moral ambiguities" of the war; one delegate explained the deletion in the words: "When a man lays down his life for another man's freedom, that's not morally ambiguous."[15] Billy Graham spoke from the heart of the southern religious community when he said: "The church should not answer questions the people aren't asking. We've become advisors, social engineers, foreign policy experts, when we should be answering the questions of the soul. Christ taught that man must first be born again."[16]

To most southern church members the church was a sanctuary from the pressures and hardships of this life as well as a means of attaining glory in the next. This was especially true of the southern poor. A sympathetic northerner admitted he found it difficult to comprehend the deep and abiding religious faith of the southern tenant farmers and sharecroppers of both races, the migrant workers, and the mountain folk of Appalachia. But he warned against the tendency of outsiders to look upon these worshipers as a group of "opiated and deluded victims," or as "philosophically duped and neurotically afflicted patients." "God lives for sharecroppers, difficult though that may be for some of their distant friends and allies to accept and believe."[17]

The urban poor were just as devoted as the rural poor to their religion. An investigation in 1970 of the ten white churches serving an indigent mill section of Atlanta revealed that they included two Pentecostal, one Holiness, one Salvation Army, three independent Baptist, two Southern Baptist, and one Methodist. All were intensely fundamentalist in their theology. One of the Southern Baptist congregations even looked with suspicion on its own denomination. "We are fundamental," explained the minister. "The Southern Baptists [generally] have a tendency toward liberalism." Many of the members of these bodies appeared to have developed an ideology of withdrawal from the world because of their poverty and insecurity. Yet many others did not fit this description. "For some persons," said an observer, "involvement in their church's program is the core of their existence. Meaning and purpose of life, values to live by, encouragement in the face of constant adversity, are given through their church associations. Real joy and integrity in the lives of these individuals seems traceable to their commitment to a religious community."[18] The Friendship Baptist Church lived up to its name. On a typical

Sunday morning it was packed with happy, friendly people: an apparent anachronism in the midst of a frenetic, tension-racked world.

A few years before the outbreak of World War II Edwin McNeill Poteat, Jr., said that southern clergymen were arranged along caste lines. The Episcopalians represented the regional aristocracy, he said; the Presbyterians represented the Bourbons, or business and professional groups; and the Methodists and Baptists represented the common folk. This was a deliberate overstatement; yet it affirmed the fundamental truth that southern religion accommodated itself to social distinctions. In a different sense this remained true in the postwar years. Generally, the Episcopal church and the Pentecostal bodies were at the upper and lower extremes of the social scale. But the various religious groups embraced all classes. The Southern Baptist church was the most representative as well as the largest of the regional churches. It included congregations and rituals to suit virtually all tastes: "high-church" congregations located on the most fashionable avenues of the cities and attracting many of the wealthiest and most prestigious families; congregations for the middle class; congregations for the mill hands; small-town and rural congregations that comprised all classes; backwoods congregations made up of dirt farmers, with one of their own number parking his tractor and mounting his pickup truck to go to church and take the pulpit on Sunday. Every southerner could find a pew where he felt comfortable.

Religion continued to play a vital role in the lives of the masses of southern blacks. About 70 percent of the black church members were affiliated with one or another of the many Baptist groups, the largest of which were the National Baptist Convention, U.S.A., Incorporated, the National Baptist Convention of America, and the Progressive National Baptist Convention, Incorporated. The black Baptist churches were similar to the white Baptist groups in organization and theology, except that the blacks tended to retain a stronger Calvinism. Almost 20 percent of the black church members were Methodists, the main branches of which were the African Methodist Episcopal church, the African Methodist Episcopal Zion church, and the Christian Methodist Episcopal church. The remainder of the black believers were scattered among the other denominations of the region, with significant numbers in the black Pentecostal bodies.[19]

As in the past, the black church served not only as a source of inspiration and hope, but also as a social agency promoting recreation and diversions, family stability, community responsibility, and experience in leadership. The church continued to provide a pattern for black business and mutual aid societies. On the negative side, according to some liberal thinkers, the black church with its authoritarian ministers and elders and its anti-intellectual outlook tended to retard the education of blacks both in democratic processes and in academic fields. The black scholar E. Franklin Frazier went so far as to say that religion was responsible for the so-called backwardness of American blacks.[20]

The church traditionally sublimated the hopes and aspirations of the blacks from earthly to heavenly goals. Yet in holding forth the prospect of equality, however remote and ethereal, it doubtless helped to sustain a latent hope of equality in this life. In any case, as the dominant institution of black society, the church was destined to play a central part in the civil rights movement of the post–World War II era. The most obvious example of this is seen in the career of Dr. Martin Luther King, Jr., who was transfigured from Baptist preacher into an internationally renowned herald of racial justice. The Montgomery bus boycott owed its origin and success directly to the Dexter Avenue Baptist Church, whose leaders created the boycott organization and provided its officer cadre. The Progressive National Baptist Convention, Incorporated, was founded in 1961 by Dr. King and other civil rights advocates in protest against the conservative leadership of the parent Baptist organization. In Mississippi during the voter registration drive of the mid-1960s, the COFO civil rights workers employed the churches as rallying points of the black community. In a larger sense, the Southern Christian Leadership Conference itself was a secular manifestation of the black church.

In spite of the civil rights activities of the black church in the South, it remained essentially fundamentalist in theology and heaven-directed in its ultimate goals. The great majority of southern blacks, like the great majority of southern whites, adhered to those groups that held the most conservative theological and social views. They rejected the new "black theology" of a number of young black seminarians in the North, and instead upheld the declaration of Dr. Joseph

H. Jackson, president of the National Baptist Convention, U.S.A., Incorporated, that these teachings were actually a "gospel of blacks against whites."

Black religion generally continued to be distinguished from white religion in traditional qualities of mood and style. Except for the most fervid spiritual exercises of the white Pentecostal and Holiness groups, black worship was more emotional than white worship, closer to the verities of black life. Acknowledging these distinctions, some black religious thinkers entertained the hope that the spiritual awareness of the blacks ultimately would provide a regenerating force for the religious disaffection of whites. "[The whites] need to hear the powerful, free and prophetic preaching of black preachers," said one black minister and scholar. "The deep emotional worship experiences of black people need to be infused into our white churches."[21]

A typical southern black service was more than an intellectual examination of Scripture or a moral homily. It was an exchange of sonorous exhortation from the pulpit with ecstatic response from the congregation, often including tears, laughter, handclapping, "amens," and other expressions of assent. The usual Protestant hymns seemed to become spirituals on the tongues of black singers. A black minister in the Arkansas Delta explained the difference between black worship and white worship: "Black folks don't like lecturing from the pulpit. We are more emotional in our worship. We rejoice. We like loud music and singing. We like preaching that is spiritually invigorating and establishes rapport between the minister and the worshippers." Then he added, "Most white services, by comparison, seem more like our funerals."[22] A black Mississippi sharecropper's wife explained more poignantly what religion meant to the lowly: "I kneel all week long with the beans, but on Sunday I kneel to speak with God, and He makes my knees feel better, much better . . . [and] all of a sudden I know He's touched me and given me a little of His strength, so I can go on."[23]

Black Pentecostal and Holiness sects flourished in the post–World War II years. They were strongest in the city ghettos but were popular too with many rural blacks. Like their white counterparts, they represented an emotional intensity above that of the larger denominations. They also practiced faith healing, "speaking in tongues," prophecy, and trances. Their most spectacular form of expression was their music, rich with gospel themes set to jazz and blues, accompanied by various instruments and sometimes by frenzied dancing and handclapping.

The gravest social issues before the southern churches, both white and black, after World War II were those of racial segregation and the effects of the civil rights movement. Officially, the major denominations took positions on these matters that were moderate or, in some instances, liberal. As early as 1947 the Southern Baptist General Convention adopted a resolution calling upon members to think of and treat blacks as human beings and to work for the eradication of racial prejudice in all forms. Most of the churches endorsed the Supreme Court's 1954 public school desegregation ruling. The Southern Baptist General Convention that year said the decision was in harmony with the constitutional guarantee of equal freedom to all citizens, and with the Christian principles of equal justice and love for all men. The Southern Presbyterian General Assembly adopted a similar statement and later condemned racial discrimination in employment, politics, education, and religion. The various church conferences continued at intervals to make comparable pronouncements. A number of ministers of the Churches of Christ affirmed their belief in racial religious brotherhood. A small amount of desegregation occurred in the 1960s among the Pentecostal bodies; one of the four major groups, the Church of God, admitted blacks. Most of the Pentecostal groups eventually issued cautious statements to the effect that God is no respecter of persons.

Affirmations of racial equality and brotherhood were doubtless sincere on the part of a majority of the church convention delegates. But proclamations of this kind were no more effectual than exhortations against sin in general. The very assemblies that denounced racial discrimination in the abstract often shied away from concrete proposals to combat specific discriminatory practices. Moreover, the resolutions taken by assemblies of church notables frequently did not represent the beliefs of the rank and file of the membership. The congregational autonomy of the Southern Baptists turned these proposals into mere expressions of purpose, without any binding effect upon individual churches or members. Although the assemblies and synods of the Methodists and Presbyterians had more theoretical authority, actually they were unable or unwilling to enforce their

decisions upon local groups. The Churches of Christ had no ecclesiastical authority above the congregational elders. If, as con-
troversially suggested, the lack of an established authoritarian church
in the Old South prevented religion from mitigating the evils of
slavery, it could be said that the absence of such a church in the recent
South prevented religion from banishing racial discrimination and
segregation.[24]

The vigor and means of resistance to desegregation varied according to the denomination, the geographic location of the specific congregation, the economic and social level of the local membership,
and the proportion of blacks in the surrounding population. On some
occasions during the late 1950s and early 1960s state conventions
and synods of the lower South rejected desegregation outright. Ministers who endorsed it often found themselves out of the pulpit. In
1963 a group of twenty-eight Methodist clergymen in Mississippi
openly condemned segregation; five months later only nine of them
were in their original locations. Laymen who disregarded the racial
barriers suffered boycotts in their businesses or professions; their
families were socially ostracized. Black pray-ins and kneel-ins were
sometimes turned away on the church steps by angry deacons who
were thought to be armed. Most white congregations used subtler and
less direct but equally effective measures to discourage blacks from
attending their gatherings.

The most stringent policies of racial segregation and white supremacy came from the independent groups that had already broken
away from the major denominations on grounds of liberal apostasy.
Among these sects persisted a strong belief in the scripturally ordained inferiority of blacks. A convention in 1969 of some 200 Baptist delegates from Florida justified racial separatism with the following resolution: "Both Hebrew and Christian civilizations of the
past and every denomination of Christianity during the last 1900
years prior to this century have held to the concept that segregation
of the races in social, religious and marital life is of divine command."[25]

Even where the white churches adopted no measures against
black attendance, the aloofness of white communicants and the lack
of social affinity between the races were strong deterrents to black
membership. President James McBride Dabbs of the Southern
Regional Council anticipated this difficulty when he voiced the fear

that white churches might receive blacks as members, but treat them "coldly and impersonally." Black observers were painfully aware of the realities of white standoffishness. Said one of them, "The door to WASP church society (other than at worship) is nowhere near so open as many well-intentioned whites think they have made it."[26] Another black writer scoffed at so-called integrated Sunday schools, retreats, and conferences that, he said, often comprised 500 whites and 2 blacks.[27] There was also an ominous trend of whites abandoning congregations when they came to be attended by more than a few blacks.

Nor did the blacks themselves manifest any widespread desire to give up their own churches in order to join the whites. Despite the efforts in the 1960s of small groups of black activists to penetrate the white churches, the masses of the blacks continued to assert an independence in religion that harked back to their voluntary withdrawal during Reconstruction. While refusing to adopt an explicit black theology, they nevertheless continued to cherish their denominational and congregational autonomy as an important form of black expression and community. "No other movement . . . gathers as many people as regularly as the church," wrote a black religious scholar. "No other movement talks to, dialogues with, and influences as many people as the black church does."[28] Blacks were also repelled by the "coldness" of white worship; those who ventured into the white churches missed the higher emotional charge of their own services. They went away, said one of them, "hungry in spirit."[29]

For whatever reasons, southern churches held the color line more intractably than any other institutions that served the general public. David E. Harrell, Jr., estimates that in 1968 the number of American blacks worshiping with whites was not appreciably greater than the number twenty years before.[30] Although some blacks in the late 1960s and early 1970s came into the white congregations, the movement across the boundaries was virtually a movement in one direction; almost no whites went into black congregations. Thousands of assemblies remained absolutely separated by race; other thousands of white churches had so few black members that they would hardly be found by an observer. The dual system of churches was not significantly affected by the token amount of mixing that occurred. Plans in 1973 by liberal groups in eight of the leading white and black denominations to form an organization called the Consultation on Church Union had to be shelved because of the disfavor of most local members. According to a perceptive saying, "From 11 to 12 on Sunday morning is the most segregated hour of the week in the South."

Religion continued to play a more conspicuous role in the everyday affairs of the South than perhaps it played in the affairs of any other major part of the country. So pervasive was its influence and so intimate its connection with the other aspects of regional life that in 1962 Samuel S. Hill, Jr., gave southern religion the name "Culture-Protestantism." Ten years later John Lee Eighmy selected for his history of the Southern Baptists the suggestive title *Churches in Cultural Captivity*. Southern state legislatures and local authorities reflected more directly than governing bodies elsewhere the church views on sex, divorce, abortion, pornography, drugs, alcohol, education, child rearing, dress, and general behavior.[31] The Southern Baptist church and the state and local authorities sometimes formed so close a liaison that neither was aware of its existence, and both could honestly denounce a union of church and state as a violation of one of the most venerable of American principles.

Religion was to a marked extent responsible for what was called in 1969 the "family-centered, work-oriented ethic" that remained strong in the South at a time when it appeared to be flagging in the North. A Calvinistic disbelief in the perfectibility of man persisted in the region's skepticism concerning government programs for the uplift of society. Kenneth K. Bailey thoughtfully points out that amid a present nationwide and worldwide waning of faith in progress, southerners more than other Americans are prepared both by history and religion to perceive "the enormity of the human predicament and the inadequacies of their efforts to improve it."[32]

Religion in the 1970s was still a powerful conservator of regional distinctiveness.

VIII.

After the Southern Renaissance

Southern literature and fine arts in the postwar years were as subject as regional politics, economics, education, or religion to impulses from beyond the borders of the South. The growth of university programs in literature, theater, art, music, and architecture tended to draw these forms of regional expression into the national or even the international mainstream of culture. An almost universal literacy combined with the spread of libraries and the sale of relatively inexpensive paperbound books to bring about a virtual revolution in southern reading habits; no longer apt was the gibe that more southerners wrote books than read them. The ubiquitous radio and television had their effects, good and bad, upon the tastes of the region. The new wealth enabled the South to indulge its artistic yearnings in a measure never before possible. Out of it all came a unique medley of styles, indigenous and imported, traditional and novel, trite and original, vulgar and chaste, ugly and beautiful. They were the modes and tones of the recent South.

Words remained the primary means of intellectual, spiritual, and aesthetic expression. Although in most places during the twentieth century, oratory had lost much of its appeal, the politicians, lawyers, and preachers of the South still relied heavily upon it to impart their messages and assert their personalities. Modern communications provided them with an infinite audience. Whatever differences might exist among such fellow southerners as Sam Ervin, Billy Graham, and Martin Luther King, Jr., they shared the regional cult of the spoken word.

Journalism also continued to be an important outlet for the regional mood. Every southern city published one or more newspapers of national scope, though none of them matched the major northern journals in the comprehensiveness of their reporting or the perceptiveness and cogency of their editorials. Among the regional newspapers that came nearest to these standards were the *Louisville Courier-Journal*, the *Atlanta Constitution*, and the *Houston Post*, all founded in the nineteenth century. Southern journalism enjoyed the advantages and suffered the afflictions of journalism elsewhere; it tended to become merely a purveyor of news columns and syndicated comments sent down by the Associated Press and United Press International.

Virtually gone was the fiery personal journalism that turned many nineteenth-century southern editorials into challenges to duels or provocations to homicide. Still, on such explosive issues as school desegregation or bussing, many southern editors, especially in the small cities and towns, continued to show the old-time spark. The small-town southern weeklies were perhaps the nation's most down-to-earth journals in their advertisements, local events columns, and homespun editorials. Where else was a reader likely to find homilies on the rewards of thrift and industry, notices of family visits and homecomings, and accounts of birthday parties all in a single issue?

The recent South was not the "graveyard of magazines" that the pre–Civil War South is said to have been. A significant number of periodicals were now published in the region. The most distinguished journals of literary criticism, general commentary, and history were established before World War II. Among these were the *Sewanee Review*, published by the University of the South; the *South Atlantic Quarterly*, published by Duke University; the *Virginia Quarterly Review*, published by the University of Virginia; the *Southern Review*, a venerable journal that resumed publication in 1965 by Louisiana State University; and the *Southern Historical Review*, published by the Southern Historical Association. Every state historical society also published its own journal of local history.

The most popular southern magazine was *Progressive Farmer*, a longtime favorite among the rural inhabitants of the South. In 1974 it had a circulation above 1 million. The second most popular southern magazine was a newcomer, *Southern Living*, introduced in 1966 by the publishers of *Progressive Farmer*. It combined lively text with colorful illustrations to celebrate all aspects of life in the area. By 1974 it also had a circulation above 1 million. *New South*, published in Atlanta 1946–1973 by the Southern Regional Council, was primarily devoted to liberal social commentary. It was superseded by *Southern Voices* under the same auspices.

But the presence of these magazines failed to give the South any significant measure of journalistic independence. Most of them existed only through university subsidies and they chiefly served a limited clientele of scholars. The bulk of southern readers got their news and commentary from magazines published in New York, the journalistic capital of the South as well as of the nation. What a southerner said during the Civil War could as truly be said by her descendant today: "We hope [someone] will be able to get *Harper's* to us [now it might also be *Time* or *Playboy*].... The literature of the North is to us what the 'flesh pots of Egypt' were to the wandering Israelites—we long for it."[1]

In one branch of literature—imaginative writing, especially fiction—the South still was unexcelled. Stimulated by the contrast and paradox of southern change and continuity and perhaps sheltered by a certain "culture lag" from the outside pressures of literary convention, southern novelists continued to draw upon the southern mystique to sustain a regional literature of national and international acclaim.

Many of the major figures of the earlier period were still alive and productive. Faulkner's *Intruder in the Dust* came out in 1948. It was the story of a black man of towering character, wrongfully accused of murder, saved from a lynch mob through the intervention of "good" Mississippi whites. Speaking through a leading figure of this work, the author expressed an enlightened southerner's sense of southern destiny and his recipe for racial justice, and indicated the interdependence of the two. "We alone in the United States . . . are a homogeneous people.... Only a few of us know that only from homogeneity comes anything of a people or for a people of durable and lasting value.... We—he and us [blacks and whites]—should confederate: swap him the rest of the economic and political and cultural privileges which are his right, for the reversion of his capacity to wait and endure and survive. Then we would prevail; together we would dominate the United States."[2] Faulkner wrote several other novels before his death in 1962, most of them sequels to earlier works. His last book, *The Reivers* (1962), was a comical work including some reminiscence about his own youth.

Robert Penn Warren of Kentucky more than any other figure bridged the prewar and postwar generation gap in southern letters. Beginning his career as a member of the Vanderbilt Fugitives, he later taught at Louisiana State University where he helped edit the old *Southern Review*. In 1942 he left the South to teach in northern universities, but the South remained the setting for his books. *All the King's Men* (1946) grafted onto the story of Huey Long's career a philosophical musing on the human condition. It won for the author the Pulitzer Prize for fiction. *Brother to Dragons* (1953) was a book-length poem about a historical event, the murder of a Kentucky slave, with emphasis on original sin and human depravity; *Band of Angels* (1955) recounted the tragic experience of a beautiful octoroon girl during the Civil War and Reconstruction; *The Cave* (1959), based on the death of Floyd Collins in a Kentucky cave, was primarily concerned with the commercial exploitation of tragedy; *Wilderness* (1961) was the story of the disillusionment of an immigrant volunteer in the Union army during the Civil War; *Flood* (1963) was a pensive satire on the displacement of a southern town, including its history and memories, its cemetery dead and its Confederate monument, to make way for progress in the form of a TVA lake; *Meet Me in the Green Glen* (1971) was a brooding tale about the conviction and execution by southern authorities of an Italian-American falsely accused of murder because he had committed the indiscretion of making love to a southern Anglo-Saxon woman. Meantime, Warren won the Pulitzer Prize in poetry for a collection entitled *Promises* (1957). He was the only holder of both the Pulitzer Prize for fiction and the Pulitzer Prize for poetry.

Among other outstanding southern writers active both before and after the war were John Crowe Ransom, Allen Tate, Caroline Gordon, Andrew Lytle, James Agee, Jesse Stuart, Carson McCullers, Katherine Anne Porter, and Eudora Welty. Miss Welty was possibly the most widely hailed of this group. Her brief novel *The Ponder Heart* (1954) was an exquisite piece of southern humor; *Losing Battles* (1970) was a story matchlessly presented in dialogue showing the clannishness and frontier qualities persisting in the twentieth century among the hill-country folk of northern Mississippi; *The Optimist's Daughter* (1972) explored southern class distinctions through an examination of the marriage of a "poor white" girl to an aging member of the Mississippi gentry. Also a master of the short story, perhaps more than any other writer Miss Welty revealed both the lofty and the base in southern life without resorting to chauvinism, caricature, or apology.

Drawing inspiration from the senior writers of the South were scores of talented younger authors who rose to prominence after World War II by developing the themes and settings of their native region. Among the more noteworthy of this group were Peter Taylor, Madison Jones, and Jesse Hill Ford of Tennessee; Reynolds Price of North Carolina; Harper Lee of Alabama; Shirley Ann Grau and Walker Percy of Louisiana; James Dickey and Flannery O'Connor of Georgia; and William Styron of Virginia.

The postwar writer who most profoundly expressed the Southern Gothic form was Flannery O'Connor of Georgia. Her two novels, *Wise Blood* (1952) and *The Violent Bear It Away* (1960), and her brilliantly executed short stories—first published in magazines, then in collections under the titles *A Good Man Is Hard To Find* (1955) and *Everything That Rises Must Converge* (1965)—were tragicomic morality plays on man's fall, redemption, and faith in God Almighty. From the vantage of a Roman Catholic versed in the "Culture-Protestantism" of the South, Miss O'Connor used religious fundamentalism of baroque intensity to satirize the hollowness of modern rationalism.

Miss O'Connor's most substantial work, *The Violent Bear It Away*, described a contest of wills between a fanatical old man obsessed with the determination to have his feeble-minded grandson baptized, and the child's guardian uncle, an enlightened schoolteacher whose religion was that of social progress and who considered baptism a ridiculous survival from the dark and superstitious past. Superficially, the author appeared to be mocking the fundamentalists; actually she was mocking their antagonists, the sociologists, psychologists, and other modern liberals who blithely dismiss the phenomenon of sin as the product of inadequate education or faulty life adjustment.

Asked once about her pursuit of the grotesque in southern life, Miss O'Connor replied tartly that to nonsouthern critics every theme adopted by a southern writer was grotesque, unless it actually was grotesque, in which case it was called southern realism. The author's untimely death in 1964 of lupus cut off one of the most promising careers in the annals of southern literature.

William Styron of Virginia was considered by some critics the figure most likely to lead in sustaining the importance of the southern literary mode in American letters. Styron's *Lie Down in Darkness* (1951) was a story of family disintegration told in stream-of-consciousness style as its southern protagonist followed the hearse bearing to the grave the body of his daughter, a suicide because she had been too weak and selfish to cope with life in New York City. *Set This House on Fire* (1960) examined the futile efforts of an artist of southern origin to escape the hold of his native region by working and playing in Europe. Finally, repelled by episodes of sexual exploitation and homicide, he returned to Charleston where he recovered his own serenity through that of the enchanting old southern city. In *The Confessions of Nat Turner* (1967) Styron recreated in fiction the life of the famous Virginia slave insurrectionary. Though written with compassion and a sense of atonement, this work aroused severe controversy because it pictured Turner as squeamish about killing whites and obsessed with sexual fantasies involving white women. It also was attacked because it attributed Turner's failure to the timidity or apathy of most of the slaves themselves, who were represented as refusing to join the rebellion and, in some instances, as actually helping to suppress it.

Among the most celebrated poets of the recent South was Randall Jarrell, a native of Nashville and a student of the Vanderbilt Fugitives. Remarkably sensitive to the sounds and impulses of nature, Jarrell was said by Marianne Moore to carry on conversations with birds and other animals and then to translate their language into English in such works as "A Country Life" and "The Mockingbird."[3] After World War II in his collections *Losses* (1948), *The Woman at the Washington Zoo* (1960), and *The Lost World* (1965), he increasingly gave aesthetic expression to the horrors of war and to a deep foreboding concerning the destiny of mankind. The title poem of *The Lost World* opened:

There off Sunset, in the lamplit starlight,
A scientist is getting ready to destroy
The World. . . .[4]

Jarrell died in 1965 in an automobile accident. The South produced many other talented poets, including James Dickey, James Whitehead (born in Saint Louis, but educated and now living in the South, and steeped in its culture), Miller Williams of Arkansas, and Dabney Stuart of Virginia. But perhaps because the poetic form is less dependent than fiction upon social convention, southern poetry was less distinctively regional than southern fiction. It was also considered by some critics to be less mature.

Black writers made noteworthy contributions to the outpouring of southern literature in the postwar years. Under the influence of the civil rights movement, they strove far more consciously than in the past to create an exclusively black perspective for their literary expression. They did not wish to merge into the mainstream of southern or American literature, to become black Faulkners or Hemingways. Instead, they turned to black traditions and denied that their writings were of the same order as those of the whites. "In the future," said a black poet, "the only relevant literature will be that which has gone to the heart of Blackness. . . . The black experience seems the most intense experience in the modern world. It is better that black people write it ourselves rather than have it written for us exploitatively." Most black literature understandably became an instrument as well as a product of the struggle for equality and recognition. The new black poetry was especially adapted to this end. "Our weapons are cultural, our poems," said a black editor and critic. "Our poems exist primarily for and go directly to our central human needs, the people, our *shauku* (strong desire). Our minds are the strategy-drawing-boards of a social revolutionary battleground!"[5]

Scores of blacks, many of them either in or of the South, wrote impassioned verse that found its way into the anthologies of the period. Their works often seethed with rage, racial hatred, or disdain for whites, sometimes expressed through obscenity. A few examples show the prevailing style. Julia Fields of Alabama expressed in one of her poems entitled "Black Students" the feelings of irrelevance and futility aroused in the students of her race by the white man's education being imparted to them:

> One lone case of white Encyclopedia Britannica stands
> Untouched, But there is no picture of Christ hanging
> With Messianic, tortured blue eyes
> Muttering "I's lynched, I dies." [6]

Worth Long, a native of North Carolina and one-time official of the Student Nonviolent Coordinating Committee, charged his lines with fury and militancy. In "Arson and Cold Lace" he said:

> We have found you out
> False faced America. . . .
>
> Hot flames must devour
> The kneeling and fleeing
> and torture the masters. . . . [7]

Etheridge Knight, born in Mississippi, began writing poetry while serving a sentence in an Indiana prison. Afterward he taught at Rutgers University and at Lincoln University in Missouri. Among his more vehement works is "Dark Prophesy: I Sing of Shine." Presumably looking toward a reversal of ethnic roles in American life, it celebrated the imagined exploits of a black stoker named Shine in escaping from the sinking *Titanic* and described his jeers at the panic of the white passengers, his scornful rejection of their offers of wealth and sexual favors in return for assistance, and finally

> how Shine swam past a preacher afloat on a board
> crying save me nigger Shine in the name of the Lord—
> how the preacher grabbed Shine's arm and broke his stroke—
> how Shine pulled his shank and cut the preacher's throat—
> Shine swam on—Shine swam on—
> And when the news hit shore that the titanic had sunk
> Shine was up in Harlem damn near drunk—
> and dancing in the streets.
> damn near drunk and dancing in the streets. [8]

Nikki Giovanni, born in Tennessee, wrote poetry of "muted militancy" expressing the ambivalence of many blacks toward the whites. In "Categories" she said:

and sometimes on rainy nights you see
an old white woman who maybe you'd
   really care about
except that you're a young Black woman
whose job it is to kill maim or seriously
make her question
the validity of her existence. . . .[9]

Black novelists and short-story writers in or born in the South were as active after the war as black poets. Though their prose usually was less vehement than black poetry in the expression of social attitudes, the two forms nevertheless displayed many of the same qualities. Richard Wright, whose *Native Son* (1940) had made him the most distinguished black novelist of the prewar years, remained productive until his death in 1960. Though he lived and wrote in Chicago, New York, and Paris, his works continued to reflect the imprint of the South, where he was born and spent his early childhood. In *Black Boy* (1945), an autobiography, he acknowledged this bond by saying, "There had been slowly instilled into my personality, black though I was, the culture of the South."[10] In an assortment of postwar novels, including *The Outsider* (1953), *The Long Dream* (1958), and *Lawd Today* (1963), and in polemical essays, including *Black Power* (1954) and *White Man, Listen!* (1957), he expressed the growing estrangement from American values that in 1947 caused him to leave the country to live in Europe.

Among the more notable of the many recent black writers of fiction were Margaret Walker and Albert Murray, born in Alabama; John A. Williams, born in Mississippi; Ernest J. Gaines, born in Louisiana; Julian Mayfield, born in South Carolina; Alice Walker of Georgia; and Ralph Ellison, born in Oklahoma. Margaret Walker, who had previously made her mark in poetry with *For My People* (1942), now brought out her first novel, *Jubilee* (1966), a story of the tribulations of a southern slave woman of mixed blood living through the final years of bondage, the Civil War, emancipation, and Reconstruction. Albert Murray in numerous short stories proved himself a master of black speech, perceptions, and humor. In a book of essays, *The Omni-Americans: New Perspectives on Black Experience and American Culture* (1970), he avoided the racial chauvinism that marred the works of some of his contemporaries.

Julian Mayfield in *The Hit* (1957) and *Long Night* (1959) dealt with the problems of southern blacks and their descendants transplanted in Harlem. *The Grand Parade* (1962) was a novel for the times; it analyzed the affairs of an eastern city in the throes of school desegregation and pressure politics. Alice Walker's *The Third Life of Grange Copeland* (1971) exposed the brutalizing effects of poverty and oppression on the family life of Georgia blacks.

Ernest J. Gaines and John A. Williams were among the postwar black novelists who most directly addressed their works to racial antagonism and discord. In *Of Love and Dust* (1967) Gaines presented an account of conflict and reciprocal sexual exploitation between blacks and whites on a Louisiana plantation. Though the black hero ultimately dies at the hands of a brutal Cajun overseer, this occurs only after the hero has avenged his earlier mistreatment by making love to the overseer's wife. Other stories by Gaines on the trials of blacks in the rural South include *Catherine Carmier* (1964), *Bloodline* (1968), and *The Autobiography of Miss Jane Pittman* (1971). Williams was perhaps the angriest of the black novelists. In *The Man Who Cried I Am* (1967) he described a conspiracy of the white nations of the world to hold the continent of Africa in perpetual subjection and a plan by the United States government to end "once for all" this nation's minority problem by exterminating its black population. His *Sons of Darkness, Sons of Light* (1969) visualizes a solution to the hardships of his race through the adoption of the Mosaic principle of an eye for an eye and a tooth for a tooth.

The outstanding black writer of the postwar era, and one of the most capable of all American writers, was Ralph Ellison. Educated in part at the Tuskegee Institute in Alabama, Ellison in his twenties went to New York and met Richard Wright, who inspired him to become a writer. Less prolific than many of his fellow authors, Ellison has produced only two major books: *Invisible Man* (1952), a novel, and *Shadow and Act* (1964), a volume of interviews and essays on his political, social, and aesthetic views. But *Invisible Man* is unique: in 1953 it earned the National Book Award for Fiction, and in 1965 it was selected by a *Book Week* poll of critics, authors, and editors as the most distinguished single work published in America since 1945. Like Wright, Ellison recognizes his ties to the regional culture.

Invisible Man is the story of a young southern black exiled to New

York through the intrigue of an Uncle Tomish but Machiavellian southern black college president. Unable to shed completely the influence of his southern upbringing or to cope fully with the difficult ethnic, class, and political design of his adopted city, the protagonist eventually drops out of the society altogether to become an "invisible man." Like the novel's black matriarch from the South, he is in New York but New York is not in him. The work is a vivid exposition of the surreal existence of a black from the rural South transplanted to the frenetic and alien world of the urban North. A strong countertheme is that of abiding racial identity and pride. From still another perspective, the novel reveals the sense of alienation that threatens all American life; ironically, much of it would be as applicable to a displaced southern rural white as to the black man who is its main character. In spite of his literary realism, the author has not given way to the rage of the black militant writers. Instead, he has remained at heart an idealist. "Fully aware of the limitations placed upon the Negro in America, [he] has nevertheless chosen to emphasize those positive elements of Negro life that have helped to keep American culture rich and varied."[11] This is the spirit of his book of essays also.

Unquestionably the southern literature of the postwar years differ in many ways from the region's earlier writings. Recent southern letters reflect the impact on the regional culture both of outside forces and of stirrings within the southern heart. Many of these works are concerned with the effects of urbanization, migration, and civil rights, and with the various other issues that engage the region's consciousness. Southern literature since the war, like southern life, has been in constant flux.

Southern writing appeared to deteriorate in quality as it increased in volume. On the eve of World War II Carson McCullers said the region's writers had reached the limits of their particular mode; that as yet no southern Tolstoi or Dostoevski was on the horizon. Twenty years later Professor Walter Sullivan, of Vanderbilt University, said the Southern Renaissance had ended in the mid-forties. No postwar writing, he believes, including that of Faulkner, is as good as Faulkner's earlier works, because the recent literature has lost the spiritual dimension, the "sense of a divine reality."

Other critics are of the opinion that much of the new southern literature suffers from a subordination of art to the presumed ends of social justice by presenting most or all whites as being pervasively evil and most or all blacks as being pervasively good. In the words of Robert Penn Warren, this attitude still refuses to recognize the black as a man. "It recognizes him only as a Negro—if sometimes as a Negro Jesus Christ. And that is the worst condescension of all."[12] Perhaps these are the things that Katherine Anne Porter had in mind when she attributed Eudora Welty's literary insights partly to her having escaped a "militant social consciousness in the current radical-intellectual sense." Yet she grounded her writings, explained Miss Porter, on ancient and indispensable moral law.[13]

Whatever the merits of recent southern literature, it was still distinctively southern. Faulkner and his generation of writers continued to exert heavy influence upon southern letters, because, said a perceptive critic, "though there is change, there is also continuity, resistance to change, conditions that remain the same even though other factors may change utterly. So it is an oversimplification to say that Faulkner's South is no longer the present-day South, and therefore that the insights whereby Faulkner gave order and meaning to his experience will no longer suffice."[14]

Despite the innumerable evidences of modernization in southern life today, the region's scholars appear to agree that the southern literary imagination is fired by elements of the past that remain alive in the present. Paying recognition to the operation of these forces upon his own works, Reynolds Price says that within five hundred yards of his residence in North Carolina live people, white and black, who could carry on mutually intelligible dialogues with their great-grandparents. A brief automobile drive takes him to the home of his aunts, who submerge him in memories of the past—"each word as rigid in its place and function as a phrase of the Mass, as productive of promise, release, joy." The sight of his three-year-old niece listening to these ceremonies causes him to ask, "How can I guess what strata are slowly, immovably depositing in her?"[15]

In comparison with the works of nonsouthern writers, southern letters continued to emphasize the traditional themes of history, family, religion, sense of place, race, violence, and the inherent sinfulness of man. These characteristics appear in the driven protagonists of the militant black writers, or in Jesse Hill Ford's unremitting white supremacist who happily anticipates a racially segregated sanctuary in the hereafter, no matter whether in heaven or in hell. They appear in the flawed heroes of Robert Penn Warren's imagination, or in Flannery O'Connor's implacable fundamentalist who disdains the marvels of the jet age with the sneer, "A buzzard can fly."

In the midst of an unprecedented rootlessness and feeling of alienation, writers of the South were especially preoccupied with the importance of place and kin in sustaining the human spirit. One sees this in Ralph Ellison's lonely young black in New York City who is comforted in body and soul by eating the hot, baked "Car'lina" yams purchased from an aged black street vendor; in Walker Percy's aimless movie addict who ultimately settles down by marrying his own cousin and accepting the immemorial family and regional philosophy of his aunt; in William Styron's wanderer who, unlike the disenchanted expatriates of Ernest Hemingway's works, finally returns to Charleston to "find himself." Pointing to the mellow beauty of the city's harbor, flowers, and shaded old mansions, he exclaims: "Look at the sky. Did you ever see anything so clean and beautiful? . . . You'll search a long way for that kind of purity. Look at that brickwork. Why, one of those houses is worth every cantilevered, picture-windowed doghouse in the state of New Jersey."[16] These regional qualities endured even the rage of the black militants. Etheridge Knight's poem "The Idea of Ancestry" begins:

> Each Fall the graves of my grandfathers call me,
> the brown hills and red gullies of mississippi send
> out their electric messages, galvanizing my genes.
> Last yr /like a salmon quitting the cold ocean—
> leaping and bucking up his birthstream/ I hitchhiked
> my way from L.A. . . .[17]

IX.

Music & the Visual Arts

The South after World War II was the scene of an unprecedented stirring of interest and activity in the fine arts. A combination of increased prosperity, expanded programs of formal education in the arts, and the aesthetic stimulation of broader travel and improved communications brought an awakening in this field that was as widespread if not as profound as that of the southern literary renaissance. Also, southern arts received support from the National Endowment for the Arts, a federal agency created in the 1960s to provide money to the states by more or less matching funds appropriated locally. Every state established an arts commission to use these federal and state funds. By the early 1970s the state commissions were sponsoring hundreds of performances and exhibits annually throughout the South.[1] The region teemed with artists and art consumers of one kind or another.

The affinity between southern drama and southern literature remained close. The three southern dramatists whose works most vividly illustrated this kinship were Thomas Lanier "Tennessee" Williams, a native of Mississippi; Lillian Hellman, born and reared in New Orleans; and Paul Green of North Carolina. Williams was possibly the most celebrated American playwright of the era. He became famous with the production of *The Glass Menagerie* (1945), the drama of an emotionally fragile girl who sought escape from reality through her assortment of animal figurines. In *A Streetcar Named Desire* (1947) Williams portrayed an encounter between a lusty young Polish-American laborer of New Orleans and a neurotic woman of the decayed plantation aristocracy. *Cat on a Hot Tin Roof* (1955) told a story of parental aspiration and marital felicity threatened by the protagonist's sense of guilt and resort to alcohol. The script for the film *Baby Doll*

(1956), combining two of Williams's earlier short pieces, examined the infantile behavior of a young wife with unawakened but powerful appetites. Williams's underlying theme was that of people seeking withdrawal from life in romantic fantasy, but forced by brutal experiences to abandon their illusions. His concern for love and beauty in a materialistic world was, like Faulkner's, often obscured by the violence and degradation of his characters and situations. In his later works, many of them set outside the South, Williams became even more sensational. Critics came to believe that he partly admired the very forces of evil that his victims cried out against.

Lillian Hellman was also one of the most respected figures in American theater and was perhaps without peer among women dramatists. *The Children's Hour* (1934), a tragedy concerned with juvenile malice, established Miss Hellman in the New York theater. Among the best of her numerous works was a triad on her native region. *The Little Foxes* (1939) and *Another Part of the Forest* (1947) portrayed the repudiation by the New South's moneymakers of the Old South's code of valor and honor. *Toys in the Attic* (1958) exposed the destructive forces sometimes generated by love through the experience of an affluent young southerner whose affections were torn between his elder maiden sisters and his insecure child bride. All of Miss Hellman's pieces, many of which were on nonsouthern themes, were moving studies of human failings.

Paul Green, the acknowledged master of the outdoor drama, was the most eminent southern playwright who lived and worked in his native region. His first major open-air production, *The Lost Colony* (1937), told the story of Sir Walter Raleigh's vanished settlement on Roanoke Island. *The Common Glory* (1947) presented Jefferson's fight for democracy during the birth of the republic. In the next years Green wrote numerous comparable works for historic places throughout the South, including *Wilderness Road, The Confederacy, Texas,* and *Trumpet in the Land*. He looked upon the South as a uniquely favorable place for this kind of presentation, because, he explained, "Our very existence as a people here in the South has been something of an epic tragic drama—a sort of huge and terrifying Job story, if the truth were acknowledged."[2]

Theater in the South continued to depend strongly upon the drama departments of the universities and colleges. The schools most active in this field at the beginning of the era were the universities of North Carolina, Virginia, South Carolina, and Louisville, and the Northwestern State College of Louisiana. All of them emphasized native folklore in their productions. By the early 1970s most of the region's institutions of higher learning offered courses of instruction in acting, producing, directing, and designing for the stage.

Despite an increased interest in universal dramatic themes and techniques, the most distinguished southern programs still turned to local history and lore. North Carolina maintained its prewar standing in this endeavor. The Carolina Playmakers of the University of North Carolina were the leading collegiate theater company of the region. Paul Green was a product of the early Playmakers. In the 1960s the university theater program added the Institute of Outdoor Drama. Under the direction of Mark Sumner it conducted research on outdoor drama, published bulletins, and supervised productions throughout the country. An estimated 4 million spectators attended outdoor dramas between 1937 and 1970.[3]

North Carolina also took the lead in state-sponsored dramatic enterprises. In 1961 the legislature designated the Flat Rock Playhouse as the state theater of North Carolina. This theater was the base of the Vagabond Players, an experimental group that had been brought down from New York by the director, Robroy Farquhar, before World War II. Under the new arrangement, the state supported the actors in making tours under the name Vagabond Touring Company and in providing instruction and other services for drama teachers and drama clubs throughout North Carolina. In 1965 the state opened in Winston-Salem the North Carolina School of the Arts, the first state-supported institution in the nation devoted exclusively to training professional talent in drama, music, and dance.

By the 1970s most of the major cities of the South had professional theater companies. Dallas kept its prewar reputation for dramatic endeavor with the success of Margo Jones's Theater, until her death in 1954, and with the development in 1959 of the Dallas Theater Center. Under Paul Baker's direction, the center by 1970 was presenting more than 440 performances annually, with a selection that ranged from musical comedy to Shakespeare. The center also operated in connection with Trinity University of San Antonio a graduate program in the fine arts and conducted numerous courses in drama for the children, teachers, and citizens of the area. A point of special pride for the center was its Kalita Humphreys Theater, the only public theater building designed by Frank Lloyd Wright. Houston's Alley Theater, founded in 1947 by Nina Vance and later directed by William Trotman, was considered by some critics the best performing arts institution in the South. During the 1960s it attracted national recognition and a subsidy of $3.5 million from the Ford Foundation. Other noteworthy professional theaters included Theatre Atlanta, Repertory Theater in New Orleans, Actors Theatre in Louisville, Front Street Theater in Memphis, Barter Theater in Abingdon, Virginia, and Asolo Theater in Sarasota. The Free Southern Theater of New Orleans represented a commendable achievement in black theater. Under black direction and drawing upon local black talent, it received some municipal and private support, but depended primarily on box office receipts.

Architecture was the one southern art form with a tradition as old and rich as that of southern literature, if not older and richer. But architecture in the postwar South too often surrendered unconditionally to the demands of technology. This was especially true of residential architecture, which in the Old South had been distinguished by its gracious style and sensible adaptation to climate, terrain, and vegetation but now tended to become monotonously utilitarian and dull. Cooled and heated as units by air conditioners and gas or electric furnaces and heavily insulated against both outside heat and cold, most of the dwellings built after World War II had low ceilings and few and miniature windows. Family rooms and "dens," which were almost always equipped with television sets and record players, and often with bars, replaced spacious hallways and verandahs as the centers of family conversation and informal social activity in the hot season.

The new dwellings were more efficient and, throughout most of the year, more comfortable than the grandest mansion of an antebellum planter. Southern lawns still boasted a distinctive appearance given by the stately pines of the hill and coastal country, the dense groves of hardwood and the rich grass of the river valleys, and the majestic live oaks, Spanish moss, and profusion of semitropical flowers of the lower South. But the houses now were so perennially closed and the occupants so habitually inside them that the grounds lost much of their original purpose as living space. Increasingly they became merely ornamental settings to be admired from passing automobiles or from the "picture windows" of the houses they surrounded. This may have been a perverse representation of the architectural dictum that form follows function. Or possibly it was proof that in practice function more often follows form.

Despite its functional uniformity, recent southern residential architecture displayed a great variety of modes and appearances. In the new subdivisions, especially in the affluent ones, houses reflecting Frank Lloyd Wright's influence, with bold intersecting planes and ingenious cantilevers, were artfully blended into hillsides, ravines, or woods. These stood side by side with white-columned "traditionals" reminiscent of Tara in *Gone with the Wind*. Except for the surroundings and the proportion of plantation-house imitations, most of the houses were quite similar to those in other parts of the country. But the early 1970s brought hints of impending change. The threat of fuel and power shortages caused one student of southern domestic architecture to anticipate hopefully a return to earlier principles of adaptation to the weather in the design of southern homes.[4] It would be ironic if the southern climate, once the chief influence in the growth of a regional consciousness and culture but later somewhat neutralized by technology, should again oblige the South to create a truly regional domestic architecture.

The new southern urban business architecture was symbolic of the South's recently acquired prosperity and self-confidence. Towering, functional, glittering, it was perfectly designed to attract the rural and small-town population away from their less exciting dwellings, shops, and offices even as it also beckoned to tourists and newcomers to the area. Atlanta in the Southeast and Houston in the Southwest were leaders in this architecture, though Dallas, New Orleans, Miami, Memphis, and various other cities within the region could claim primacy in one aspect or another of it.

Perhaps the single most important figure contributing to the new architecture was John Portman of Atlanta. Born in South Carolina but reared in Atlanta and trained professionally at the Georgia Tech school of architecture, Portman fully reflected the spirit and personality bequeathed to his city by the great nineteenth-century New South advocate Henry W. Grady. Asked why he chose Atlanta for his work, Portman replied: "It's my home. Its surge forward has cor-responded with my career. Primarily, it's the people here."[5] Also, he explained, Atlanta is favored with rolling hills, luxuriant trees and other vegetation, and abundant rainfall. Influenced by the earlier architecture and living arrangements of his native region and by his observation of Scandinavian city design, he sought to create environ-ments that attract gatherings of people. He especially admired the Tivoli Gardens of Copenhagen, where he said he had never seen any-one without a smile; he compared them in principle with the southern porches of yesterday where everyone sat and talked.[6]

Portman's Peachtree Center, located on and named for the city's most celebrated street, made a major contribution toward keeping downtown Atlanta alive and vibrant. The twenty-two-floor Merchan-dise Mart, completed in 1961, was the commercial heart of the center, but the Hyatt Regency hotel across the street from the mart was the showplace that drew the crowds. Opened in 1967, the hotel had 1,000 rooms, arranged around the outer walls of the building. The rooms were reached through ivy-hung terraces surrounding a spacious interior courtyard that rose breathtakingly from the lobby at ground level to the translucent roof twenty-three stories above. Streamlined glass elevators flashed up and down like silent rockets in full view of lobby and terraces. An unenclosed lobby restaurant created something of the atmosphere of a French sidewalk café; a lobby cocktail lounge shaped like a parasol, and so named, rested on its access stem but appeared to hang by a slender cable from the distant ceiling. On the roof of the building revolved a circular restaurant and cocktail lounge that seemed to hover like a flying saucer over the hotel and the city. Attached to the main structure was the hotel tower, a gleaming cylin-drical annex of equal height containing 200 additional rooms. The Hyatt Regency represented a spectacular blend of technological in-genuity, aesthetic aspiration, and downright ostentatiousness. It was so popular that many other southern cities, including Houston, built similar hotels.

The Peachtree Center in 1974 embraced some twenty acres and was still expanding. It included three office buildings in addition to the structures already described. Some of the buildings were connected by pedestrian bridges at great heights; one of them spanned Peachtree Street at twenty-three stories. Between two of the office towers was a plaza with trees and shrubs growing in planters. Like a Charleston or New Orleans courtyard or a Savannah square, it offered relief from the bustle and tension of the street. In the middle of the plaza was a sunken restaurant connected with the basements of the adjacent buildings. Massive sculpture of abstract or mechanistic design complemented the buildings and grounds of the center. Portman hoped that his architecture would lead the way in reviving the inner city of Atlanta.

If the emphasis in Atlanta's new commercial architecture was on downtown concentration, that of Houston was on a modified dispersal, or "nodal" pattern. True, within the past ten years downtown Houston had built a score or more steel and glass skyscrapers, and the immense Houston Center under construction was expected ultimately to cover thirty-four city blocks. The center's master architect, William Pereira of Los Angeles, likened his projected creation to an ancient Mayan city with promenades, greenery, and fountains at upper levels among a warren of hotels, office towers, and apartment buildings soaring to great heights. Already most of the major structures of downtown Houston were connected by underground pedestrian tunnels and by walkways far above the streets. So complete was the tunnel system that one authority on urban planning said the entire complex ought to be treated as an architectural unit.[7]

But Houston's extensive net of expressways built in the 1960s led to a scattering of its business centers and commercial architecture into clusters somewhat in the manner of Los Angeles. Many of the striking new office towers were located away from the downtown area. Perhaps nothing better illustrated the spirit of the perennial Texas boom city and its vast hinterland than the Galleria, a shopping center near the city's most affluent residential suburb. The Galleria was a superarcade three levels high and connected with well over a hundred business establishments, including the Houston branch of the famous Neiman-Marcus department store of Dallas. A luxury hotel catered to out-of-town customers who came to buy from the adjoining stores. The middle of the arcade was a great concourse, open from the bottom level to the vaulted skylight at the top and partly occupied by an ice-skating rink visible from all levels. Here one might sit in air-conditioned comfort sipping a beverage at a balcony restaurant and watch pretty girls cutting figures on artificial ice while outside the summer temperature stood at 100 degrees.

Some of the most noteworthy architecture created in the South in the postwar years was built on college and university campuses to accommodate their great expansion and to satisfy the demand for physical surroundings to stimulate student minds. Borrowing from the practices of commercial architecture in the conservation of ground space, many of the educational institutions built high-rise dormitories, libraries, and office towers that differed little in appearance from the downtown skyscrapers. One of the most distinctive pieces of regional campus architecture was the massive and fortresslike LBJ Library on the University of Texas grounds in Austin. Opened in 1971, the $18.6 million structure housed Johnson's presidential papers.

Among the aesthetically satisfying and functional buildings on southern campuses were the student center at Louisiana State University in Baton Rouge and the Robert W. Woodruff Library of Advanced Studies at Emory University in Atlanta. Attractively placed in a grove of live oak trees, the Louisiana State University student center was thoroughly modern in its use of steel and glass walls; yet it retained a strong element of the North Italian Renaissance style featured in the older buildings on the campus. It contained a theater and a display hall in addition to the customary cafeteria, bookstore, ballroom, and meeting rooms. The Emory University library was a handsome ten-story building supported by slender concrete arches that went up to the roof, with walls of black steel panels. It was surrounded by a broad concrete plaza reached by a bridge spanning the wooded ravine beside the building. A terrace outside the glass walls on the top floor offered a view of the Atlanta skyline. Virtually every college and university in the region had new buildings that would compare favorably with these few examples.

Many of the buildings for public assembly and diversion could be included among the more spectacular pieces of southern architecture during the postwar era. The Atlanta Memorial Arts Center, a colonnaded structure opened in 1968, was the home of the High Museum, the Atlanta School of Art, the Alliance Theater Company, and the Children's Theater. The Houston Contemporary Arts Museum, which opened in 1972, was perhaps the most unusual building of its kind in the region. Designed in the shape of a parallelogram to accommodate exceptionally lengthy exhibits along its main diagonal, the building had outer walls of vertical steel strips; its interior supports, concrete floors, and heating and cooling pipes were exposed so as to be in harmony with the experimental and improvisational nature of the exhibits and activities. So casual was the entire scene that an uninformed visitor might have had difficulty knowing whether a tall metal frame in one corner of the museum was a repairman's scaffold, a building truss, or an art object on display.

Yet in southern architecture as in all other forms of southern expression, a strong nostalgia for the old persisted in the midst of a yearning for the new. The building of many residences to resemble plantation mansions was one evidence of this enchantment with forms out of the past. More significant were the region's efforts to preserve or restore houses actually built in the past. Every southern city had some kind of program for accomplishing this purpose, though unfortunately they often were countered by the American urge to tear down and build afresh. For example, admirers of the French Quarter of New Orleans were appalled at the encroachment of motels on that historic site; the construction in the 1960s of an expressway along its front was only narrowly averted by citizen protest and court action.

In spite of all hazards, numerous southern cities, including Charleston, Savannah, New Orleans, Beaufort (South Carolina), Natchez, and Macon, still contained scores of houses, churches, and public buildings representing the grandeur of an earlier age. Also, hundreds of genuine antebellum plantation mansions throughout the region yet survived the elements and human vandalism though, sad to say, one by one they were falling. In 1961, for instance, Greenwood mansion at St. Francisville, Louisiana—said to have been the most photographed house in a state rich in such showplaces—was destroyed by lightning. Some of the great old houses were kept up by local associations formed for this purpose; others were turned over to the National Trust for Historic Preservation. Most of them were preserved by individual owners, who frequently met the expense by opening them to the public and charging admission fees. Possibly the most notable example of an individual undertaking of this sort was the restoration of the Rosedown mansion and grounds at St. Francisville, with its marvelous collection of shrubs and flowers from all over the world. A wealthy Texas couple purchased the place in the 1950s and devoted themselves to its revival.

The restoration of Williamsburg, capital of colonial Virginia, was the most publicized undertaking of this nature in the entire United States. Supported liberally with funds donated by John D. Rockefeller, the work was well under way before World War II and was largely complete by 1960. Many of the most important buildings, including the Capitol and the Governor's Palace, had long since disappeared and had to be entirely reproduced. Painstaking research assured restorations and reconstructions of remarkable fidelity to the original buildings. Colonial Williamsburg was a major historical and architectural accomplishment and throughout the postwar era one of the most popular tourist attractions in the South.

Savannah's program of revival compared most favorably with that of Williamsburg. Neglected, frayed, and altered as it was, more of old Savannah than of old Williamsburg was yet standing; hence in Savannah the emphasis was on preservation rather than reproduction. Historic Savannah Foundation was formed in 1955 to save the old city from further decay and to adapt its configuration and architecture to the needs of the present. The foundation's aim was to restore and preserve both the historic buildings of Savannah and the essence of the city plan used in 1733 by the founder, General James Oglethorpe. Developed around a system of twenty-four open public squares dotted with live oak trees, flowers, and occasional pieces of statuary, the old city provided elbow room for its inhabitants. The restoration plan, nearing completion in 1974, was exceptionally practical as well as aesthetically appealing, because the increased population density made elbow room more important than ever. In observing the businessmen, secretaries, laborers, and other city dwellers relaxing on benches under the trees and chatting or eating sandwich lunches, one had the conviction that the squares were more than pretty little parks; they were an organic part of the city's living space.

Identifying 1,100 buildings of historical and architectural significance and arming itself with an effective zoning ordinance, the Savannah organization carried out its object through the purchase and resale of selected properties to individuals who agreed under covenant to restore them according to rules approved by an official Architectural Review Board. Where the initial building had already been destroyed, new construction had to be compatible with the surrounding architecture though not necessarily a copy of the original. By 1973 more than 70 percent of the designated houses were restored and occupied. So successful was the Savannah project that it became a model for other cities. It made General Oglethorpe a hero of today's urbanologists. One of them said: "The great tragedy is that Savannah was not on the main line for immigrants who headed west. Otherwise, they might well have imitated this sort of urban plan elsewhere, and other cities wouldn't have the urban sprawl that we are all so concerned about now."[8]

The visual arts were traditionally the South's weakest form of aesthetic outlet. The most distinguished painting and sculpture in the region were done by nonsoutherners; to achieve excellence or fame in these fields, southerners usually had to leave the South and adopt techniques developed elsewhere. Among the epithets fixed upon the South by Henry L. Mencken was "The Sahara of the Bozart" (1920). He of course exaggerated in saying the South had no art galleries, that no artist ever gave an exhibition, and no one was interested in such things. A few of the major cities had art museums of varying size and quality. But a southern critic and museum director said that as late as 1950 the Southeast, by and large, was lamentably short in the creative arts; a museum, he explained whimsically, "was a place where the family put things that were not good enough to keep and too good to throw away."[9]

Probably the visual arts in the 1970s were still the South's weakest form of aesthetic outlet. Certainly they continued to receive less recognition than southern literature and perhaps less than southern architecture, theater, or music. For example, most of the sculpture used by John Portman to enhance his Atlanta architecture was imported from Europe.

Yet the visual arts in the South experienced something of a renaissance of their own after World War II. All the major art museums of the region, including those of Richmond, Atlanta, New Orleans, Houston, and Dallas, either moved into new and larger buildings or made significant additions to their original space and holdings. By the 1970s all had collections containing works by the world's masters. Through improved communications and an interest generated in the schools and colleges, and through their enlarged programs of activities, the museums established a degree of contact with the public that was unprecedented for the South. The Virginia Museum of Fine Arts, a state-supported institution located in Richmond, offered an outstanding example of such services. In addition to its permanent and special exhibitions, it sponsored dramatic productions, professional dance events, chamber music concerts, films, and courses in art, acting, directing, and voice.[10] Its "art-mobiles" carried exhibits throughout the state. It published nine bulletins annually, and it maintained an art reading and research library of better than 20,000 volumes. By 1973 the museum's various activities together attracted almost 1.3 million visitors annually. The other leading museums of the region had comparable if less extensive programs and recorded annual attendances in the hundreds of thousands.

Interest in art and support for the development of museums and galleries reached beyond the larger cities. Assisted by federal subsidies and by local business subscriptions, many of the smaller cities built museums and stocked them with collections. In 1956 the state of North Carolina opened the North Carolina Museum of Art at Raleigh, thus following the lead of Virginia, the only other state with a state-supported museum. By the early 1970s the states of the former Confederacy had more than 170 museums and galleries of all sizes and grades.

Art departments in the colleges and universities along with institutions devoted exclusively to the arts helped to bring qualified artists into the region, to train southern artists, and to awaken a segment of the population to the importance of art in improving their lives. The college and university art programs grew along with the general expansion of the educational institutions. All the leading museums offered art training. Among the more important institutions engaged wholly in art education were the Memphis Academy of Art, the Atlanta School of Art, and, in a folksier medium, the Penland School of Crafts in western North Carolina. More than 160 programs of art instruction were active in the region.

Hundreds, even thousands, of painters and sculptors plied their arts in the postwar South. An estimated 200 or more artists practiced permanently in the one state of North Carolina; the number in other southern states appeared to be comparable. In quality and technique they ranged from the highly trained independent professionals and members of university staffs to the folk artists and "primitives" who relied chiefly on self-education or on an intuitive sense of design and color.

Lamar Dodd of Georgia exemplified the teacher-artist in southern life. He was believed by some to be the most important figure in postwar art in the South. Trained as a painter at the Art Students League of New York, he returned to his native region in the mid-1930s and soon became head of the art department of the University of Georgia. During the next thirty years he developed there one of the most extensive and most active art programs in the nation. He also continued to paint: at first local scenes and landscapes; later, European settings. In 1963 he was one of seven painters invited by the National Aeronautics and Space Administration to record the manned orbital flight of Astronaut Gordon Cooper; six years later Dodd was among the artists who recorded the Apollo 11 moon mission. His work was represented in more than a score of the leading museums and galleries of the country; he received the acclaim of the nation's critics and was honored with countless awards and citations. His career illustrated a virtually unexceptional tendency among southern university artists: that of shedding their regionalism in favor of universalism and abstraction. Yet, said a perceptive commentator, Dodd seldom painted in pure abstraction; his style was fundamentally graphic. Certainly his perception of color, space, and design was influenced by his life in the South.[11]

John McCrady of Oxford, Mississippi, and New Orleans was one southern artist whose work remained explicitly southern. He tried his brush in New York in the early 1930s, but he was unable to shut the vision of Oxford out of his mind. Returning there he painted the city's public buildings and the houses and churches of the surrounding countryside. On the eve of World War II he was acclaimed by critics as one of the nation's outstanding regionalists. He established an art school in New Orleans where he painted scenes of the coast and of Louisiana life. In the 1960s he turned back to Oxford as the source of his inspiration. He died in 1969. McCrady's expressed ambition was to portray "an order that ennobled the humblest scenes, recasting mere realism into what we call Art." Measured by the works of the abstractionists, his paintings appeared almost photographic. Yet he succeeded in capturing the spirit behind the commonplace objects of his native state. A visiting journalist observed that his paintings illuminated the "enduring verities" of the country darkened by the shadows conjured by Faulkner's pen.[12]

Southern primitive painters were to the visual arts what the folk singers, players, and dancers were to music. Clementine Hunter of the Cane River country of Louisiana may have been the most remarkable member of this group of artists. An elderly and illiterate black woman who said she was born in 1883, Mrs. Hunter picked up a discarded brush in the early 1950s and began to paint scenes of weddings, baptisms, funerals, cotton picking, and many other activities among the rural blacks of the state. She worked by sheer intuition. She said she could not paint a tree by looking at one; she had to do it as she imagined it, or as the Lord told her to do it.[13] Her paintings were hung in museums throughout the country. One of them served the photographer Edward Steichen to illustrate the meaning of a picture, its inner vision distinguishing it as a work of art. Needless to say, Clementine Hunter became known as a black Grandma Moses. Every state had its primitives, white and black, who recorded life as they saw it, remembered it, or imagined it.

Music after World War II, as before, was the most popular of the fine arts in the South. Along with the other arts it received unprecedented support in money and enthusiasm. Television, record players, and tape players now joined radio as means of bringing all kinds of music into southern homes. The music departments of all regional colleges and universities expanded their programs to include opera and symphony in addition to the assorted vocal and instrumental ensembles. The public schools greatly increased their musical instruction; even most elementary schools now had bands, orchestras, and choruses trained by professional teachers. All the major southern cities improved their symphony orchestras; five cities of the former Confederacy—Atlanta, Dallas, Houston, New Orleans, and San Antonio—had orchestras included among the twenty-nine "major orchestras" so designated by the American Symphony Orchestra League. Another nineteen southern orchestras were in the less distinguished "metropolitan orchestra" classification.

Through the rise of local concert associations that sold season tickets, all the larger southern cities and many smaller ones were able to enjoy performances by major artists, orchestras, and ballet troupes of the North and of Europe. The regional metropolises attracted visits also by the opera companies of Chicago and New York. Southern cities with distinguished opera companies of their own were New Orleans, Dallas, Houston, Mobile, and Miami. By 1974 the region supported nineteen local opera companies. The Southeastern Regional Ballet Association, largely under the inspiration of the Atlanta Ballet, included scores of private ballet schools throughout the area.

Despite these substantial gains in formal musical instruction and classical performance, folk music and its offshoots were still the South's most vigorous and most original kind of musical expression. Except for literature, they were the region's most spontaneous and distinctive form of cultural outlet. Black spirituals and freedom songs took on a renewed interest from the civil rights movement. Old-fashioned jazz by both black and white musicians remained popular, especially in cities such as New Orleans, traditionally the birthplace of this music, where groups of black musicians could still be heard nightly in the French Quarter's Preservation Hall and almost daily in the black funeral processions. A number of prominent early jazz figures were yet alive and active. Louis Armstrong, the great trumpeter, was a favorite entertainer until his death in 1971.

The mountainous and isolated rural areas of the South continued to preserve a tradition of white spirituals through the sacred harp groups, so called because they sang from shaped notes derived from the *Sacred Harp* hymnal of the early nineteenth century, and of white secular folk music through balladry and self-taught "hillbilly" singing and playing. Sunday afternoon "singings" of traditional Protestant hymns were still held in many small towns and crossroads communities.

The most noteworthy postwar developments in southern music were the rise of white gospel music and of country music. Gospel music was an adaptation of the old-fashioned church singings to the appetites of the masses of recently urbanized southerners of the laboring class and the lower middle class. Audiences of thousands met in municipal auditoriums to hear quartets and other small vocal and instrumental ensembles perform. Their themes were fundamentalist in theology and morals. A typical line went, "Build my mansion next door to Jesus and tell the angels I'm coming home." Tones ranged from spectacularly low basses to soaring falsetto tenors; words were homey and familiar; rhythms were doleful one moment, jazzy the next. Singers were accompanied by pianos, electric basses and guitars, drums, and other instruments already popular in country music.

Dozens of professional groups of gospel musicians sprang up. Perhaps the single most popular figure in the movement was J. D. Sumner of the Stamps Quartet. A native of Florida and a pioneer singer in gospel music, Sumner was called the world's deepest bass, a claim that may have been true. His voice was recorded down to contra C: three notes from the bottom of the piano keyboard! He helped to establish the Gospel Music Association with headquarters in Nashville, the capital of country music. By 1973 gospel music was estimated to be grossing about $50 million annually. One student of this mode called it "a truly ethnic music."[14]

The rise of country music after World War II was probably an unparalleled phenomenon in American cultural affairs. A sophisticated derivative of hillbilly music, country music during the war began to spread beyond the South in popularity. The song "You Are My Sunshine," by Jimmie Davis (soon to be elected governor of Louisiana) may have been the most frequently sung tune of the United States Army during the war. Troops arriving overseas after the initial American landings were astounded to hear it on the lips of French or Polynesian children.

With the help of radio, television, and records, country music swept the entire nation in the postwar years. Earlier the national center of hillbilly music with its Grand Ole Opry, Nashville now became the major dispenser of country music; the expression "Nashville sound" arose as a synonym of "country music." Singers such as Eddy Arnold of Tennessee, Ray Price of Texas, Johnny Cash of Arkansas, and Loretta Lynn of Kentucky were among the most popular entertainers of the era. The recording industry threatened to abandon Tin Pan Alley of New York in favor of Music Row in Nashville. By 1973 the seventy-four studios located there together made 90 percent of all country music records and brought in $200 million annually. Approximately 2,000 musicians performed in Nashville, and nine country music television shows originated in the city. A Country Music Association founded in 1958 became the Country Music Foundation six years later and erected a Country Music Hall of Fame, a combination of shrine and museum, which attracted 200,000 visitors a year. In 1973 it contained exhibits on twenty "immortals" of the hillbilly and country music genre.[15]

The sentimental lyrics and pleasing rhythms of country music suited the postwar mood. Despite its rural southern origins it appealed to multitudes of urban nonsoutherners also, because it affirmed traditional American virtues and values. It was a secular form of gospel music, upholding fundamentalist theological and moral views and lamenting instances of their decline. It expressed without inhibition the joys of love fulfilled, family unity, hard work, and clean living; it described with equal candor the pain of love unrequited, marital infidelity, divorce, crime, and poverty. It was the southern folk culture given aesthetic form: a lament against the mass culture, rootlessness, and alienation of modern urban America.

The many southern achievements in the fine arts after World War II failed to give the region claims to national leadership except in those fields where it was already recognized: imaginative literature, the preservation of antebellum architecture, and folk drama and music. Of the 787 painters and sculptors selected for inclusion in the current *Dictionary of Contemporary American Artists* fewer than 50 were born in the South. Of almost 200 pictures in a *Time-Life* book on twentieth-century American paintings, none were by southerners. Most of the superior artists of southern birth practiced outside their native region and in styles not discernibly associated with the South. Virtually all the directors of southern symphony orchestras were nonsoutherners; the principal actors in the performances of the leading southern theaters were usually imported from the New York talent pool; the principal singers in most southern operatic productions were brought down from the Metropolitan Opera of New York.

Perhaps an even greater weakness of the classical arts in the South was their failure to exercise a profound influence on the attitudes and behavior of society. Such a shortcoming was not new. Soon after World War II Francis Butler Simkins observed genteel Virginians discussing houses and livestock between dances by a distinguished ballet group on tour. His mind turned back to a pre–Civil War scene at the famous resort White Sulphur Springs, Virginia (now West Virginia). Bacon was the topic of a serious conversation overheard here by an English writer. Believing the planters of the company to be as intellectual as Thomas Jefferson, he assumed their subject was Sir Francis Bacon. He discovered he was wrong; they were discussing pork.[16] In the late 1960s a student of modern drama lamented the failure of the messages of the theater to "flow into the life of the [southern] community."[17] And Paul Green deplored the insistence of southerners upon military or other violent dramatic themes. The modern South was no more inclined to surrender its folkways to the fine arts than was the Old South to philosophy.

X.

Change & Tradition in Southern Society

Southern society after World War II underwent the most severe stress of its entire history. Despite the trials of the Civil War and the upheavals of Reconstruction, neither of these experiences had threatened the core of the traditional southern society with the force of the recent political, economic, and social changes. Yet countless landmarks of sectional distinctiveness remained. The changes themselves took place in a manner peculiar to the South. Moreover, the primary institutions and modes of conduct survived, even where drastically modified. Every study of southern behavior and attitudes in the 1960s and 1970s indicated the persistence of the old in the midst of the new.[1]

Southern class structure endured the effects of industrialization, urbanization, and prosperity. Descendants of the antebellum planters still formed a small but select gentry even if overshadowed by others with more money or more political influence. The planter offspring usually lived on income from inherited property or by such professions as law, medicine, or the military. But tradition was the mainstay of their survival as a class. Southerners continued to draw a sharper distinction than nonsoutherners between the expressions "good family" and "good people." This was especially true in such enclaves of old southern values as Charleston, where, according to one observer, the very names of individuals tended to become genealogical incantations: for example, Pinckney Ravenel Rutledge or Ravenel Rutledge Pinckney. Though less pronounced in less historic places, the principle of guarding family name and prestige was strong everywhere. A scholar reared in New Orleans described this trait: "Even most Boston Brahmins can hardly imagine the intense awareness of the past long dead and the preoccupation with matters of family, ancestry, and local history particularly among older women of the Southern patriciate."[2]

The aristocratic tradition was not altogether the product of self-admiration. Most white southerners of all classes, and at least some black southerners, still venerated the region's plantation past and conferred a certain respect upon its heirs. At their worst, these aristocrats by popular consent represented a pretentiousness that failed to conceal their lack of wealth or power. At their best, they continued to represent a welcome exception to the mass, with emphasis upon personal honor and integrity, valor, graciousness of manners, and the perfection of "good living," as opposed to the mere accumulation of money or the cultivation of utilitarian competence.[3] They believed, said a sympathetic but critical analyst, "that who you are, if not superior to what you are, transcends at least the standard of what you have."[4]

Eclipsing the old plantation elite in everything but tradition and family pride were the wealthy businessmen, who had begun to arise before World War II and whose numbers were multiplied by the prosperity of the 1950s and 1960s. The New South ideal of progress through commerce and industry now came into its own and spread from the metropolises to the smaller cities and eventually into the towns and villages. At the top of the economic and social pyramid were the millionaire and multimillionaire entrepreneurs in mineral recovery, manufacturing, marketing, and life insurance. Oil was the source of the most sensational wealth, especially among the swashbuckling prospectors of Texas. Such men as H. L. Hunt, Sid W. Richardson, and Clinton W. Murchison stood at the head of a list of Texas "Big Rich" who would have been at ease among the Rockefellers, Vanderbilts, and Carnegies of an earlier age. Spreading down from the multimillionaires was a substructure of lesser business figures—self-made, rugged proprietors of small, independent enterprises in furniture, clothing, refining, and food processing. Serving the needs of these manufacturers and marketers was a multitude of contractors, truckers, machinery and appliance agents, employees of service firms, and wholesalers and retailers.

The blending of the regional economy into the national economy greatly increased the number of native southerners and newcomers associated with national corporations. These employees of General Motors, Standard Oil, Du Pont, Lockheed, and the like were scattered throughout the society at all levels. Corporate executives and regional managers lived in the most exclusive neighborhoods and moved in social circles with the entrepreneurs and most distinguished professional men. The corporation engineers, geologists, and lower-echelon administrators made up a significant part of the southern "white-collar" class. They together with the rank and file of the lawyers, physicians, accountants, small businessmen, and teachers populated the sprawling middle-class suburbs that grew around the cities.

Next in order were the armies of "blue-collar" workers, the mechanics, carpenters, pipe fitters, electricians, machine operators, and assembly line workers of the expanding cities and industries. Unlike many of their fellow laborers in other parts of the country, who often were from the immigrant population, these southerners were of the same origins as their superiors in the business and social hierarchy; they were chiefly new arrivals from the hundreds of thousands of surrounding small farms that were now disappearing under the economic and social forces of the times. Many of them came also from the neighboring small towns. They lived in the previously middle-class and now frayed sections of the cities, which became available to them because of the exodus of former residents to the suburbs, or in the lower priced new residential developments in the less scenic or less convenient areas on the outskirts of the cities.

But class distinctions were still observed in the midst of social flux, and the southern sense of hierarchy remained strong. The innumerable whites who rose to prosperity from humble origins quickly took on the airs and practices of the establishment and guarded their new status as jealously against the lower economic and social orders as the baronial planters of the Old South were said to have done. Many of them built houses that looked like plantation mansions and filled them with antique furniture, or with reproductions of antique furniture. If all did not become Episcopalians, as some did, they moved into the "high church" congregations of the other denominations. They began to send their children to exclusive private schools. They changed from Populist to Bourbon in their political outlook. Frequently some member of the family undertook to trace the family tree in an effort to establish a legitimate heritage from the Virginia or South Carolina gentry.

All classes retained a certain rural outlook and style, though by 1970 approximately 65 percent of the southern population was officially classified as urban. A primary reason for the rural tone was that the great majority still lived outside the large cities. Only about 25 percent of the total population lived inside cities of as many as 100,000 residents, while 40 percent lived in suburban areas or in the more than 4,500 cities and towns of fewer than 100,000. The suburbs were generally conservative in social and political attitudes and shared many of the values and beliefs of the rural and small-town population. Indeed, most southern cities themselves were hardly cities at all by nonsouthern standards; they were still more like overgrown country towns. No city in the states of South Carolina, Mississippi, and Arkansas had a population as high as 200,000. Southern cities also preserved a rural flavor because most of their residents were from the surrounding countryside and still had countless friends and relatives there. Visits back and forth kept common interests alive. Even such southern metropolises as Atlanta and Houston seemed quaintly uncrowded and relaxed in comparison with the leading metropolises of the East, Midwest, or Pacific Coast. Southern cities lacked what James Dickey called the "frenetic, urban sensibility" of a Pittsburgh or a Detroit.

Finally, better than 35 percent of the southern population was still officially classified as rural, that is, actually living in the country or in towns or villages with populations under 2,500. Though four out of five of these people now held their chief employment in the factories, stores, or offices of nearby cities or towns, driving automobiles to and from work every day, they remained country folk in outlook and behavior as well as in residence. The small portion of the population still making a living on the farm kept its division into planters, yeoman farmers, and tenants, with social distinctions to match.

An important cause also of this persistently rural outlook was the emphasis on family that survived the disruptive forces of modern life. Southern families were exceptionally cohesive; divorce was less popular than in other major areas; parental authority tended to be

stronger. Domestic training and family lore, more often than elsewhere reinforced with a hickory switch, still impressed upon southern
children an assortment of distinctive if not ineradicable attitudes,
tastes, loyalties, and mannerisms. A southern-born scholar writing
in the mid-1960s commented upon the reluctance of southerners
to espouse ideas that might stir up disagreement among their extended, close-knit families of uncles, aunts, siblings, and cousins.[5]

The family was the citadel of the color line. "Family life in
Brazil cannot be defined in racial terms," said a sociologist, "but this
is precisely how it is defined in the South. White and Negro Southerners do have kin across the color line but they are not publicly recognized, and we may not expect the fundamental social structure of
southern society to change appreciably until and unless the family
finally yields to desegregation."[6] Interracial marriage was the strongest of southern taboos. Occasional marriages of this nature took place
as a result of the desegregation of schools and other public institutions
and of the federal courts' striking down laws against such unions. But
the number was too small to have any significant effect on the color
line.

To a considerable extent the entire southern community kept a
familylike quality, so much so that James McBride Dabbs called
it a "kinship-oriented society." This was possible because, in spite of
the stream of outsiders coming into the region after World War II,
the southern people retained much of their homogeneity. In 1970 the
South was substantially higher than the rest of the country in the
proportion of inhabitants whose parents were born in the same state
as the child. In six former Confederate states more than 98 percent
of the population was from "native parentage" as compared with
83.5 percent in the entire nation.

Also, newcomers into the region still demonstrated a marked
capacity to "go native." Their children born in the South were hardly
if at all distinguishable from other southern children; their grand-
children doubtless will be absolutely indistinguishable. Walker Percy
in the mid-1960s described the "almost familial ambit" of Mississippi
in terms that would have been more or less applicable to the entire
South. "The whole Delta, indeed of white Mississippi, is one big
kinship lodge," he said. "You have only to walk into a restaurant
or a bus station to catch a whiff of it. There is a sudden kindling

of amiability, even between strangers. The salutations, 'What you say now?' and 'Y'all be good,' are exchanged like fraternal signs. The presence of fraternity and sorority houses at Ole Miss always seemed oddly superfluous."[7]

All the southern traits of class and family were held by the region's blacks, along with various other characteristics derived from their own experience. Though blacks left the South in great numbers during and after World War II—approximately 1.5 million each decade between 1940 and 1970—the area still had the nation's greatest concentration of Americans of African descent. The more than 10 million blacks in the old Confederate states in 1970 accounted for almost half the nation's blacks and for better than 20 percent of the region's total population. Because of economic pressure and social preference the movement of blacks from southern farms into southern cities went on steadily. On the eve of World War II approximately 35 percent of the region's blacks were city dwellers; by 1970 approximately 67 percent of southern blacks were classified by the census taker as urban. About 56 percent of them lived in metropolitan areas, with 41 percent collected within the central cities. Blacks now made up more than half the population of Atlanta, and they were approaching the halfway mark in a number of other southern cities.

Profound changes took place in the lives of black city dwellers. The upper and middle classes expanded significantly both in numbers and in wealth, thus reflecting the growth of black insurance companies, banks, savings and loan associations, and a wide variety of small business enterprises, all primarily serving a black clientele. By 1970 the North Carolina Mutual Life Insurance Company, a black organization with headquarters in Durham, held assets worth over $118 million; in 1972 the Atlanta Life Insurance Company announced assets of better than $80 million, plus an unassigned surplus of more than $14 million. Auburn Street in Atlanta, where many of the city's flourishing black businesses were located, was called the "richest Negro street in the world." Every major southern city had prosperous black owners and managers of thriving companies, along with a professional class of successful physicians, lawyers, ministers, and professors in the black colleges and universities. Handsome and exclusive black residential neighborhoods, some of them with swimming pools and golf courses, marked the rise of the black bourgeoisie.

Table 8

POPULATION OF THE SOUTH 1940, 1970

	Total[a] 1970	% change since 1940	White 1970	% change since 1940	Black 1970	% change since 1940
Alabama	3,444,165	+ 22	2,533,831	+ 37	903,467	− 8
Arkansas	1,923,295	− 1	1,565,915	+ 7	352,445	− 27
Florida	6,789,443	+258	5,719,343	+314	1,041,651	+103
Georgia	4,589,575	+ 47	3,391,242	+ 66	1,187,149	+ 9
Louisiana	3,641,306	+ 54	2,541,498	+ 68	1,086,832	+ 28
Mississippi	2,216,912	+ 2	1,393,283	+ 26	815,770	− 24
N. Carolina	5,082,059	+ 42	3,901,767	+ 52	1,126,478	+ 15
S. Carolina	2,590,516	+ 36	1,794,430	+ 65	789,041	− 3
Tennessee	3,923,687	+ 35	3,293,930	+ 37	621,261	+ 22
Texas	11,196,730	+ 75	9,717,128	+ 77	1,399,005	+ 51
Virginia	4,648,494	+ 74	3,761,514	+ 87	861,368	+ 30
Total South	50,046,182	+ 57	39,613,881	+ 73	10,184,467	+ 15
United States	203,211,926	+ 54	177,748,975	+ 50	22,580,289	+ 76

Source: U.S., Bureau of the Census, *Sixteenth Census of the United States, 1940: Population*, vol. 2, pt. 1, p. 52; *1970 Census of Population*, vol. 1, parts for individual states.
[a]Includes white, black, and other nonwhite.

Employment opportunities created by the civil rights acts of the 1960s along with the rising demand for labor drew blacks into jobs never before open to them in the South. The textile mills, for example, began to hire black operatives, not only because the law required it, but because their workers were leaving for the higher wages of the new plastics and electronics factories. The many industries that had traditionally held blacks to the most menial jobs now began to upgrade a number of their positions. Fear of the adverse economic consequences of racial strife and black boycotts caused many southern business and community leaders to undertake to preserve racial harmony; by the late 1960s most of the states and many communities had created interracial committees that attempted to relieve the urgent problems of black employment, relations with the police, and general living conditions. Virtually every southern business and industry was now hiring blacks in at least limited numbers for a variety of jobs that spread from the janitorial level through the secretarial and assembly line positions and into the lower administrative ranks. Local authorities added blacks to police and fire department forces and assigned them to clerical positions in the courthouses and government offices.

Although racial friction still existed in the South, it tended to fade in the public mind during the late 1960s in comparison with the violence, arson, and looting of the black riots in the northern and western cities. Appalled by these upheavals, some students of racial matters, including such eminent spokesmen as Roy Wilkins of the NAACP and the sociologist Gunnar Myrdal, went so far as to predict that the South would outpace the North in establishing harmony between the races. Increased opportunities for black employment in the South joined with the relative calm of the area to cause a significant reverse migration of blacks from North to South. In the early 1970s an estimated average of about 100,000 blacks a year was reported to be moving into the region, a number that probably exceeded the rate of those leaving during the same period. But these figures were uncertain and controversial. Estimates by the Bureau of the Census showed that between 1970 and 1972 the black population of the greater South decreased from 53 percent to 52 percent of the total American black population, thus indicating a continued excess of outward movement.

In spite of the many improvements in the situation of the blacks, they remained as a class at the bottom of the regional economic and social scale. In 1966 the median income of black families was estimated to be only 51 percent as high as that of white families; in 1972 it had risen to 55 percent. Favorable as this advance unquestionably was, it brought little comfort to most blacks. Much of the gain turned out to be the result of a higher proportion of employed black wives than of white wives. Ominously, as inflation elevated the "poverty line"—defined in 1973 by the Office of Economic Opportunity as $4,275 annual income for an urban family of four—the proportion of blacks below it increased far more rapidly than the proportion of whites. And recession unemployment among the blacks was higher than among whites. The plight of rural blacks, who still made up roughly one-third of the region's total black population, was especially severe, because of their virtual peonage on the white man's land or in his shop or, worse, because of the unemployment brought on by mechanization and conversion to grazing. Thousands of black children in the isolated countryside were found to be seriously undernourished.[8]

Nor did the comparative racial harmony of the South and the collapse of legal segregation indicate the disappearance of actual segregation. The vast majority of the members of the two races lived as far apart in the 1970s as they had in the 1940s. Possibly they lived farther apart. The black influx into the cities accelerated the white exodus to the suburbs and left extensive ghettos where checkerboard neighborhoods once existed. Atlanta was the leading example of this transformation within the old Confederate states; some observers foresaw the day when this city would be all black. The same trend was at work in most other southern metropolises.

The rural and small-town South showed a far greater amount of genuine desegregation in public places than was to be seen in the cities. But in the small towns and the countryside the rigidity of a caste system grounded upon the conjunction of race, poverty, and tradition was largely unshaken. A careful study of the blacks in South Carolina, a state of small cities and towns and a large rural population, concludes that the civil rights movement of the 1960s caused little fundamental change in the race relations of this state. At the beginning of the 1970s, the author says, blacks had little prospect "that their needs would be realized in the near future. . . . Public policy was still more concerned with neutralizing their aspirations than with helping them realize them."[9] Paradoxically, where things had changed the most they seemed to have changed the least.

If modern southerners in the midst of economic and social transition managed to perpetuate numerous traditional distinctions of class and race, they also preserved a great body of traits common to all levels of the regional population. Unconscious as well as conscious ties with the past held strong. Southerners remained conservative in lifestyle as in public attitude. Even southern liberals were scarcely so by outside standards. James McBride Dabbs said: "Northern liberals are much more typical of the modern world. Southern liberals are hardly liberals at all. . . . The Southerner retains a sense of community—he's critical, but not willing to chuck the whole thing. . . . Southern liberals are really conservatives."[10] Observation of the regional characteristics in, and outlook toward, personal and domestic relationships, manners and speech, and athletics and recreation indicates the South has kept a style of its own.

Violence was still very much a part of the regional way of life. In 1972 the southern murder rate was almost 40 percent higher than that of the West, the major area that came nearest to matching the South in this unenviable record. Some of the regional violence was accountable to racial discord and the anger stirred by the civil rights movement. But the homicide rates within the races of the South were also higher than those elsewhere. Was this the result of the southern habit of owning firearms? Most residents of the area did so; virtually every household in the rural and small-town South had a closetful of shotguns and rifles, and many had a pistol for good measure. Or did southerners own and use weapons because they were by nature or circumstance violent? Was violence impressed into the southern personality by the prevalence of corporal punishment during childhood? At least one study suggested this possibility. Was Wilbur Cash right in attributing personal violence in the South partly to the intemperance of the southern weather: the languorous heat of summer followed by the crashing thunderstorm? Whatever caused the violence, it seemed to persist.

Doubtless the regional tendency toward personal violence underlay its continued emphasis on force as an agent of national policy. Southerners exhibited a collective "military-patriotic" personality that placed them in the forefront of support for the armed services and of a strong American presence overseas. One analysis of the army's officer corps in the early 1970s estimated that four out of five of its active generals were born in small southern towns. Representing less than 23 percent of the nation's population, soldiers from the old Confederate states received better than 29 percent of the Congressional Medals of Honor awarded during the Vietnam war. This seemed a natural heritage of a people bred to revere military heroes as the greatest historic figures.[11]

Southern manners and southern violence were at the opposite poles of regional behavior; it has been said that a southerner would remain polite until he was angry enough to kill. The regional code of manners remained recognizable, though eroded by the frictions of the new industrial progress and by the "candor" of many of the young. Especially in circles away from the business centers of the major cities, or away from the more "enlightened" university campuses, one still observed a certain quaint deference of man to woman, of youth to age, of student to teacher; the attentive ear still caught the "yes sir" or the "no ma'am" that so long had been hallmarks of southern courtesy. Quite possibly the rituals and restraints of etiquette, deeply ingrained in southerners of both races, helped to keep the civil rights confrontation from becoming uglier than it was. At one point in negotiating with the segregationist members of the Board of Commissioners of Prince Edward County, Virginia, a civil rights leader commented that she was dealing with gentlemen.[12] Blacks who returned to the region from elsewhere frequently referred to the greater ease of communication and personal relationship in the South. Beset as it was on every front, the old chivalry had not yet surrendered; it was another vestige of the "culture lag" between the South and the rest of the nation.

The primary source of all southern social conventions was still the home, for it continued to be the center of most social activity except among the young singles. Dining out, nightclubbing, and theatergoing among the married folk were largely confined to an affluent minority in the larger cities. Home cooking still presented a sharp contrast to the fare of the mediocre if not dismal restaurants of most southern cities and towns. Perhaps the culinary South was no longer as clearly defined as it once was; yet southern wives still prided themselves on special family recipes. Despite many compromises with the science of nutrition and with the convenience of the frozen and prepackaged groceries of the supermarkets, they were yet able to prepare such historic regional delicacies as hot breads, country-cured ham, and pecan pie. Innumerable southern tables at frequent intervals still served corn bread, black-eyed peas, and fried chicken or ham in the ordinary family diet. Renamed "soul food" among the blacks, and whimsically called this by many whites as well, these dishes came to enjoy considerable popularity in restaurants throughout the country. An entire new industry grew up to meet the regional, and to some extent national, demand for fried catfish. Even clay eating, a habit presumably adopted among some poor southern whites and blacks in response to malnutrition, seemed to have become a culture trait that refused to yield to improved diets. Stories were told of southern migrants to the North who had friends mail them table clay from choice locations in Mississippi.

The central figure in the southern home was the southern lady. An institution that had endured the travail of war, Reconstruction, and all the rest of the regional experience, she refused to disappear from the modern scene. A recent critic has attempted to destroy the image of the southern belle by reducing her to a purely ornamental figure without brains, substance, or even sensuality.[13] A serious evaluation of southern women would reveal that they have never been the vaporous creatures portrayed in sentimental lore but have always borne their share of the burdens and responsibilities of life. The South has had its quota of mother O'Haras and Melanies as well as its Scarlets and Aunt Pitty Pats. Southern women in the 1960s and 1970s hearkened to the practical aspects of the Women's Liberation Movement, including such demands as those for equal economic opportunities, day-care centers for working mothers, and greater participation in the political process.[14] But they did not renounce either their femininity or their southernness. They retained enough of what William Alexander Percy once called a "morning-glory air" to make a southern Bella Abzug impossible to imagine.

Southern speech in the 1970s remained as distinctive as southern manners, southern cooking, or any of the other characteristics that continued to set the region apart from the rest of the country. In spite of the recent immigration of hundreds of thousands of newcomers, and in spite of a half-century of listening to the brisk syllables of northern radio announcers and a quarter-century of northern television commentators, southern children still grew up speaking southern. They still drawled their vowels, dropped their r's, said "creek" instead of "crick" (or brook), and addressed one another as "y'all." Blacks from the South who applied for jobs outside the region were said to be handicapped by dialectalia—the most sophisticated name ever invented for the southern accent. The region was full of expressions of strictly local coinage and meaning. More than a century ago Union soldiers from the far North could hardly believe that Confederates from the Deep South spoke the same language as they. Doubtless a northern visitor today would be less impressed by the regional differences in cadence and intonation. But he could not fail to notice them.

Southern forms of recreation also distinguished the region, though southerners enjoyed many of the same diversions enjoyed by all Americans. For example, they embraced television with the uncritical devotion of the rest of the country. Yet to the close observer there were subtle distinctions of tone and mood.

Considering the strictures of their orthodox Protestant churches, southerners were perhaps freer in indulging in many of the pleasures of the flesh. Wilbur Cash in the 1930s was struck by the South's ability to reconcile love of pleasure with the exercise of religious puritanism; forty years later he would have been even more intrigued by this paradox. Gradually the southern states relaxed their laws against the sale of alcoholic beverages; in the late 1960s Mississippi, the last state to do so, repealed its statewide prohibition statute. The hard-drinking state of Texas long kept a law forbidding the sale of alcoholic drinks in public places; but the law permitted a subterfuge whereby these drinks could be dispensed in private clubs, and so-called private clubs flourished everywhere in the Lone Star State. New Orleans with its French Quarter and Mardi Gras celebration remained an entertainment Mecca where throngs of tourists reared in a Calvinistic atmosphere vicariously discharged their pent-up hedonistic impulses. The strong influence of the Southern Baptist church and other denominations of conservative social outlook in Kentucky did not prevent this state from being a leading producer of Bourbon whiskey, cigarette tobacco, and race horses for parimutuel betting. The Kentucky Derby with its pageantry, gaiety, and flow of mint juleps was something of a Mardi Gras of the border South.

Southerners kept their enthusiasm for sports and outdoor exercise. The regional passion for athletics, especially college football, reached new heights during this period. Virtually all the colleges and universities either built new stadiums or greatly expanded their old ones. Southerners were convinced that their football teams played the best game in the nation; indeed, a football argument was one of the surest tests for establishing regional loyalty. Lighter on the average than opponents from other places, southern teams emphasized speed, deception, passing, and adroit ball-handling. Also, in the eyes of a northern journalist, southern football reached "levels of meaning, intensity, and violence entirely foreign to other regions."[15] Southern contenders in intersectional rivalries won often enough to give a measure of support to the boasts of their partisans. Oklahoma earned the national championship in 1950, 1955, and 1956; Tennessee in 1951; Auburn in 1957; Louisiana State in 1958; Alabama in 1961, 1964, and 1965; and Texas in 1963 and 1969. Alabama again was rated the top team of 1973 and 1974 before losing hard-fought postseason games.

Regional teams in other sports did not enjoy a comparable success and prestige. For example, Kentucky was the only school of the Southeastern Conference whose basketball teams were traditionally able to compete successfully in intersectional rivalries; they won national championships four times during the 1950s and 1960s and won National Invitational Tournaments three times. Southern basketball improved in the 1960s and 1970s, especially after the southern schools began to admit black athletes. In addition to their teams in the major sports, southern colleges and universities turned out representative and sometimes outstanding teams or performers in the so-called minor sports, including track, swimming, boxing, wrestling, tennis, golf, and gymnastics.

The regional interest in athletics, along with the growth of southern cities and the rise of southern prosperity, caused for the first time a number of major league professional teams to be located in the South. By the 1970s there were major league football teams in Atlanta, Houston, Dallas, Miami, and New Orleans; major league baseball teams in Atlanta, Houston, and Arlington (Texas); and major league basketball teams in Atlanta, Houston, Greensboro, Dallas,

Louisville, Memphis, and Norfolk. The South provided its share of players to the major league teams in all these sports, whether located in the region or elsewhere.

Almost all kinds of amateur sports had their devotees in the South. All the cities and many towns had leagues of softball and bowling teams. Thousands of golf courses and tennis courts were crowded with users. Municipal recreation departments and local chapters of the YMCA sponsored youth programs in the major sports and in many of the minor ones. Soccer enjoyed a limited popularity on southern high school and college campuses and in the major cities. Even such winter sports as ice skating and skiing made some headway in the South, though they usually required artificial ice or snow.

A remarkable increase in water sports occurred during the postwar years. Because of the long hot season, swimming in the region's countless rivers, lakes, and ponds had always been a favorite exercise and the period between the two world wars saw a great proliferation of community and privately operated swimming pools. During the 1950s and 1960s the backyard swimming pool became both a convenience and a status symbol among the well-to-do; the residential subdivision or apartment house pool served the same purposes for the somewhat less well-to-do. All motels of any claim to distinction installed pools of their own. In the earlier years boating and water skiing were largely confined to the coastal waters and the larger lakes and rivers. The postwar affluence changed this. By the 1960s the yards and garages of prosperous residential neighborhoods everywhere were cluttered with power boats and cabin cruisers. On weekends and holidays roads were jammed with boats in tow to automobiles, and waterways swarmed with craft. Even in small lakes and streams of the most remote and land-locked places one saw bronzed, bikini-clad young men and women flashing on water skis like Floridians.

The South was the acknowledged center of stock car racing—a sport matching Fords, Chevrolets, Dodges, and other passenger cars supercharged to reach speeds above 175 miles per hour in contests of as much as 600 miles. Scores of thousands of spectators gathered at the oval tracks to enjoy the ceremonial parade of pretty girls aboard floats and to cheer the daredevil antics of such favorite drivers as Glenn "Fireball" Roberts (who died in a crash in the 1960s), Robert G. "Junior" Johnson, Fred Lorenzen, and Richard Lee Petty. Tom

Wolfe saw in stock car racing an authentic expression of the ethos of the rural South; he celebrated the courage of the drivers and called them the last American heroes.

The most venerable, most thoroughly native, and most widespread sports of the South remained hunting and fishing, which were pursued with as much enthusiasm in the post–World War II years as in the pre–Civil War period. The region still contained such vast areas of open field and forest that hunting was the prerogative of Everyman. Wild animals abounded from the lowly cottontail rabbit or the sulling 'possum to the dangerous wild boar or the majestically antlered deer. Hunting was open to all classes and ages of both races, from wealthy Virginians in fancy attire riding blooded horses behind pedigreed dogs in the fox chase to poor whites and blacks tramping the woods with single-barreled shotguns in the crooks of their arms and flea-bitten hounds barking up squirrel trees. Except for the poorest of the poor, game was no longer an essential part of family diet; but countless southerners still ate it as a delicacy.

Fishing was even more widespread than hunting. No other major region possessed such a combination of lakes, ponds, streams, and coastline. It would be difficult to find a spot in the entire Southeast, except in the major cities, beyond walking distance from a fishing creek or pond. The state of Florida alone claimed over 300 species of freshwater and saltwater fish. Equipment could be as simple as a cane pole cut on the creekbank, a few feet of string, a bead of lead for a sinker, a hook, and a worm or cricket for bait: total expense, a few pennies. Or it could include motorboats and elaborate tackle together costing hundreds or thousands of dollars. Every person in the entire South who liked to fish could do so, and millions took advantage of the opportunity. Perhaps no other population in the world spent so high a proportion of its time in this activity.

Examination of the South's social and recreational activities during the quarter-century after World War II reveals countless changes in and additions to the old modes of behavior. New classes rose to prominence; a revolution occurred in the situation of the black community; innovations took place in the life-style and diversions of the population. Yet these changes came no nearer to destroying sectional distinctiveness than did comparable developments in southern industry, agriculture, religion, education, fine arts, or politics. The new dominant classes inherited old customs and preferences. Official policies of racial equality and desegregation benefited the blacks but did not break the color line in the actual living arrangements of the masses of the inhabitants. The migration of population to the cities and suburbs did not destroy the rural outlook, nor did the emergence of new domestic relationships eliminate the family as the most cohesive unit of southern society or the home as the center of southern traits and attitudes. Southern courtesy, southern food, southern speech, southern athletic chauvinism, and southern sectional consciousness persisted in the midst of expanding tastes and altered mannerisms. Significantly, the immemorial sports of hunting and fishing were still the most popular and lasting kinds of southern recreation.

XI.

The Enduring South

The South by the mid-1970s was obviously approaching the close of an economic, political, and social era. Its postwar industrial and financial surge was giving way to a nationwide and worldwide energy shortage and recession. Its traditional advantages in Congress through the rules of seniority and unlimited debate were eroding swiftly and seemed likely to be gone altogether by the end of the decade. The activist stage of the civil rights movement was over, leaving the South, ironically, the most desegregated and racially harmonious part of the country. Old desegregation battlegrounds such as Birmingham, Jackson, and Selma were almost smugly quiet while Boston responded with violence to court-ordered school desegregation there, and the authorities of Chicago, Detroit, and Los Angeles shuddered at the prospect of what might happen if these cities should be compelled to follow suit.

If this was indeed the end of an epoch, where then did the South stand after thirty years of prodigious and often turbulent change? Economically, the region was closer than ever to the national level. Yet one must admit that behind the glittering facade of industrial and commercial expansion the regional economy still had a great deal in common with that of the 1940s. True, its balance had shifted radically from agriculture to industry, and now that life in the region was more comfortable because of air-conditioning and insecticides, and healthier because of improved medical services, many of the administrative offices of the national corporations had moved south, attracted by the milder winters, cleaner atmosphere, less congested streets, and more relaxed living conditions here. But it was still very much a colonial economy. Southern per capita income and wealth were still significantly below those of the nation at large. Also, southern industry, perhaps because of its so recent and rapid growth, appeared to be more grievously hurt by the recession. Certainly the South was less of an economic problem than it had previously been, but according to the usual measurements it was still the nation's economic problem number one.

The South was affected in a special way by the energy shortage and by environmental pollution. As a land of sunshine it would benefit immensely from the efficient harnessing of solar energy, but this seemed unlikely to occur within the twentieth century. If worst came to worst, in the present crisis the South would enjoy an undeniable if unwelcome advantage over the North; that is, summer life in Georgia without air-conditioning would be more tolerable than winter life in Michigan without heat. With conditions as they actually were in the 1970s, the South appeared highly fortunate as the nation's major producer of oil and coal; but these fuels were needed mainly for use elsewhere and were owned primarily by corporations that belonged chiefly to nonsoutherners. Abnormal demand for southern fuels threatened to deplete and ravage the area, draining off most of the profits along with the resources themselves. The southern environment was still somewhat less polluted than that of the North because the South was still less industrialized, its backwardness an unearned blessing in this respect. But the region was catching up. It was time for southerners to reconsider the warnings of the Southern Agrarians in *I'll Take My Stand* (1930), especially that of John Crowe Ransom, who described a progressive, industrialized society as one always winning "Pyrrhic victories at points of no strategic significance" in a losing war with nature.

The decline in the 1970s of conservative southern leadership in Congress and the election of a number of relatively liberal governors and state legislators appeared to herald a new day in southern politics. Up to a point it was a new day. But despite its traditional Democratic solidarity and white exclusiveness, southern politics in the twentieth century had never been of one mind. Rather, it was always a mixture of radicalism, liberalism, and conservatism, and it often elected radicals or liberals to power. The major difference now was the presence of large numbers of blacks at the polls and of a few in office. Without question, black political influence was making itself felt in the region. But neither ancient nor recent southern history suggested the masses of white and black voters could be formed into any kind of permanent coalition—liberal or conservative. Governor Wallace and other office-holders of similar view were obliged to modify their rhetoric and tactics to meet the new conditions, but these leaders neither disappeared from the scene nor altered their fundamental principles. Wallace on the eve of the 1976 presidential campaign appeared still to be the most formidable political force in the South.

The greatest observable difference between southern life today and yesterday was in its racial practices and attitudes. To the casual eye, racial segregation was virtually dead, integration triumphant. Legally and officially this was certainly the situation. It was also true that the outlook of whites and blacks toward each other was changed. Whites no longer took black inferiority and deference for granted; blacks no longer took white supremacy as a matter of course. A southern Rip Van Winkle awakening in the mid-1970s from a thirty-year sleep would not have believed his senses.

But actually the color line was still there beneath the surface of southern affairs. Only through massive programs of bussing was significant desegregation brought about in the most desegregated of southern institutions, the public schools, and even this accomplishment was seriously threatened by the flight of whites from the centers of urban black population and the movement of rural blacks into the cities. School desegregation in the South appeared jeopardized also by recent unfavorable federal court decisions and a rising nationwide popular opposition to bussing for this purpose—unless the national conscience should turn out to demand desegregation through bussing in the South while favoring segregated neighborhood schools elsewhere.

In the sectors of southern life beyond the reach of laws and courts the two races remained pretty much apart. Southern cities began to rival northern ones in residential segregation; southern churches were largely separate along racial lines, apparently by common consent; family and personal relations seldom crossed the ethnic barrier. Yet a new mood of accommodation was discernible in both races, both sensing that neither could permanently prosper or be happy with the other in poverty or misery. Thus the South appeared to be establishing an arrangement of racial accord on the soundest of foundations, the self-interest of each of the races. If the whites now recognized that desegregation would not cause the sky to fall, the blacks recognized, or perhaps had always known, that desegregation of itself was neither a guarantee of the good life nor preferable to it. For the blacks as a group remained at the bottom of the economic scale, and they, far more often than whites, were the victims of recession unemployment.

Regional institutions of mind and spirit showed the effects of a quarter-century of prosperity, growth, and the impulse toward national conformity. Outwardly they resembled closely their counterparts throughout the country. Yet there remained subtle inner distinctions. Southern churches were still more conservative in their theology and outlook on life, more concerned about the winning of souls to Christ than about the reform of society. If northern and southern communicants were now closer together on this point, it was fully as much because of a rising nationwide acknowledgment of man's earthly imperfectibility as of a southern conversion to the Social Gospel. Southern faith in formal education as a means of both individual improvement and sectional progress remained high, but it was no longer higher than that of nonsoutherners. The South was no longer willing to spend a greater proportion of its income on the schools, although on the average they were still inferior to the schools elsewhere. Impressive advances occurred in the promotion of the formal arts, but the freshest and strongest modes of expression were still those growing out of the folk culture. In spite of everything, modern Menckens could still find reasons to look upon the South as the Bible Belt and the Sahara of the Bozart.

The South of the 1970s was far more industrial, commercial, mobile, and urban than the South of the 1940s. The southern population was now more cosmopolitan because of a substantial postwar immigration from other parts of the country. But the greater ruralness, homogeneity, and folksiness of the region were not gone. To a remarkable extent southern society still seemed like a giant family, or, more precisely, like two giant families distinguished by color, capable of assimilating newcomers and new ideas without giving up their own tastes and traditions. Strangely, this ancient southern trait was quite in line with a new national mood. In a day of waning faith in the melting pot, of rising emphasis on ethnicity and cultural pluralism, the South happened to have two of the largest and most durable ethnic groups in the country: southern blacks and southern whites.

This study has emphasized the paradox of southern continuity in the midst of immense regional change. Manifestations of both appear in census reports and other statistical compilations, accounts of political campaigns and voting behavior, church and school records, literary and artistic productions, newspapers and comparable forms of eyewitness narrative, and personal observation. They can be tabulated, measured, classified, analyzed, seen, felt, or heard.

These objective differences between the South and the rest of the nation take on an added dimension from the subjective distinctions that have survived the changes of the postwar years or, in some cases, have even been nourished by them. More than a decade ago Francis Butler Simkins pointed out that "facts" and statistics alone cannot fully identify the South. He warned against the fallacy of confusing "facts" with truth. The South, he said, is an attitude of mind and a pattern of behavior just as much as it is a territory.[1] Even those students of the regional scene today who minimize or dismiss the remaining overt regional differences acknowledge the presence of an Enduring South through a particular state of mind.

This state of mind, the South's perception of itself and the nation's perception of the South, has always been an important element in the actual distinctiveness of the region. The pre–Civil War literary and popular views of the South as a land of gracious and open-handed Cavaliers and the North as a land of grasping and bigoted Puritans, or obversely, the South as a land of Simon Legrees and the North as a land of undiluted freedom and promise, helped exaggerate if not create real psychological differences between the two societies.[2] Wilbur Cash's *The Mind of the South* (1939), as the title indicates, emphasized that a peculiar regional experience had produced a peculiar regional mentality. Recent scholarship suggests that the ultimate distinctiveness of the South may lie, not in its empirical dissimilarities from other regions, but in its unique mythology: those images of the region that give "philosophical meaning to the ordinary facts of life."[3]

The flesh and blood South since World War II has reenacted virtually all the roles assigned to the mythic South both by southerners and nonsoutherners. Students of the regional phenomenon are agreed on the historical existence of a Defensive South, a South that came into being and remained alive largely because of the threat, either real or fancied, of the majority North. Observers of the angry southern response to the civil rights movement of the 1950s and 1960s had an uncomfortable sense of déjà vu as they reflected upon the regional behavior during the antislavery crusade a century before. Most of the southern states in the recent crisis attempted to put into legal effect a form of Calhoun's doctrine of state nullification. Conceivably the more vehement states were deterred from a resort to secession only by the lessons of history. Obviously, the Defensive South was still alive.

Closely akin to the concept of the Defensive South is that of the Benighted South.[4] Having committed the two cardinal sins in the national mythology—slavery and secession—the South compounded these ancient wrongs by its dogged modern resistance to racial desegregation. Whereas the national self-perception until very recently was one of innocence and a regenerate society, the southern self-perception was thought to be clouded with a subconscious sense of guilt.[5] For the rest of the nation, the Benighted South also provided a convenient easement of conscience: a scapegoat, a "moral lightning rod" for grounding any bolts of guilt that might otherwise have hit outside the regional strike zone.[6] Some critics even went so far as to blame the South for the racial difficulties occurring elsewhere during the 1960s.

But the national problems of the period caused subtle changes in the mythology of southern regionalism. Honest observers were aware of the existence of widespread racial discrimination and de facto segregation outside the South. The congestion, pollution, poverty, and violence of the great northern and Pacific Coast metropolises combined with the energy shortage to cast doubt on the time-honored American faith in progress. Failure in the Vietnam war challenged the national myth of invincibility; both the war experience and the exposure of racism throughout the country tainted the myth of national innocence. In 1970 Paul Gaston felt obliged to say that regional distinctions were receding because the entire American society was absorbing the elements of pathos, frustration, and human weakness traditionally associated only with the South.[7] More recently John Egerton described a reciprocal process in which the South was being Americanized, the nation southernized.[8] In other words, the Benighted South appeared to be blending into a Benighted Nation.

At the same time, the concept of a Benighted Nation gave birth to an extraordinary compensatory regional myth, that of the Redemptive South. Its chief votaries were a group of liberal scholars, journalists, politicians, and business and professional men who caught a vision of southern industrial expansion minus pollution, of southern urban development free of pathological crowding. In 1969 a number of persons holding these views formed themselves into the L. Q. C. Lamar Society, an association dedicated to work toward such goals. It took its name from a renowned nineteenth-century Mississippian who had been an ardent secessionist and Confederate, but who later led a movement for racial accommodation and sectional reconciliation.[9] Members of the society expressed the hope also that the emerging South would solve the oldest and most vexing of southern problems and lead the way in solving one of the most vexing if not the oldest of northern problems, that of race. "It may be the South," said the journalist Marshall Frady, "where the nation's general malaise of racial alienation first finds resolution. Not in the order of division prophesied by the old segregationist apologists but in the formal advent of a single people unique and richly dimensioned."[10]

The growth of southern industry and the unprecedented affluence of the postwar years also rekindled the persistent myth of a coming Abundant South. Since the pitching of the first English camp on Roanoke Island almost four centuries ago southerners and outside observers alike have predicted that the South was about to become a New World Eden. In the late 1950s Walter Prescott Webb reaffirmed this belief in an address fittingly titled "The South's Call to Greatness: Challenge to All Southerners." Naming the South's unsurpassed natural resources, its coastlines, rivers, water power, climate, fertile soil, timber, and metal and mineral reserves, and reviewing the recent gains in manufacturing, agriculture, per capita income, bank deposits, and ownership of corporate stock, he declared the region to be on the threshold of a new age. Chance and circumstance, he said, had combined to give the South an unparalleled opportunity to fulfill its ancient dream of plenty.[11] At least until the energy crisis and recession of the 1970s dimmed economic prospects everywhere, southern political and civic leaders, chambers of commerce, industrial commissions, and indeed the population generally believed the realization of this vision was at hand.

Traces of many other mythological Souths still lingered in the southern and American minds: the Romantic South of white-columned mansions, gallant horsemen, and beautiful, fragile ladies; the Tragic

South of defeat on the battlefield, military occupation and humiliation, racial violence, and poverty; the Fundamentalist South of wild-eyed street-corner evangelists, faith healing, and religious hysteria. The list could be extended indefinitely.

The matrix of the southern state of mind was, however, the Historical South, the South of a unique past as understood by southerners. Every mythologist discovered support for his regional image in this history. Obviously, spokesmen of a Defensive South, a Romantic South, a Tragic South, or a Benighted South could find ample evidence here for their points of view. Exponents of a Redemptive South were not without their historical resources also. They appealed to the immortal rhetoric of Jefferson the Virginian or to the example of Lamar practicing moderation under stress. Ironically, they found a perverse blessing even in the South's racial history, believing that southern whites and blacks, having shared the stage, however unequally, in the bitter drama of slavery, war, Reconstruction, poverty, violence, and pain, were now better equipped than other Americans to establish a true racial brotherhood.[12]

But the history embraced by most southerners went beyond the findings of academicians. It was a history partly imbibed from parents, grade school teachers, associates, local raconteurs and preservers of community lore, and from diaries, letters, and personal relics either in archives or museums or in private possession. History with a southern accent radiated also from the mansions and public buildings still standing from a bygone and romantic age, and from the battlefields, ruins, and other reminders of wars, especially of The War, fought on southern soil.

Southerners generally continued to revere the heroes of the Confederacy, even if the present southerners no longer endorsed the causes for which those men fought. Southern children appeared to be as captivated as any previous generation by the Civil War; invariably they looked upon the blue-clad troops as "the enemy." According to Henry Steele Commager, one could still study the Civil War in southerners of today because they retained "the psychology and vocabulary of the period."[13] Atlanta's love affair with the moving picture *Gone with the Wind* was seemingly as strong as ever, not that the cult of this film was confined to Atlanta or the South. The popular white southern interpretation of Reconstruction was still that of a chamber of horrors. Outsiders continued to say southerners lived in the past. Not so, replied the poet Miller Williams: the past lived in southerners.[14]

So powerful was the traditional outlook on southern history that it gripped even many of those who were devoted to regional change. Southern reformers after World War II, like the spokesmen of a New South after the Civil War and Reconstruction, often linked their objective to the Old South with bonds of sentiment, romanticizing the plantation society of long ago and the Lost Cause of the Confederacy, thus forming a "vital nexus" between the epochs.[15] The liberal mayor of Atlanta, William B. Hartsfield, believed the nation's two epic films were *The Birth of a Nation* and *Gone with the Wind*. On the living room wall of James McBride Dabbs, the late president of the Southern Regional Council and one of the foremost advocates of racial desegregation and understanding, hung a plaque of grateful recognition from the Detroit chapter of the NAACP. Displayed beneath it was a pair of crossed Confederate rifles.[16]

Notes

PROLOGUE

1. *The Mind of the South* (New York, 1941), "Preview."
2. *Intruder in the Dust* (New York, 1948), p. 153.
3. *Life and Labor in the Old South* (Boston, 1929), p. 3.
4. V. O. Key, Jr., *Southern Politics in State and Nation* (New York, 1949), p. 315.
5. Quoted in George B. Tindall, *The Emergence of the New South* (Baton Rouge, La., 1967), pp. 687–88.
6. Hodding Carter, Jr., *Southern Legacy* (Baton Rouge, La., 1950), p. 27.
7. Louis D. Rubin, Jr., *The Faraway Country: Writers of the Modern South* (Seattle, Wash., 1963), p. 131.
8. *Southerners and Other Americans* (New York, 1973), p. viii.
9. "Iowa, North Carolina, and the Humanities," *North Carolina Historical Review* 23 (April 1946): 222–27.
10. "The Enigma of the South," *Yale Review* 51 (Autumn 1961): 150–51.
11. Quoted in Tindall, *Emergence of the New South*, p. 700.
12. Quoted ibid., p. 716.

I. THE POSTWAR ECONOMIC DRAMA

1. *Sales Management*, July 15, 1970, p. 50.
2. Robert Cooney, "The Modern South: Organized Labor's New Frontier," *American Federationist* 68 (May 1961): 15.
3. Donald F. Roy, "Change and Resistance to Change in the Southern Labor Movement," in John C. McKinney and Edgar T. Thompson, eds., *The South in Continuity and Change* (Durham, N.C., 1965), p. 243.
4. *Business Week*, July 3, 1971, p. 46.
5. "Improving the Southern Environment," *New South* 25 (Fall 1970): 65.
6. Association of Southern Agricultural Workers, *The South on the March* (n.p., n.d.), p. 10.
7. Quoted in Thomas D. Clark, *The Emerging South* (New York, 1961), p. 90.
8. Minor S. Gray to the author, June 23, 1969.
9. *The New York Stock Exchange Fact Book* (New York, 1973), pp. 50, 55.
10. Quoted in Francis Butler Simkins, *A History of the South*, 2d ed. (New York, 1953), p. 593.

II. THE CHALLENGE TO RACIAL INEQUALITY

1. Robert C. Weaver, "The Economic Status of the Negro in the United States," *Journal of Negro Education* 19 (Summer 1950): 240.
2. *New York Times*, October 30, 1947.

3. Quoted in Benjamin Muse, *Ten Years of Prelude: The Story of Integration since the Supreme Court's 1954 Decision* (New York, 1964), pp. 21–22.

4. Hubert H. Humphrey, ed., *School Desegregation: Documents and Commentaries* (New York, 1964), pp. 23–29; Muse, *Ten Years of Prelude*, pp. 1–15.

5. Dan Wakefield, "Respectable Racism: Dixie's Citizens Councils," *Nation*, October 22, 1955, p. 339.

6. Quoted in Muse, *Ten Years of Prelude*, p. 20.

7. Humphrey, *School Desegregation*, pp. 29–31.

8. Quoted in Wakefield, "Respectable Racism," pp. 339–41.

9. Hodding Carter III, *The South Strikes Back* (New York, 1959), pp. 21–48; Numan V. Bartley, *The Rise of Massive Resistance: Race and Politics in the South during the 1950's* (Baton Rouge, La., 1969), pp. 108–50; Reed Sarratt, *The Ordeal of Desegregation: The First Decade* (New York, London, 1966), pp. 298–306.

10. Robert McKay, "Little Rock: Power Showdown," *Nation*, September 28, 1957, p. 189.

11. Muse, *Ten Years of Prelude*, pp. 122–45; Sarratt, *Ordeal of Desegregation*, pp. 159–63.

12. *Facts on File Yearbook*, 1958, p. 315.

13. Bartley, *Rise of Massive Resistance*, pp. 251–92; Muse, *Ten Years of Prelude*, pp. 187–90.

14. *Facts on File Yearbook*, 1959, p. 438; Robert C. Smith, *They Closed Their Schools: Prince Edward County, Virginia, 1951–1964* (Chapel Hill, N.C., 1965), pp. 151–207, 258.

15. James G. Cook, *The Segregationists* (New York, 1962), p. 3.

16. Margaret Anderson, *The Children of the South* (New York, 1968), pp. 57–65; Robert Coles, *Children of Crisis: A Study of Courage and Fear* (Boston, Toronto, 1964), pp. 72–146, and *Children of Crisis: Migrants, Sharecroppers, Mountaineers* (Boston, Toronto, 1967), pp. 382–93.

III. THE ACHIEVEMENT OF LEGAL EQUALITY

1. Martin Luther King, Jr., *Stride toward Freedom: The Montgomery Story* (New York, 1958), pp. 71–89; Lawrence D. Reddick, *Crusader without Violence: A Biography of Martin Luther King, Jr.* (New York, 1959), pp. 112–56.

2. "The Angry South," *Atlantic Monthly* 197 (April 1956): 33. Also Calvin M. Logue, *Ralph McGill: Editor and Publisher*, 2 vols. (Durham, N.C., 1969), 1: 118–26, 180–211.

3. Quoted in Benjamin Muse, *Ten Years of Prelude: The Story of Integration since the Supreme Court's 1954 Decision* (New York, 1964), p. 258.

4. *New York Times*, August 29, 1963.

5. *Facts on File Yearbook*, 1964, pp. 205, 220–21. Also Benjamin Muse, *The American Negro Revolution: From Nonviolence to Black Power, 1963–1967* (Bloomington, Ind., 1968), pp. 75–93.

6. Len Holt, *The Summer That Didn't End* (New York, 1965), pp. 13, 31–42, 76–94. Also Muse, *American Negro Revolution*, pp. 139–43; Elizabeth Sutherland, ed., *Letters from Mississippi* (New York, 1965), pp. 1–63, 188–94.

7. *New York Times*, March 16, 1965.

8. Quoted in Muse, *American Negro Revolution*, p. 244.

9. Ibid., pp. 180–81, 201–2, 286, 314, 290–317. Also *New York Times*, summers of 1965–1967, especially July 24–25, 1967.

10. Quoted in Muse, *American Negro Revolution*, p. 250.

11. Lerone Bennett, Jr., *What Manner of Man: A Biography of Martin Luther King, Jr.* (Chicago, 1968), p. 238.

12. *New York Times*, April 4, 1968.

IV. THE POLITICS OF TRANSITION

1. Quoted in Francis Butler Simkins and Charles P. Roland, *A History of the South* (New York, 1972), p. 590.

2. Ibid.

3. Quoted in Amile B. Ader, *The Dixiecrat Movement: Its Role in Third Party Politics* (Washington, D.C., 1955), p. 10.

4. Quoted in Virginius Dabney, *Virginia: The New Dominion* (Garden City, N.Y., 1971), p. 539.

5. Alberta Lachicotte, *Rebel Senator: Strom Thurmond of South Carolina* (New York, 1967), p. 71.

6. Quoted in Simkins and Roland, *History of the South*, p. 592.

7. *New York Times*, September 19, 1952.

8. Ibid., September 27, 1957.

9. *Newsweek*, October 24, 1960, pp. 42–44.

10. W. Wayne Shannon, "Revolt in Washington: The South in Congress," in William C. Havard, ed., *The Changing Politics of the South* (Baton Rouge, La., 1972), p. 637.

11. Joseph L. Bernd, "Georgia: Static and Dynamic," in Havard, *Changing Politics of the South*, p. 297.

V. THE POLITICS OF ACCOMMODATION

1. "The South: A Shifting Perspective," in William C. Havard, ed., *The Changing Politics of the South* (Baton Rouge, La., 1972), p. 36.

2. *The New Republic*, September 10, 1962, p. 6; *U.S. News & World Report*, December 9, 1963, pp. 36–37; *Ebony* 19 (January 1964): 82.

3. Benjamin Muse, *The American Negro Revolution: From Nonviolence to Black Power, 1963–1967* (Bloomington, Ind., 1968), pp. 268–70.

4. Marshall Frady, *Wallace* (New York, 1968), p. 137.

5. Ibid., p. 139.

6. George B. Tindall, *The Disruption of the Solid South* (Athens, Ga., 1972), p. 43; *Facts on File Yearbook*, 1968, pp. 358–59; *New York Times*, August 20, 1968.

7. *Facts on File Yearbook*, 1968, pp. 54, 422.

8. Malcolm Jewell, "Recent Southern Politics" (an address delivered before the University Club, University of Kentucky, Spring 1972).

9. Douglas Kiker, "Russell of Georgia: The Old Guard at Its Shrewdest," *Harper's Magazine* 233 (September 1966): 106.

10. V. O. Key, Jr., *Southern Politics in State and Nation* (New York, 1949), p. 374; W. Wayne Shannon, "Revolt in Washington: The South in Congress," in Havard, *Changing Politics of the South*, p. 648. For the percentages on the roll

calls, see *Congressional Quarterly Almanac*, 1959, p. 141; ibid., 1960, p. 117; ibid., 1972, p. 66.

11. Voter Education Project, *Black Elected Officials in the South* (Atlanta, Ga., 1973); *Southern Voices* 1 (March–April 1974): 80; Bill Schemmel, "Atlanta's 'Power Structure' Faces Life," *New South* 27 (Spring 1972): 65.

12. Thomas Powers, "Letters from a Lost Campaign: The Unreported Story of Charles Evers' Race for the Mississippi Governorship," *Harper's Magazine* 244 (March 1972): 29.

13. Ibid., pp. 29–31; Lester Salamon, "Mississippi Post-Mortem: The 1971 Elections," *New South* 27 (Winter 1972): 45, 47.

14. John Nordheimer, "Florida's 'Supersquare'—A Man to Watch," *New York Times Magazine*, March 5, 1972, pp. 54–56.

15. Ibid., p. 11.

16. *Time*, June 25, 1973, p. 18. Also ibid., March 25, 1974, p. 23; *U.S. News & World Report*, November 19, 1973, p. 35; *Harper's Magazine* 248 (April 1974): 65–72; *Louisville Courier-Journal*, March 29, 1974.

17. *Time*, March 25, 1974, p. 23.

VI. TURBULENT PROGRESS IN EDUCATION

1. *New York Times*, August 27, 1967.

2. Henry Leifermann, "Southern Desegregation," *Atlantic Monthly* 223 (February 1969): 19.

3. Winifred Green, "The Struggle for Freedom: Public Education in the South," *New South* 25 (Fall 1970): 86–90.

4. M. Hayes Mizell, "The Myth of Quality Education," *New South* 36 (Winter 1971): 26–33.

5. Leifermann, "Southern Desegregation," p. 20; *Montgomery Advertiser*, July 19, 1973; *U.S. News & World Report*, May 20, 1974, p. 29.

6. *New South* 27 (Spring 1972): 72.

7. *U.S. News & World Report*, August 16, 1971, p. 38; *Louisville Courier-Journal*, March 10, 1973; *Montgomery Advertiser*, July 19, 1973.

8. Clarence A. Bacote to author, July 25, 1973 (personal interview); Robert H. Brisbane to author, July 26, 1973 (personal interview).

9. Southern Regional Education Board, *Annual Report 1971–72* (Atlanta, Ga., 1972), pp. 2–5; Redding S. Sugg, Jr., and George Hilton Jones, *The Southern Regional Education Board* (Baton Rouge, La., 1960), pp. 39–41, 48–55; *Louisville Courier-Journal and Times*, March 17, 1974.

10. *Time*, March 1, 1971, p. 56.

11. Black institutions offering the top graduate and professional degrees are among exceptions to the general weakness of these colleges.

12. *Bulletin of the American Association of University Professors* 60 (June 1974): 200–226; National Center for Educational Statistics, *Library Statistics of Colleges and Universities* (Washington, D.C., 1972), pp. 6–16.

13. Virginius Dabney, "The Good Southern Universities," *Harper's Magazine* 230 (March 1965): 86; Kenneth D. Roose and Charles J. Anderson, *A Rating of Graduate Programs* (Washington, D.C., 1970), pp. 11–13; *U.S. News & World Report*, January 4, 1971, pp. 70–71.

14. *Graduate and Professional Education, 1980* (New York, 1970), pp. 15–16.

15. Bernard D. Karpinos, "Mental Test Failures," in Sol Tax, ed., *The Draft: A Handbook of Facts and Alternatives* (Chicago and London, 1967), pp. 52–53.

16. *New York Times,* July 19, 1971.

17. U.S., Bureau of the Census, *1970 Census of Population: General Social and Economic Characteristics: United States,* p. 493.

VII. RELIGION & CONTROVERSY

1. "An Agenda for Research on Religion," in Edgar T. Thompson, ed., *Perspectives on the South: Agenda for Research* (Durham, N.C., 1967), p. 198.

2. Edward B. Fiske, "The Closest Thing to a White House Chaplain," *New York Times Magazine,* June 8, 1969, pp. 27–116.

3. David E. Harrell, Jr., *White Sects and Black Men in the Recent South* (Nashville, Tenn., 1971), pp. 21–22.

4. "Southern Baptists and the Bible," *Christianity Today,* April 25, 1969, pp. 34–35.

5. O. P. Baird, "The Consequences of Denying Supernatural Inspiration," *Gospel Advocate,* January 25, 1968, pp. 49–53.

6. John Vander Ploeg, "Pulpits without Power," *Presbyterian Journal,* April 17, 1968, p. 18.

7. *Lexington Herald-Leader,* March 4, 1973. Also *Louisville Courier-Journal,* April 9, 1973; *Christianity Today,* April 28, 1972, p. 42. Weston La Barre, *They Shall Take Up Serpents: Psychology of the Southern Snake-Handling Cult* (Minneapolis, Minn., 1962), pp. 88–109, 126–62, offers a Freudian interpretation of this phenomenon in which the snakes are seen as phallic symbols and the rituals as subliminal masturbatory experiences.

8. Quoted in John Shelton Reed, *The Enduring South: Subcultural Persistence in Mass Society* (Lexington, Mass., Toronto, London, 1972), p. 61.

9. Ibid., pp. 57–81. An excellent series of tables is here accompanied by textual analysis on surveys of regional and national religious attitudes from the late 1940s to the early 1970s.

10. Quoted in Marshall Frady, "God and Man in the South," *Atlantic Monthly* 219 (January 1967): 40.

11. Dean M. Kelley, *Why Conservative Churches Are Growing* (New York, 1973), pp. 25–27.

12. *Southern Churches in Crisis* (New York, 1967), pp. 112–14.

13. *Presbyterian Journal,* January 17, 1968, p. 1.

14. *Southern Baptist Convention 1967 Annual* (Nashville, Tenn., 1968), p. 75.

15. *Christianity Today,* July 2, 1971, pp. 32–33.

16. Quoted in Frady, "God and Man in the South," p. 40.

17. Robert Coles, "God and the Rural Poor," *Psychology Today* 5 (January 1972): 33. For other sympathetic interpretations of the religion of the southern poor by this author, see *Children of Crisis: A Study of Courage and Fear* (Boston, Toronto, 1964), pp. 10, 97–98; and *Children of Crisis: The South Goes North* (Boston, Toronto, 1967), pp. 617–51.

18. Harry Lefever, "The Church and Poor Whites," *New South* 25 (Spring 1970): 26, 32.

19. Membership numbers in the South are unavailable. In 1972 the nationwide memberships were: National Baptist Convention, U.S.A., Inc., 6.3 million; Na-

tional Baptist Convention of America, between 3.5 and 4 million; Progressive National Baptist Convention, Inc., 550,000; African Methodist Episcopal church, 1.6 million; African Methodist Episcopal Zion church, 850,000; Christian Methodist Episcopal church, 500,000. Perhaps half or more of the aggregate were in the former Confederate states.

20. *The Negro Church in America* (New York, 1963), p. 79.

21. Thomas Kilgore, Jr., "The Black Church: A Liberating Force for All America," *Ebony* 25 (August 1970): 108.

22. *U.S. News & World Report*, September 25, 1972, p. 48.

23. Coles, "God and the Rural Poor," p. 33.

24. Stanley M. Elkins, *Slavery: A Problem in American Institutional and Intellectual Life* (Chicago, 1959), pp. 27–29, advances this theory concerning the weakness of southern churches in the slavery question.

25. Harrell, *White Sects and Black Men in the Recent South*, p. 60.

26. Henry H. Mitchell, "Negro Worship and Universal Need," *Christian Century*, March 30, 1966, p. 396.

27. James H. Cone, "Toward a Black Theology," *Ebony* 25 (August 1970): 115.

28. Kilgore, "Black Church," p. 107.

29. Mitchell, "Negro Worship and Universal Need," p. 396.

30. *White Sects and Black Men*, pp. 41–42.

31. Attitudes of the Southern Baptist church appear in the Southern Baptist Convention annuals for the period 1950–1971. For example, see *Southern Baptist Convention 1971 Annual* (Nashville, Tenn., 1971), pp. 69–72, which records, among others, resolutions condemning the use of alcohol as a beverage, opposing the use of tax money for the support of any kind of private or church-related schools, and denouncing abortion except in certain circumstances such as rape, fetal deformity, or "carefully ascertained evidence of the likelihood of damage to the emotional, mental, and physical health of the mother."

32. *Southern White Protestantism in the Twentieth Century* (New York, 1964), p. 167.

VIII. AFTER THE SOUTHERN RENAISSANCE

1. Quoted in John Q. Anderson, ed., *Brokenburn: The Journal of Kate Stone, 1861–1868* (Baton Rouge, La., 1955), p. 270.

2. *Intruder in the Dust* (New York, 1948), pp. 153–54.

3. "Randall Jarrell," *Atlantic Monthly* 220 (September 1967): 98.

4. *The Complete Poems* (New York, 1969), p. 290.

5. Quoted in Clarence Major, ed., *The New Black Poetry* (New York, 1969), p. 140; ibid., p. 12.

6. Ibid., pp. 49–50.

7. Ibid., p. 84.

8. Stephen Henderson, *Understanding the New Black Poetry* (New York, 1973), p. 331.

9. *My House: Poems* (New York, 1972), p. 29.

10. *Black Boy: A Record of Childhood and Youth* (New York, 1945), p. 298.

11. James A. Emanuel and Theodore L. Gross, eds., *Dark Symphony: Negro Literature in America* (New York, 1968), p. 253.

12. *Who Speaks for the Negro?* (New York, 1965), p. 439.

13. Katherine Anne Porter, *The Collected Essays and Occasional Writings of Katherine Anne Porter* (New York, 1970), p. 286.

14. Louis D. Rubin, *The Curious Death of the Novel: Essays in American Literature* (Baton Rouge, La., 1967), p. 286.

15. "Dodo, Phoenix, or Tough Old Cock?" in H. Brandt Ayers and Thomas H. Naylor, eds., *You Can't Eat Magnolias* (New York, 1972), p. 75.

16. *Set This House On Fire* (New York, 1959), pp. 48, 52.

17. Quoted in Henderson, *Understanding the New Black Poetry*, p. 326.

IX. MUSIC & THE VISUAL ARTS

1. Paul Green to the author, August 14, 1973 (personal interview); Gordon Holl to the author, August 23, 1973 (personal interview).

2. "Symphonic Outdoor Drama," in Robert West Howard, *This Is the South* (Chicago, 1959), p. 251; also to the author, August 14, 1973 (personal interview).

3. Mark R. Sumner to the author, August 13, 1973 (personal interview); Mark R. Sumner, *A Selected Bibliography on Outdoor Drama* (Chapel Hill, N.C., 1971), pp. 1–16.

4. John W. Linley to the author, August 28, 1973.

5. *Louisville Times*, December 22, 1972.

6. "Revitalizing Downtown with Atlanta's John Portman, Architect and Entrepreneur," reprinted from *World* (Winter 1971), n.p.

7. Donald Williams to the author, July 13, 1973 (personal interview).

8. *Newsweek*, February 7, 1972, pp. 50–51.

9. John Richard Craft to the author, August 21, 1972.

10. William Gaines to the author, August 16, 1973 (personal interview).

11. Lamar Dodd to the author, July 27, 1973 (personal interview); Lloyd Goodrich, *Lamar Dodd: A Retrospective Exhibition* (Athens, Ga., 1970), p. 16.

12. *Cape Bretan Post*, October 22, 1966, in Mississippi Artists File, University of Mississippi Library, Oxford, Miss.

13. Clementine Hunter to the author, July 8, 1973 (personal interview).

14. Betsy Farlow, "The Untouchables: Aspects of White Gospel Music," presented in April 1973 at Austin Peay University, Clarksville, Tenn., before the South Central Chapter of the American Musicological Society.

15. Danny R. Hatcher to the author, August 23, 1973 (personal interview); Hubert Long, "The Long Look at Country, Before and Aft"; "Country Television Shows"; "Country Music Hall of Fame Members"; "The Country Music Foundation"; "The Origin of Country Music," all in Country Music Hall of Fame Library, Nashville.

16. Francis Butler Simkins, "The Education That Doesn't Educate: The Persistence of Virginia Folkways," undated manuscript in possession of the author.

17. Julius Novick, *Beyond Broadway: The Quest for Permanent Theaters* (New York, 1968), p. 18.

X. CHANGE & TRADITION IN SOUTHERN SOCIETY

1. John C. McKinney, "Continuity and Change in Sociological Perspective," in John C. McKinney and Edgar T. Thompson, eds., *The South in Continuity and Change* (Durham, N.C., 1965), p. 3. Also John Shelton Reed, *The Enduring*

South: Subcultural Persistence in Mass Society (Lexington, Mass., Toronto, London, 1972), pp. 1–104.

2. Alfred O. Hero, Jr., *The Southerner and World Affairs* (Baton Rouge, La., 1965), p. 296.

3. Ibid.

4. William F. Guess, "South Carolina's Incurable Aristocrats," *Harper's Magazine* 214 (February 1957): 46.

5. Hero, *Southerner and World Affairs*, p. 361.

6. Edgar T. Thompson, "The South in Old and New Contexts," in McKinney and Thompson, *South in Continuity and Change*, p. 476.

7. "Mississippi: The Fallen Paradise," *Harper's Magazine* 230 (April 1965): 170.

8. U.S., Bureau of the Census, *Current Population Reports: The Social and Economic Status of the Black Population in the United States, 1972*, p. 18; *Time*, September 3, 1973, pp. 74–75; *Atlanta Journal and Constitution*, June 17, 1973; Steve Van Evera, "A Family Assistance Plan: 40 Acres and a Mule?" *New South* 26 (Fall 1971): 71–72.

9. I. A. Newby, *Black Carolinians: A History of Blacks in South Carolina from 1895 to 1968* (Columbia, S.C., 1973), pp. 359–60.

10. Quoted in John Egerton, "A Visit with James McBride Dabbs," *New South* 24 (Winter 1969): 44.

11. Lewis H. Lapham, "Military Theology," *Harper's Magazine* 243 (July 1971): 76; *The World Almanac and Book of Facts, 1972* (New York, 1972), pp. 462–63.

12. Robert C. Smith, *They Closed Their Schools: Prince Edward County, Virginia, 1951–1964* (Chapel Hill, N.C., 1965), p. 246.

13. Marshall Frady, "Skirmishes with the Ladies of the Magnolias," *Playboy* 19 (September 1972): 121–222.

14. Sara Murphy, "Women's Lib in the South," *New South* 27 (Spring 1972): 45.

15. Peter Schrag, "A Hesitant New South: Fragile Promise on the Last Frontier," *Saturday Review*, February 12, 1972, p. 55.

XI. THE ENDURING SOUTH

1. *The Everlasting South* (Baton Rouge, La., 1963), pp. 17, 20; *A History of the South* (New York, 1953), p. ix.

2. William R. Taylor, *Cavalier and Yankee: The Old South and American National Character* (New York, 1961); Howard R. Floan, *The South in Northern Eyes, 1831–1860* (Austin, Tex., 1958); David Brion Davis, *The Slave Power Conspiracy and the Paranoid Style* (Baton Rouge, La., 1969).

3. George B. Tindall, "Mythology: A New Frontier in Southern History," in Frank E. Vandiver, ed., *The Idea of the South: Pursuit of a Central Theme* (Chicago, 1964), pp. 1–15.

4. George B. Tindall, "The Benighted South: Origins of a Modern Image," *Virginia Quarterly Review* 40 (Spring 1964): 281–94.

5. C. Vann Woodward, *The Burden of Southern History* (Baton Rouge, La., 1960), pp. 19–21.

6. C. Vann Woodward, "From the First Reconstruction to the Second," *Harper's Magazine* 230 (April 1965): 133.

7. Paul M. Gaston, *The New South Creed: A Study in Southern Mythmaking* (New York, 1970), p. 245.

8. *The Americanization of Dixie: The Southernization of America* (New York, 1974).

9. H. Brandt Ayers and Thomas H. Naylor, eds., *You Can't Eat Magnolias* (New York, 1972), pp. 317–71.

10. "Discovering One Another in a Georgia Town," *Life*, February 12, 1971, p. 46D.

11. Delivered before the Seventh Annual Conference of the Texas Council for Social Studies, San Marcos, Texas, June 29, 1959.

12. Terry Sanford, "The End of the Myths: The South Can Lead the Nation," in Ayers and Naylor, *You Can't Eat Magnolias*, pp. 317–29.

13. Quoted in *New York Times*, April 26, 1971.

14. "The Dominance of Southern Writers," *LSU Alumni News* 41 (September 1965): 3.

15. Gaston, *New South Creed*, pp. 153–86.

16. Roger Williams, "GWTW: A Civic Love Story," *New South* 26 (Winter 1971): 72; John Egerton, "A Visit with James McBride Dabbs," *New South* 24 (Winter 1969): 46.

Bibliographical Note

The most thorough works on the South during the first half of the twentieth century are C. Vann Woodward, *Origins of the New South, 1877–1913* (Baton Rouge, La., 1951), and George B. Tindall, *The Emergence of the New South, 1913–1945* (Baton Rouge, La., 1967)— volumes 9 and 10 of the planned 10-volume *History of the South* series published under the editorship of Wendell H. Stephenson and E. Merton Coulter by the Louisiana State University Press. General histories of the region that extend into the period after World War II include William B. Hesseltine and David L. Smiley, *The South in American History*, 2d ed. (Englewood Cliffs, N.J., 1960); John S. Ezell, *The South since 1865* (New York and London, 1963); Thomas D. Clark and Albert D. Kirwan, *The South since Appomattox* (New York, 1957); Monroe L. Billington, *The American South: A Brief History* (New York, 1971); and Francis Butler Simkins and Charles P. Roland, *A History of the South* (New York, 1972).

Wilbur Cash, *The Mind of the South* (New York, 1941), is a brilliant if controversial psychoanalysis of the society of the region. Other important works dealing in whole or in part with the South during the period prior to that of this study include Howard W. Odum, *Southern Regions of the United States* (Chapel Hill, N.C., 1936); Rupert B. Vance, *Human Geography of the South* (Chapel Hill, N.C., 1932); William T. Couch, ed., *Culture in the South* (Chapel Hill, N.C., 1934); Allen Tate, ed., *A Southern Vanguard* (New York, 1947); Hodding Carter, Jr., *Southern Legacy* (Baton Rouge, La., 1950); and Gunnar Myrdal, *An American Dilemma* (New York, 1944).

Useful works devoted wholly or in part to the South since World War II include Thomas D. Clark, *The Emerging South* (New York, 1961); C. Vann Woodward, *The Strange Career of Jim Crow* (New York, 1957), and *The Burden of Southern History* (Baton Rouge, La., 1960); Louis D. Rubin, Jr., and James J. Kilpatrick, eds., *The Lasting South* (Chicago, 1957); Howard Zinn, *The Southern Mystique* (New

York, 1964); James McBride Dabbs, *The Southern Heritage* (New York, 1958), and *Who Speaks for the South?* (New York, 1965); Robert Howard West, ed., *This Is the South* (Chicago, 1959); Ralph McGill, *The South and the Southerner* (Boston, 1963); Avery Leiserson, ed., *The American South in the 1960s* (New York and London, 1964); Alfred O. Hero, Jr., *The Southerner and World Affairs* (Baton Rouge, La., 1965); John C. McKinney and Edgar T. Thompson, eds., *The South in Continuity and Change* (Durham, N.C., 1965); Harry S. Ashmore, *An Epitaph for Dixie* (New York, 1958); Charles L. Weltner, *Southerner* (Philadelphia, 1966); Willie Morris, *North toward Home* (Boston, 1967); Frank E. Smith, *Look Away from Dixie* (Baton Rouge, La., 1966); John Egerton, *A Mind to Stay Here: Profiles from the South* (New York, 1970), and *The Americanization of Dixie: The Southernization of America* (New York, 1974); Pat Watters, *The South and the Nation* (New York, 1969); H. Brandt Ayers and Thomas H. Naylor, eds., *You Can't Eat Magnolias* (New York, 1972); and George E. Mowry, *Another Look at the Twentieth-Century South* (Baton Rouge, La., 1973).

Contemporary periodicals and newspapers are indispensable sources of information on the recent South. Among the most useful periodicals are *Time, Newsweek, Harper's Magazine, Atlantic Monthly, U.S. News & World Report, Saturday Review, Facts on File Yearbook, Southern Living, New South, Southern Voices, Journal of Southern History, Industrial Development and Manufacturers Record, Sales Management,* and *Business Week.* Among the more informative newspapers are the *New York Times, Louisville Courier-Journal, Atlanta Constitution,* and *New Orleans Daily Picayune.*

Essential official documents include the various publications of the United States Bureau of the Census, especially the population census of 1970, the agricultural census of 1969, and the manufacturing census of 1967. The *Statistical Abstract of the United States* (published annually), the *Annual Survey of Manufactures,* and the *Survey of Current Business* (published monthly) are invaluable for a study of the recent South.

The best bibliographical guides to southern history are Arthur S. Link and Rembert W. Patrick, eds., *Writing Southern History: Essays in Historiography in Honor of Fletcher M. Green* (Baton Rouge, La., 1965), a comprehensive work; O. A. Singletary and Kenneth K. Bailey,

The South in American History (Washington, D.C., 1965), a brief but excellent essay; and Thomas D. Clark, ed., *Travels in the New South: A Bibliography*, 2 vols. (Norman, Okla., 1962), vol. 2, *The Twentieth-Century South, 1900–1955*, an extensive survey of accounts by travelers in the region.

For analyses of southern industry since World War II, see Frederick L. Deming and Weldon A. Stein, *Disposal of Southern War Plants* (n.p., n.d.); Glenn E. McLaughlin and Stefan Robock, *Why Industry Moves South* (n.p., 1949); James G. Maddox et al., *The Advancing South: Manpower Prospects and Problems* (New York, 1967); Research Department, Federal Reserve Bank of Atlanta, *Statistics on the Developing South* (Atlanta, Ga., 1972); F. Ray Marshall, *Labor in the South* (Cambridge, Mass., 1967); John Fischer, "Georgia: Mother of Social Invention," *Harper's Magazine* 244 (March 1972): 10–20; James Clotfelter, "The South and the Military Dollar," *New South* 25 (Spring 1970): 52–56; Osborn Segerberg, Jr., "Power Corrupts," *Esquire* 77 (March 1972): 138–95 passim; Robert Cooney, "The Modern South: Organized Labor's New Frontier," *American Federationist* 68 (May 1961): 15–19; Linda L. Liston, "The Southeast: Economic Imperatives Bow to Environmental Integrity," *Industrial Development and Manufacturers Record* 140 (September–October 1971): 6–21; and Frank E. Smith, "Improving the Southern Environment," *New South* 25 (Fall 1970): 63–69.

Studies dealing in whole or in part with southern agriculture include Association of Southern Agricultural Workers, *The South on the March* (n.p., n.d.); Dorothy and Joseph Dowdell, *Tree Farms: Harvest for the Future* (Indianapolis, Ind., 1965); Roscoe R. Snapp and A. L. Neumann, *Beef Cattle* (New York, London, Sydney, 1960); Joseph Berger, *The World's Major Fibre Crops: Their Cultivation and Manuring* (Zurich, 1969); Fred C. Elliot, Marvin Hoover, and Walter K. Porter, Jr., *Advances in Production and Utilization of Quality Cotton: Principles and Practices* (Ames, Ia., 1968); J. W. McKie and K. L. Anderson, *The Soybean Book* (n.p., n.d.); Wayne M. Cox, "The New Face of Southern Agriculture: The Southeast," *Farm Chemicals* 130 (March 1967): 30–37; and Zenas Beers, "The New Face of Southern Agriculture: The Delta," *Farm Chemicals* (October 1967): 33–38. The United States Department of Agriculture, *Agricultural Statistics*, published annually, is a useful source.

The literature on racial affairs and civil rights in the recent South is immense. All of the general histories of the region deal with this topic. Specialized works most helpful to this study include Benjamin Muse, *Ten Years of Prelude: The Story of Integration since the Supreme Court's 1954 Decision* (New York, 1964), and *The American Negro Revolution: From Non-violence to Black Power, 1963–1967* (Bloomington, Ind., 1968); Hodding Carter III, *The South Strikes Back* (New York, 1959); Numan V. Bartley, *The Rise of Massive Resistance: Race and Politics in the South during the 1950's* (Baton Rouge, La., 1969); Neil R. McMillen, *The Citizens' Council: Organized Resistance to the Second Reconstruction* (Urbana, Ill., 1971); Robert C. Smith, *They Closed Their Schools: Prince Edward County, Virginia, 1951–1964* (Chapel Hill, N.C., 1965); Robert Coles, *Children of Crisis: A Study of Courage and Fear* (Boston, Toronto, 1964), and *Children of Crisis: Migrants, Sharecroppers, Mountaineers* (Boston, Toronto, 1967); Lawrence D. Reddick, *Crusader without Violence: A Biography of Martin Luther King, Jr.* (New York, 1959); C. Eric Lincoln, ed., *Martin Luther King, Jr.: A Profile* (New York, 1970); Thomas R. Dye, *The Politics of Equality* (Indianapolis, Ind., 1971); Frederick M. Wirt, *Politics of Southern Equality: Law and Social Change in a Mississippi County* (Berkeley, Calif., 1970); Len Holt, *The Summer That Didn't End* (New York, 1965); Elizabeth Sutherland, ed., *Letters from Mississippi* (New York, 1965); Robert Sherrill, *Gothic Politics in the Deep South: Stars of the New Confederacy* (New York, 1968); Donald R. Matthews and James W. Prothro, *Negroes and the New Southern Politics* (New York, 1966); Carl T. Rowan, "Martin Luther King's Tragic Decision," *Reader's Digest* 91 (September 1967): 37–42; David Halberstam, "The Second Coming of Martin Luther King," *Harper's Magazine* 235 (August 1967): 39–51.

Any study of southern politics since World War II must begin with V. O. Key, Jr., *Southern Politics in State and Nation* (New York, 1949), and must include William C. Havard, ed., *The Changing Politics of the South* (Baton Rouge, La., 1972), the most exhaustive work to date on the subject. Other informative books include Numan V. Bartley and Hugh D. Graham, *Southern Politics and the Second Reconstruction* (Baltimore and London, 1975); Alberta Lachicotte, *Rebel Senator: Strom Thurmond of South Carolina* (New York, 1967); George B. Tindall, *The Disruption of the Solid South* (Athens, Ga.,

1972); Virginius Dabney, *Virginia: The New Dominion* (Garden City, N.Y., 1971); Donald S. Strong, *Urban Republicanism in the South* (University, Ala., 1960); Numan V. Bartley, *From Thurmond to Wallace: Political Tendencies in Georgia 1948–1968* (Baltimore and London, 1970); Frank E. Smith, *Congressman from Mississippi* (New York, 1964); Bernard Cosman, *Five States for Goldwater: Continuity and Change in Southern Presidential Voting Patterns* (University, Ala., 1966); Charles O. Lerche, Jr., *The Uncertain South: Its Changing Patterns of Politics in Foreign Policy* (Chicago, 1964); Matthews and Prothro, *Negroes and the New Southern Politics*; and Marshall Frady, *Wallace* (New York, 1968).

Among the most informative studies on southern education since World War II are Ernst W. Swanson and John A. Griffin, *Public Education in the South Today and Tomorrow* (Chapel Hill, N.C., 1955); Division of Surveys and Field Services, George Peabody College for Teachers, *High Schools in the South: A Fact Book* (Nashville, Tenn., 1966); Sam P. Wiggins, *Higher Education in the South* (Berkeley, Calif., 1966); Southern Regional Education Board, *Fact Book on Higher Education in the South* (Atlanta, Ga., 1968), and *Annual Report 1971–1972* (Atlanta, Ga., 1972); United States Office of Education, *Biennial Survey of Education: Statistics of Higher Education, 1947–1948* (Washington, D.C., 1948); American Council on Education, *A Fact Book on Higher Education* (Washington, D.C., 1972); John P. Dyer, *Ivory Towers in the Market Place* (Indianapolis, Ind., 1956); Alvin Renetzky, ed., *Yearbook of Higher Education, 1969* (Los Angeles, Calif., 1969); United States Department of Health, Education and Welfare, *Racial and Ethnic Enrollment Data from Institutions of Higher Learning, Fall 1970* (Washington, D.C., 1970); Southern Regional Education Board, *The Negro and Higher Education in the South: A Statement* (Atlanta, Ga., 1967); National Center for Educational Statistics, *Library Statistics of Colleges and Universities* (Washington, D.C., 1972); Kenneth D. Roose and Charles J. Anderson, *A Rating of Graduate Programs* (Washington, D.C., 1970); Lewis B. Mayhew, *Graduate and Professional Education, 1980* (New York, 1970); Horace M. Bond, *The Education of the Negro in the American Social Order* (New York, 1966); and Virginius Dabney, "The Good Southern Universities," *Harper's Magazine* 230 (March 1965): 86–94.

The story of religion in the recent South is in George Gallup, Jr., and John O. Davies III, *Religion in America: The Gallup Opinion Index, Report No. 70* (April 1971); John Shelton Reed, *The Enduring South: Subcultural Persistence in Mass Society* (Lexington, Mass., Toronto, London, 1972); John Lee Eighmy, *Churches in Cultural Captivity: A History of the Social Attitudes of Southern Baptists* (Knoxville, Tenn., 1972); Samuel S. Hill, Jr., *Southern Churches in Crisis* (New York, 1967); Constant H. Jacquet, Jr., ed., *Yearbook of American Churches* (Nashville, Tenn., 1972); Frank S. Mead, *Handbook of Denominations in the United States* (Nashville, Tenn., 1970); Kenneth K. Bailey, *Southern White Protestantism in the Twentieth Century* (New York, 1964); Joseph R. Washington, Jr., *Black Religion: The Negro and Christianity in the United States* (Boston, 1964), and *Black Sects and Cults* (Garden City, N.Y., 1972); Joseph H. Fichter and George L. Maddox, "Religion in the South, Old and New," in McKinney and Thompson, eds., *The South in Continuity and Change*; Donald W. Shriver, Jr., "Southern Churches in Transition," *New South* 25 (Winter 1970): 40–47; Marshall Frady, "God and Man in the South," *Atlantic Monthly* 219 (January 1967): 37–42; Harry Lefever, "The Church and Poor Whites," *New South* 25 (Spring 1970): 20–32; Robert Coles, "God and the Rural Poor," *Psychology Today* 5 (January 1972): 31–41; and James McBride Dabbs, "Gentlemen Cry Peace," *Christian Century*, March 23, 1966, pp. 365–66.

This treatment of recent southern literature depends heavily upon the actual writings of southern novelists and poets. Among the great number of critical studies of recent southern literature the following works were most helpful: Louis D. Rubin, Jr., and Robert Jacobs, eds., *Southern Renascence: The Literature of the Modern South* (Baltimore, Md., 1953), and *South: Modern Southern Literature in Its Cultural Setting* (New York, 1961); Louis D. Rubin, Jr., *The Faraway Country: Writers of the Modern South* (Seattle, Wash., 1963), and *The Curious Death of the Novel: Essays in American Literature* (Baton Rouge, La., 1967); Tindall, *The Emergence of the New South*, chapters 9 and 19; Louise Y. Gossett, *Violence in Recent Southern Fiction* (Durham, N.C., 1965); Carson McCullers, *The Mortgaged Heart* (Boston, 1971); Frederick J. Hoffman, *The Art of Southern Fiction: A Study of Some Modern Novelists* (Carbondale, Ill., 1967); George Core, ed., *Southern Fiction Today: Renascence and Beyond* (Athens, Ga., 1969); Leon V. Driskell, *The Eternal Crossroads: The Art of Flannery O'Con-*

nor (Lexington, Ky., 1971); Sherley Anne Williams, *Give Birth to Brightness: A Thematic Study in Neo-Black Literature* (New York, 1972); Clarence Major, ed., *The New Black Poetry* (New York, 1969); Stephen Henderson, *Understanding the New Black Poetry* (New York, 1973); James A. Emanuel and Theodore L. Gross, eds., *Dark Symphony: Negro Literature in America* (New York, 1968); Floyd C. Watkins, *The Death of Art: Black and White in the Recent Southern Novel* (Athens, Ga., 1970); Walter Sullivan, "Southern Writers in the Modern World: Death by Melancholy," *Southern Review* 6 (Autumn 1970): 907–19; Cleanth Brooks, "Regionalism in American Literature," *Journal of Southern History* 26 (February 1960): 35–41; Reynolds Price, "Dodo, Phoenix, or Tough Old Cock?" in Ayers and Naylor, eds., *You Can't Eat Magnolias*, pp. 71–81; and Alice Walker, "The Black Writer and the Southern Experience," *New South* 25 (Fall 1970): 23–26.

The fine arts are the most neglected topic of life in the recent South. There is no comprehensive treatment of the subject. The author of this volume has undertaken with trepidation to offer an essay grounded principally upon observation, personal interviews, and reflections. Among the more useful literature devoted in whole or in part to the subject are Mark R. Sumner, *A Selected Bibliography on Outdoor Drama* (Chapel Hill, N.C., 1971); Walter Spearman, *The Carolina Playmakers: The First Fifty Years* (Chapel Hill, N.C., 1970); Richard Moody, *Lillian Hellman: Playwright* (New York, 1972); A. Lawrence Kocher and Howard Dearstyne, *Colonial Williamsburg: Its Buildings and Gardens* (Williamsburg, Va., 1949); *Historic Preservation Plan for the Central Area General Neighborhood Renewal Area, Savannah, Georgia* (Savannah, Ga., n.d.); Ola Maie Foushee, *Art in North Carolina* (Chapel Hill, N.C., 1972); Lloyd Goodrich, *Lamar Dodd: A Retrospective Exhibition* (Athens, Ga., 1970); Jerry Bywaters, *Texas Painting & Sculpture: 20th Century* (Dallas, Tex., 1972); High Museum of Art, Atlanta, *Georgia Artists* (Atlanta, Ga., 1972); Jack A. Morris, Jr., and Robert Smeltzer, *Contemporary Artists of South Carolina* (Greenville, S.C., 1970); *American Art Directory* (New York, 1970); Paul Cummings, *A Dictionary of Contemporary American Artists*, 2d ed. (New York, 1971); editors of Time-Life Books, *American Painting 1900–1970* (New York, 1970); Philip Hart, *Orpheus in the New World: The Symphony Orchestra as an American Cultural Institution* (New York, 1973); William Ferris, *Mississippi Folk Voices* (n.p., n.d.); Harold Courlander, *Negro Folk Music U.S.A.* (New York, 1963); John Lovell, Jr., *Black Song: The Forge and the Flame* (New York, London, 1972); Bill C. Malone, *Country Music U.S.A.: A Fifty-Year History* (Austin, Tex., and London, 1968); "Aims and Purposes of Historic Savannah Foundation, Inc., May 24, 1973," Historic Savannah Foundation, Inc., Savannah; Paul Green, "Symphonic Outdoor Drama," in Robert West Howard, ed., *This Is the South* (Chicago, 1959); Mark R. Sumner, "State Theater of North Carolina," *Southern Theater* 11, no. 4 (1967); Betsy Farlow, "The Untouchables: Aspects of White Gospel Music," copy of unpublished paper in possession of the author; William C. Martin, "At the Corner of Glory Avenue and Hallelujah Street," *Harper's Magazine* 244 (January 1972): 95–99; and Roger Griffin Hall, "Are the Bozarts Blooming?" in Ayers and Naylor, eds., *You Can't Eat Magnolias*, pp. 83–98. The artists' files of the various museums and university libraries of the South are rich in information on individual artists.

The most informative studies of the society and social diversions of the recent South include McKinney and Thompson, eds., *The South in Continuity and Change*; Hero, *The Southerner and World Affairs*; Reed, *The Enduring South*; Robert Coles, *Farewell to the South* (Boston, Toronto, 1972); Lewis M. Killian, *White Southerners* (New York, 1970); I. A. Newby, *Black Carolinians: A History of Blacks in South Carolina from 1895 to 1968* (Columbia, S.C., 1973); Walter B. Weare, *Black Business in the New South: A Social History of the North Carolina Mutual Life Insurance Company* (Urbana, Ill., Chicago, London, 1973); Willie Morris, *Yazoo: Integration in a Deep-Southern Town* (New York, 1971); Rupert B. Vance, "The Sociological Implications of Southern Regionalism," *Journal of Southern History* 26 (February 1960): 44–56; Gabriel Moore, "Conversation with James Dickey," *New South* 27 (Winter 1972): 66–70; James McBride Dabbs, "The New South's Inner Frontier," *New South* 24 (Fall 1969): 30–39; Steve Van Evera, "A Family Assistance Plan: 40 Acres and a Mule?" *New South* 26 (Fall 1971): 70–74; Lewis H. Lapham, "Military Theology," *Harper's Magazine* 243 (July 1971): 73–85; Robert W. Twyman, "The Clay Eater: A New Look at an Old Southern Enigma," *Journal of Southern History* 37 (August 1971): 439–48; Marshall Frady, "Skirmishes with the Ladies of the Magnolias," *Playboy* 19 (September 1972): 121–222; Sara Murphy, "Women's Lib in the South," *New South* 27 (Spring

1972): 42–46; and Peter Schrag, "A Hesitant New South: Fragile Promise on the Last Frontier," *Saturday Review*, February 12, 1972, pp. 51–57.

Information and ideas on the persistence of a southern state of mind are from Reed, *The Enduring South*; Frank E. Vandiver, ed., *The Idea of the South: Pursuit of a Central Theme* (Chicago, 1964); Monroe L. Billington, ed., *The South: A Central Theme?* (New York, 1969); Woodward, *The Burden of Southern History*; George B. Tindall, "The Benighted South: Origins of a Modern Image," *Virginia Quarterly Review* 40 (Spring 1964): 281–94; C. Vann Woodward, "From the First Reconstruction to the Second," *Harper's Magazine* 230 (April 1965): 127–33; Richard King, "The Mind of the South: Narcissus Grown Analytical," *New South* 27 (Winter 1972): 15–27; and Norval D. Glenn and J. L. Simons, "Are Regional Cultural Differences Diminishing?" *Public Opinion Quarterly* 31 (Summer 1967): 176–93.

Index

Emancipation Proclamation, 36
Emory University, 157
Energy crisis, 19, 20, 186
Entertainment, 180–84
Episcopal church, 121, 122, 130
Equal Employment Opportunity
legislation, 53
Ervin, Sam, 55, 74, 75, 137; opposes
civil rights legislation, 50; role in
Watergate investigation, 96
Evers, Charles, 84–85; elected mayor of
Fayette, Mississippi, 91; candidate
for governor, 91; defeat of, 93
Evers, Medgar, 54; assassinated, 49
Everything That Rises Must Converge
(O'Connor), 141

Fair Employment Practice Commission,
33
Farming. *See* Agriculture
Farm wages, 23
Farquhar, Robroy, 152
Faubus, Orval, 38, 45; opposes school
desegregation, 39; closes Little Rock
schools, 40; supported by Arkansas
voters, 73; defeated, 82
Faulkner, William, 1, 6, 47, 140, 143,
147, 151; awarded Nobel Prize for
Literature, 7; fictional views of, on
southern homogeneity, 139; on
racial justice, 139
Fayette, Miss., 91
Federal agencies: desegregation of, 32
Federal Aid to Education Acts, 101
Federal Air Pollution Control
Administration, 13
Federal Council of Churches, 119
Federal development grants, 14
Fields, Julia, 143, 144
Fine arts, 7; drama, 150–53; architec-
ture, 153–60; visual arts, 160–63;
music, 163–66
First Baptist Church (Dallas), 123
Fishing, 183
Fisk University Jubilee Singers, 8
Flat Rock Playhouse (N.C.), 152
Florida, 21, 31, 35, 78, 114, 122, 165, 183;
personal income, 4, 27; population
growth, 15, 19, 98; as tourist
attraction, 26; school desegregation,
39, 40, 45; for Eisenhower in 1956,
64; for Nixon in 1960, 70; elects
Republican governor, 81
Florida State University, 116
Flowers, Richmond, 84

Foerster, Norman, 9
"Folk culture," 9
Folk music, 8
Folsom, James, 38, 80; Populist
outlook, 73; vetoes Alabama
interposition bills, 73; defeated, 84
Football, 181
Ford, Jesse Hill, 141, 148
Ford Foundation, 109, 153
Forest products: growth of, 14
For My People (Walker), 145
Fourteenth Amendment, 33, 35, 50
Frady, Marshall, 191
Frazier, E. Franklin, 131
Freedom Democrats, 76
"Freedom-of-choice": in school
desegregation, 102; outlawed by
Supreme Court, 103
Freedom Project, 50
Freedom Riders, 48
Freedom Workers, 51
Free Southern Theater (New Orleans),
153
French Quarter (New Orleans): 164,
180; threatened by motels, 158
Friendship Baptist Church (Atlanta),
129
Front Street Theater (Memphis), 153
Frozen citrus juice: production of, 15
Fugitives, 7, 140, 142
Fulbright, William: chairman, Senate
Foreign Relations Committee, 89;
position on Vietnam war, 90
Fulton County, Ga. *See* Atlanta, Ga.
Fundamentalism, 6, 123–24. *See also*
Religion
Fundamentalist South, 192
Furniture: production of, 14

Gaines, Ernest J., 145, 146
Galleria (Houston), 156
Galveston, Tex., 15
Gandhi, Mohandas, 43
Garbage workers (Memphis): in protest
demonstration, 57
Gardner, James, 82
Garment factories, 14
Gaston, Paul, 190
George Peabody College, 113
Georgia, 31, 63, 85, 119, 141, 145, 146,
186; growth of industry, 12, 13, 14;
poultry farming, 21; and de-
segregation, 36, 38, 39, 40, 42,
46–47; voter registration, 51, 53;
state politics of, 72; county-unit

THE IMPROBABLE ERA has been set in
Hermann Zapf's Palatino with
display in Eric Gill's Perpetua.

Composition and printing by
Heritage Printers, Inc.

Binding by The Delmar Companies

Design by Jonathan Greene